Looking at Iberia

D1825466

Hispanic Studies: Culture and Ideas

Volume 56

Edited by
Claudio Canaparo

PETER LANG
Oxford · Bern · Berlin · Bruxelles · Frankfurt am Main · New York · Wien

Santiago Pérez Isasi and
Ângela Fernandes (eds)

Looking at Iberia

A Comparative European Perspective

PETER LANG

Oxford · Bern · Berlin · Bruxelles · Frankfurt am Main · New York · Wien

Bibliographic information published by Die Deutsche Nationalbibliothek.
Die Deutsche Nationalbibliothek lists this publication in the Deutsche National-
bibliografie; detailed bibliographic data is available on the Internet
at http://dnb.d-nb.de.

A catalogue record for this book is available from the British Library.

Library of Congress Control Number: 2013942252

Cover illustration: 'Verano' © Claudia del Río, 2013.

ISSN 1661-4720
ISBN 978-3-0343-0934-9

© Peter Lang AG, International Academic Publishers, Bern 2013
Hochfeldstrasse 32, CH-3012 Bern, Switzerland
info@peterlang.com, www.peterlang.com, www.peterlang.net

This publication has been peer reviewed.

Printed in Germany

Contents

SANTIAGO PÉREZ ISASI AND ÂNGELA FERNANDES

Looking at Iberia in/from Europe

This volume focuses on some key theoretical, methodological and historical questions related with Iberian literatures and cultures, privileging a strong European component and a comparative approach. The essays gathered here are the main outcome from the Exploratory Workshop 'Looking at Iberia from a Comparative European Perspective: Literature, Narration and Identity' funded by the European Science Foundation and held at the Faculty of Arts from the University of Lisbon, on 13 and 14 October 2011. This workshop was organized in the frame of Project DIIA – Diálogos Ibéricos e Ibero-Americanos [Iberian and Ibero-American Dialogues], from the Centre for Comparative Studies, University of Lisbon, and it brought together twenty-one scholars from eleven European countries with common interests in Iberian languages, literatures and cultures, along with a shared comparative perspective towards them. The papers presented then and the lively discussion that ensued led to the common wish to transform all of our questions and reflexions into a volume that might offer a theoretical and methodological threshold for future investigations on Iberian literary and cultural phenomena.

The field of Iberian Studies, which could be defined as the methodological consideration of the Iberian Peninsula as a complex, multilingual cultural and literary system, has known an exponential development in the last years; however, it still lacks solid theoretical and methodological reflections that may guarantee its validity and its independence as a scientific area. This volume aims at contributing towards filling that void by analysing some of the key issues in Iberian Studies from a comparative European perspective. It is intended as a wide-range panorama of current Iberian Studies, with a coherent approach to literary and cultural objects that often remain hidden, marginalized or unexplored within the traditional, national and monolinguistic 'philological' studies. It is not our intention to propose a new metaphysical, extra-historical Iberian identity, but to question the established political or epistemological barriers which have often distorted the appreciation of cultural and artistic phenomena in the Iberian Peninsula.

This volume is characterized by its broad theoretical approach and its wide European origin and perspective. It brings together more traditional historical overviews and some cutting edge contemporary analysis of reception and translation issues, focusing on literature, film, editing and cultural markets, academic policies and new trends in the humanities. With its several contributions, *Looking at Iberia* offers a comprehensive outlook on a set of historical and contemporary cultural productions that testify to the inter-dependencies, conflicts, overlappings, similarities and contradictions among Iberia's linguistic, political and artistic domains. With their multiple perspectives and methodologies, the essays collected here question the concept of 'Iberia' itself: its scientific accuracy as a starting point for scientific and academic work; its relation with other, more established terms, concepts and identities, such as Spanish, Portuguese, Catalan, Basque or Galician, but also Romance, European or Western; and, more specifically, its relation with the mythical, historical or artistic (both literary and cinematographic) narratives created to support or represent such collective identities, especially since the nineteenth century up to the present.

The essays are organized around three different axes: firstly, the theoretical grounds and methodologies of Iberian Studies, and the discussion about the location of this field within the general epistemological configuration of Comparative Literature, World Literature, Area Studies or Cultural Studies; secondly, the historical images of Iberia, regarding the configuration of this geographical, political and cultural space, as viewed from the inside and from the outside, with special attention to literary and philosophical perspectives on Iberian identities and the place of political and cultural 'Iberism'; and thirdly, contemporary Iberia, with its plural identities and their artistic representation, namely in literature and cinema. These axes constitute the centre of the three sections of the book.

In the first section, all contributions consider the new theoretical grounds and methodologies of Iberian Studies. The arguments for this new field of studies stem from the realization that there are still numerous literary and cultural phenomena that need to be studied from an Iberian relational perspective, namely multilingual authors, plural identities, and frontier cases; moreover, an Iberian point of view can be applied with promising results to an even wider set of data, most of which have traditionally been considered only from a monolingual, national(ist) perspective. Iberian Studies, in this sense, should be regarded as part of Comparative Cultural Studies, in relation with the latest European approaches to Area Studies and with the idea of World Literature. They have grown on the base of Comparative Literary Studies, but increasingly encompass a wider scope of objects and cultural objects such as artworks, historiography, journalism or cinema. The critical, methodological and theoretical tools and frames developed for and within this Iberian context may therefore be reusable for other fields and geographical areas, thus contributing to a redefinition of Comparative Studies and a better understanding of the construction and representation of plural and multilingual identities through literature and the arts.

In the beginning of this first section, Santiago Pérez Isasi (University of Lisbon) offers an overall view of the field of Iberian Studies, revising tentative definitions and sketching a 'state of the art', which shows the growing interest in recent years for this area of research. He also proposes a set of future objectives for the field, such as gaining institutional and scientific recognition, and developing deeper reflections about the epistemological location and the political implications of Iberian Studies – this volume aims precisely to meet some if these points. Teresa Pinheiro (Chemnitz University of Technology) then discusses the concept of Area Studies and examines its potentialities for Iberian and European Studies, as new epistemological fields that have emerged in recent years. Remembering how the Iberian Peninsula has been studied in Germany since the nineteenth century, she points to a cross-cultural and comparative perspective that may now be privileged, eschewing a traditional national focus and opening up new possibilities of analysis for a broader range of social and artistic discourses. Considering the question of Iberian national identities,

John Macklin (University of Glasgow) proposes a new look at Iberian Modernisms, taking into account contemporary cultural and ideological concerns. He argues that this revision of modernisms, as multiple and complex processes, may be a touchstone for a more accurate study on the intertwined processes of artistic production, cultural memory and political debate in such complex cultural spaces as Iberia. The following contribution, by Gabriel Magalhães (University of Beira Interior), presents a reflection on the implications of Iberian Comparative Studies for European Studies, stressing the necessary role of the Peninsula, as a complex cultural cross-roads, in forging a counter-argument to the dominance of scientific and economic thought in contemporary academia and political life.

This first section continues with an essay by Roberto Vecchi (University of Bologna), who argues that there is a need for a revision of the traditional outlook towards Iberian 'specificities'. Evoking Gramsci's reflection on the 'South', and considering Portugal as a 'case study', he proposes a new vision of Iberia as a relational concept, which may also help a more comprehensive reconfiguration of the relationships between space and power in Europe. Then, Jüri Talvet (University of Tartu) proposes a reflection on contemporary problems of Comparative Literary Studies, noticing some lack of theoretical reflection on the complex contacts between literary products and processes. He stresses the need for some renewed perspectives on translation practices, especially when considering very distant historical and/or linguistic contexts that may envisage Iberian literary heritage as the 'other'. Finally, César Domínguez (University of Santiago de Compostela) explores the connections between the concepts of Iberian, European and World literatures. He stresses the importance of further research into the dynamics of literary edition, translation, teaching and canon formation, in order to clarify the political and cultural transfers that have occurred and keep occurring within the Peninsula and between Iberia, Europe, and a broader worldwide context.

In the second section, the essays deal with images of Iberia, regarding the historical configuration of this geographical, political and cultural space, as seen from within and from the outside, especially from other European contexts. Since Iberian Studies intend to avoid creating new mythological or ontological definitions of Iberia, thus criticizing any ideas of specificity or exoticism, the contributors in this section propose, instead, their vision of a complex cultural Iberian polysystem, in which all discourses are considered within its cultural and institutional context of production, and in relation with the difference(s) that they include, elude, hide or represent. Through the analysis of literary and philosophical perspectives on Iberian identities, be they Catalan, Galician or Portuguese, it is possible to identify different layers of cultural relationships and perceptions of 'otherness'. Moreover, it also becomes clear that some historical periods and problems have been more frequently considered from an Iberian point of view, namely the Golden Ages and, above all, the political and cultural 'Iberism' of some authors from the turn of the nineteenth to the twentieth century. A new critical outlook on these issues may open the horizon to further research the topics implicated in building these 'images of Iberia'.

This second section opens with the essay by Maria Fernanda de Abreu (New University of Lisbon), who takes José Saramago's *The Stone Raft* as a starting point to discuss the concept of Iberia as 'an identitarian mega-frame' whose singularity has been shaped in both historiographical and literary discourses, in Portugal and Spain, especially since the nineteenth century. The author describes this process of building an Iberian identity, facing both the inner diversity of the Peninsula and the wider European context, as the consequence of both 'an anxiety of difference' and 'an anxiety of unity'. Then, Ferenc Pál (Eötvös Loránd University, Budapest) explains how the image of Portugal and Portuguese history was widespread in Hungary during the nineteenth century thanks to the reading of the Portuguese Renaissance epic poem *The Lusiads*, by Camões. The literary representation of the Portuguese at that time offered an important model in central Europe. Derek Flitter (University of Exeter) deals with the opposition between North and South as a key motive in Romantic identitarian discourses developed in the Peninsula. He argues that mediaeval and early modern Spain became a locus for the rehearsal of Iberian identities within the prism of northern European Romantic theory, and states their evocation as a means of testing aesthetic limits.

Considering intra-Iberian issues, Juan M. Ribera Llopis (Complutense University of Madrid) focuses on the discourses about the Catalan linguistic and literary Regeneration produced by Castilian authors from

1877 until 1939, and identifies a general process of neutralization of any Catalan difference. His analysis shows how the concepts of 'centre' and 'periphery' define important cultural and political categories in the Iberian context. The following essay, by Leonardo Romero Tobar (University of Zaragoza), presents the main aspects of Juan Valera's theory of Iberism, in the late nineteenth century. The discrepancies between Valera's private and public writings in what concerns the project of an Iberian political union show both the inner contradictions of Iberism and the deep literary and artistic background of this movement. Finally, Maria Graciete Besse (University of Paris IV Sorbonne) proposes a reading of Portuguese reconfigurations of Iberism during the nineteenth and twentieth centuries, taking as her theoretical frame Eduard Glissant's concept of 'relation'. She notices that most literary representations of Iberian inter-relations seem to sway between utopian views of a future peninsular union and the repetition of national identitarian commonplaces, thus building a conceptual opacity that obstructs any dialogue.

The third section of the volume is devoted to contemporary Iberia, considered as a space of plural identities, where artistic representations of difference play an important role. Literature and cinema became privileged fields to depict and question the multicultural and plurilingual Peninsula. And, as the essays in this section demonstrate, contemporary Iberia cannot be seen as a closed or isolated cultural space, but should rather be regarded as a rhizome of internal and external relations: it is indeed a complex 'semiosphere' which creates multiple centres and peripheries, insularities and exiles, but which also has a strong internal coherence and cohesion that allows for its consideration as a consistent scientific object.

In the first essay of this section, Ângela Fernandes (University of Lisbon) proposes a reflection upon the place of an Iberian cultural identity within the Romance world, remembering the status of the Peninsula as a borderline location since the time it was a part of the Roman Empire. She analyses some Portuguese twentieth-century narratives and argues that the historical and mythical role of Iberia as the Western margin of Europe makes it a privileged scenery in the literary representation of cultural crossroads. In the following contribution, Jon Kortazar (University of the Basque Country) proposes a reading of *Bilbao–New York–Bilbao*, the 2008 novel by the Basque author Kirmen Uribe. Considering the complex issues dealt with in the narrative, this reading highlights the novel's 'post-national' perspective on identity, with extraterritoriality and trans-nationality being the key elements in this new kind of national identification. Helena Buffery (University College Cork) analyses the importance of translation and self-translation in the process of revival and redefinition of Catalan culture since the 1970s. She argues that, since Iberia is a multilingual zone, the attention to translation practices enables a deeper insight into the dominant moves towards collective (self)identification and (self)recognition, and this may be one of the most relevant fields of research in Iberian studies. In the last essay, Esther Gimeno Ugalde (University of Vienna) presents a panorama of contemporary Iberian cinema, noticing that there seems to be a growing interest in films that represent the Peninsula's cultural and linguistic diversity. She mentions several recent films that reflect Iberian multilingualism, and considers it worth analysing the relation between the language choice in film productions, often sponsored by regional institutions, and the will to consolidate local identities.

The rationale of Iberian Studies, as developed in this volume, may therefore be described as the constitution of a new way of looking at the Iberian complex, based on comparative methodologies, and thus aimed at overcoming binary structures as well as any sort of established frontiers. Iberian Studies deal with the cultural and artistic representations of a multiple-layered space, with a long and complex history. It is beyond doubt that more (and renewed) research needs to be done in order to bring to light not only the Iberian complexity but also the relation of the Iberian case to the global contemporary context. Being a privileged crossroads, in space and time, Iberia asks today for a new approach and hints at a new concept of cultural community, where more complex (and eventually weaker) bonds demand for a stronger and more conscious commitment from all those belonging to it.

We would like to end this brief introduction by thanking the people who made this volume possible. First of all, we thank all those who participated in the ESF Exploratory Workshop in Lisbon in October 2011, and all the contributors to this volume for their enthusiasm, generosity and committed collaboration throughout the editing process and the internal peer-review discussion. We would also like to thank the European Science Foundation (Standing Committee for the Humanities) and the Centre for Comparative Studies from the University of Lisbon for their institutional and financial support. A special word is due to Helena Carvalhão Buescu, the director of the Centre for Comparative Studies, for her continuous support since the beginning of this project. In the copy-editing process, we were happy to count on the careful and meticulous work of Marta Pacheco Pinto, Amândio Reis and Rui Vitorino Azevedo, whom we thank warmly.

PART I

The New Theoretical Grounds and Methodologies of Iberian Studies

SANTIAGO PÉREZ ISASI

Iberian Studies:
A State of the Art and Future Perspectives

I

This volume, and this chapter in particular, are based on two complementary convictions: 1) that there is a need to create or rather to consolidate Iberian Studies as a specific field of knowledge which encompasses a wide set of literary, artistic and cultural phenomena that cannot be properly understood and explained from a national perspective; and 2) that this field, despite the fact that it has not yet been named or epistemologically positioned, has seen a significant development in the last few years through the emergence of a growing number of scholarly publications.

Admittedly, Comparative Studies on the different literatures of the Iberian Peninsula and their mutual interrelations are not new. For instance, there is a long tradition of studies that compare Spanish and Portuguese authors or texts within the general field of Comparative Literature. However and in accordance with our proposal, if we consider Iberian Studies as a specific field or subfield, we see that they consist of something different to this tradition which is, needless to say, extremely valuable and useful. It could be defined as the consistent and deliberate consideration of the Iberian Peninsula as an interconnected, multilingual and multicultural political, identitarian and literary polysystem[1] or semiosphere, to use Lotman's term.[2] Thus, the literary phenomena that can be analysed

---

1   Itamar Even-Zohar, 'The Role of Literature in the Making of the Nations of Europe: A Socio-semiotic Study', *Applied Semiotics/Sémiotique appliquée* 1/1 (1996), 39–59.
2   Yuri Lotman, 'On the Semiosphere', *Sign Systems Studies* 33/1 (2005), 205–29.

within the scope of Iberian Studies are pretty much the same as those of comparative – and non-comparative – studies; it is rather the analytical perspective, as well as the theoretical and methodological frame, in which these studies are placed and understood, that has changed.

It might be considered naïve to propose the constitution of a new field devoted to the literatures of a specific European region, especially given the loss of credibility of Area Studies, at least in their traditional configuration from the second-half of the twentieth century which derived from USA foreign interests during the Cold War.[3] Secondly, there is an almost unlimited respect towards national boundaries in Literary Studies, both in their academic and scientific manifestations. And thirdly, there is a move in the opposite direction with a strong tendency towards the idea of World Literature, which dominates current Comparative Studies.[4]

However, the need for a coherent set of methodological tools and theoretical frameworks for Iberian Studies has manifested itself in very different academic contexts. It could be argued that there is indeed a crisis in Area Studies, but this has to be understood in the etymological sense of 'change' and 'transformation'; it opens a new epistemological range of options in which Iberian Studies, as we understand them, could be timely. We could propose that national boundaries do in fact have that kind of academic and scientific power which makes them seem almost self-evident and untouchable, but this does not mean that there is no place for supra- or transnational proposals such as this one, especially during a time of crisis of academic systems and programmes worldwide. Furthermore, we would suggest that the advance towards an idea of World Literature points precisely to this overcoming of national boundaries in a radical way, which does not exclude the possibility of simultaneously exploring the specific relations within significant 'regions' of that global literature, as is the case of the Iberian Peninsula.

---

3   David Szanton, ed., *The Politics of Knowledge: Area Studies and the Disciplines* (Berkeley: University of California Press, 2004).

4   David Damrosch, *What Is World Literature?* (Princeton: Princeton University Press, 2003).

II

There is in fact some evidence in academic communities from both sides of the Atlantic that support our claim for the establishment of Iberian Studies as a field. From the American academic world, for instance, Joan Ramon Resina has argued strongly for the reconfiguration of the traditional label of Hispanism.[5] He believes it should be transformed into the more encompassing 'Iberian Studies' which would include all of the literatures and cultures of the Iberian Peninsula. Resina argues that Peninsular Hispanism, with its outdated methodologies and practices and its static canonical texts, is quickly and constantly losing ground in relation to areas such as Latin-American Studies, Chicano Studies, etc. In his view, the constitution of the new field of Iberian Studies, which would translate into new methodologies, new sets of analytical tools and a new and more inclusive canon, could help regain ground and offer an attractive and academically sustainable alternative. Behind this somewhat utilitarian phrasing lies a meaningful and clearly ideological proposal: the abolition of a monolingual Spanish identity by dissolving it into a wider, multilingual and multicultural Iberian space, which, as Resina argues, will also attract more students, more research and, in the end, more funding.

Be it as it may, it is not difficult to find examples of Departments of Iberian and Latin-American Literatures and Cultures or Departments of Spanish and Luso-Brazilian Studies (terms which seem to be considered as synonyms), especially in the United States and the United Kingdom (there is Resina's Department at Stanford, but there are also others at Columbia University, Richmond University or Queen Mary at the University of London, just to name three prestigious examples).

However, as their various names show, these Departments are not devoted specifically to the peninsular part of the Iberian world, but to

---

5   Joan Ramon Resina, *Del hispanismo a los estudios ibéricos. Una propuesta federativa para el ámbito cultural* (Madrid: Biblioteca Nueva, 2009).

both Peninsular and Latin-American Spanish- and Portuguese-speaking countries. Furthermore, it is impossible not to think that in most cases this fusion of Spanish-speaking with Portuguese-speaking Literary Studies (with the more or less explicit addition of other linguistic and literary areas) into one department does not respond to deep theoretical decisions, but to more practical – even economic – considerations. In my view and in the majority of cases, the Spanish and Portuguese elements of these departments hardly work together towards the constitution of a common space of debate, research and mutual contamination. Moreover, there persists a confusion between the concept of Iberian Studies as merely 'Peninsular Hispanism' (in Faber,[6] for instance) and true *Iberian* Studies which would, by definition, also encompass Portuguese Studies.

In Europe, and especially in Spanish and Portuguese Higher Education programmes, where the division of Language and Literary Studies by national and/or linguistic criteria (e.g. Filología Hispánica [Hispanic Philology], Estudos Portugueses/Lusófonos [Portuguese/Lusophone Studies], etc.) has just recently started to be dismantled as a result of the Bologna agreement – and once again, mainly for practical and economic reasons – initiatives in this direction are still more personal and individual than collective and institutional. For now there does not seem to be any intention of integrating Iberian languages and literatures into any kind of common programme (with the exception of the few remaining Departments of Romance Philology, which are not in fact devoted to Iberia but to Romania – in its classical meaning of 'Latin-speaking world').

6   Sebastiaan Faber, 'Economies of Prestige: The Place of Iberian Studies in the American University', *Hispanic Research Journal* 9/1 (2008), 7–32.

III

In other less institutionalized aspects of the academic system, the presence of Iberian Studies, as content and not merely as a label, is more easily traceable and offers more promising signs. For instance, the last decade has witnessed a considerable number of symposia and conferences dealing with literary and cultural relations within the Iberian Peninsula, such as the RELIPES Conferences in Salamanca and Covilhã;[7] the *XXXIVe Congrès de la Société des hispanistes français* under the title *Cultures lusophones et hispanophones: penser la relation*, organized by Maria Graciete Besse;[8] the annual Forum of Iberian Studies in Oxford, or the annual Conference of the Association for Comparative Iberian Studies.[9] Once again, we should be careful with the ambiguity with which the term 'Iberian' is used in the titles of some of these meetings and symposia: mere juxtaposition does not equal comparatism. While the RELIPES meetings and the *Congrès de la Société des hispanistes français* clearly stress the idea of interrelation across national and linguistic frontiers, in other cases it could be possible to imagine a conference with 'Iberian' in its title, in which not even one paper would go beyond the established national or linguistic barriers, thus creating the image of the Iberian Peninsula as a mosaic of isolated monolinguistic pieces that were uncomfortably put together within one room. The Association for Contemporary Iberian Studies, for instance, states its core areas of activity in a non-comparative way. It is merely summative and involves the following:

7   Gabriel Magalhães, ed., *Actas do Congresso RELIPES III: 18, 19 e 20 de Abril de 2007* (Covilhã: Universidade da Beira Interior, 2007); Gabriel Magalhães, ed., *RELIPES. Relações Linguísticas e Literárias entre Portugal e Espanha desde os Inícios do Século XIX até à Actualidade* (Covilhã and Salamanca: Universidade da Beira Interior/ Celya, 2007).

8   Maria Graciete Besse, org., *Cultures lusophones et hispanophones: penser la relation* (Paris: Indigo & Côté-Femmes, 2010).

9   Association for Contemporary Iberian Studies (ACIS) <http://www.iberianstudies. net/>.

1. Geographical limits: Spain and Portugal and their dependent territories. International relations involving either country are included.
2. Historical period: approximately the past 100 years, from the beginning of the twentieth century to the present. This is not meant to exclude references to an earlier period, where appropriate.
3. Language: the Spanish and Portuguese languages, especially contemporary usage; the minority languages of the Iberian Peninsula, especially in their social and political context ('About', ACIS website).

The comparative and supranational or transnational spirit which, in our opinion, should characterize Iberian Studies is evidently and strongly present in the growing number of publications which deal with Iberian literatures and their interconnections. In Portugal, for instance, after the seminal efforts by Maria Idalina Resina Rodrigues (in such works as *Estudos Ibéricos – Da Cultura à Literatura*),[10] we can see the birth of more systematic and co-ordinated efforts, both in the research group directed by Maria Fernanda de Abreu at the New University of Lisbon, whose study on *Cervantes no Romantismo Português*[11] is a major contribution to Iberian Comparative Studies, and the research project 'Diálogos Ibéricos e Iberoamericanos' [Iberian and Ibero-American Dialogues], at the Centre for Comparative Studies of the University of Lisbon, directed by Ângela Fernandes,[12] as well as a considerable number of publications from individual researchers that

10   Maria Idalina Resina Rodrigues, *Estudos Ibéricos – Da Cultura à Literatura: pontos de encontro, séculos XIII a XVII* (Lisbon: Instituto de Cultura e Língua Portuguesa, 1987).
11   Maria Fernanda de Abreu, *Cervantes no Romantismo Português: cavaleiros andantes, manuscritos encontrados e gargalhadas moralíssimas* (Lisbon: Editorial Estampa, 1994).
12   Ângela Fernandes *et al.*, eds, *Diálogos Ibéricos e Iberoamericanos: actas del VI congreso internacional de ALEPH* (Lisbon: Centro de Estudos Comparatistas da Universidade de Lisboa/Editorial Academia del Hispanismo, 2010); Santiago Pérez Isasi, 'Imágenes de la Península Ibérica en la historiografía literaria romántica', in Maria Jesús Fernández García and María Luísa Leal, coords, *Imagologías ibéricas: construyendo la imagen del otro peninsular* (Mérida: Gabinete de Iniciativas Transfronterizas del Gobierno de Extremadura, 2012), 181–98.

deal with Spanish-Portuguese literary relations.[13] Two more recent collective publications that have dealt with Iberian relations as a research object are the journal *Colóquio/Letras*, which published a special issue entitled *Siglo de Oro: relações hispano-portuguesas no séc. XVII*,[14] and the *Revista de História das Ideias* from the University of Coimbra which devoted its 31st issue to the idea of *Ibéria*.[15]

On the Spanish side, the majority of projects and publications that interrelate Iberian literary and cultural phenomena come from the periphery of the system: either the academic periphery (for instance, the very few Departments of Romance Philology left, such as the one at the Complutense University of Madrid) or from the geographical periphery (Galicia, Catalonia, Extremadura). An example of the first kind of peripheral location is the work being developed by Juan M. Ribera Llopis at the Complutense University of Madrid (e.g., Ribera Llopis and Arroyo Almaraz[16]); as for the second, an outstanding example is the work developed at the University of Santiago de Compostela by the team co-ordinated by Fernando Cabo Aseguinolaza, Anxo Abuín and César Domínguez, with groundbreaking contributions such as *A Comparative History of Literatures in the Iberian Peninsula*;[17] the studies carried out by Víctor Martínez

13   Among others: Gabriel Magalhães, *Garrett e Rivas. O Romantismo em Espanha e Portugal*, 2 vols (Lisbon: Imprensa Nacional–Casa da Moeda, 2009); António Apolinário Lourenço, *Estudos de Literatura Comparada Luso-Espanhola* (Coimbra: Centro de Literatura Portuguesa da Faculdade de Letras da Universidade de Coimbra, 2005); Teresa Araújo, *Portugal e Espanha: diálogos e reflexos literários* (Lisbon and Faro: Centro de Estudos Linguísticos e Literários da Universidade do Algarve/Instituto de Estudos sobre o Romanceiro Velho e Tradicional, 2004).

14   *Colóquio/Letras. Suplemento – Siglo de Oro: relações hispano-portuguesas no séc. XVII* 178 (September–December 2011).

15   *Revista de História das Ideias. Ibéria* 31 (2010).

16   Juan Miguel Ribera Llopis and Antonio Arroyo Almaraz, eds, *Literaturas peninsulares en contacto: castellana, catalana, gallega y vasca* (Madrid: Universidad Complutense/Editorial Complutense, 2008).

17   Fernando Cabo Aseguinolaza, Anxo Abuín, and César Domínguez, *A Comparative History of Literatures in the Iberian Peninsula*, 2 vols (Amsterdam and Philadelphia: John Benjamins, 2010).

Gil[18] at the University of Barcelona; the book series *Relaciones literarias en el ambito hispánico*, co-ordinated by Ricardo Lafarga and Luis Pegenaute from Barcelona, which so far consists of five volumes, three of which are specifically devoted to the internal and external relations of Iberian literatures;[19] or the consistent work developed by Antonio Sáez, from both sides of the Spanish-Portuguese border, with the publication of the volume *Suroeste* as its key bibliographical reference.[20]

Publications on Iberian issues have also proliferated outside the Iberian Peninsula in these last years, both in Europe and the United States. Apart from *A Comparative History of Literatures in the Iberian Peninsula* (which has Spanish editors, but is integrated in a wider European project), other extremely valuable contributions have been published, such as the volume co-ordinated by Helena Buffery, Stuart Davis and Kirsty Hooper, entitled *Reading Iberia*, in which methodologies and concepts from Queer Studies, Memory Studies, Translation Studies or Film Studies are applied to a varied set of texts in the wider sense of the word.[21] Brad Epps and Luis Fernández Cifuentes's *Spain Beyond Spain*,[22] and Martín-Estudillo and Spadaccini's

---

18   Víctor Martínez Gil, *Portugal y Cataluña ante la modernidad: intercambios artísticos y literarios* (Badajoz: Sociedad Cultural de Conmemoraciones Culturales/MEIAC, 2010).

19   Francisco Lafarga, Luis Pegenaute, and Enric Gallén, eds, *Interacciones entre las literaturas ibéricas* (series 'Relaciones literarias en el ámbito hispánico: traducción, literatura y cultura') (Bern: Peter Lang, 2010); Luis Pegenaute, Enric Gallén, and Francisco Lafarga, eds, *Relaciones entre las literaturas ibéricas y las literaturas extranjeras* (series 'Relaciones literarias en el ámbito hispánico: traducción, literatura y cultura') (Bern: Peter Lang, 2011); Enric Gallén, Francisco Lafarga, and Luis Pegenaute, eds, *Traducción y autotraducción en las literaturas ibéricas* (series 'Relaciones literarias en el ámbito hispánico: traducción, literatura y cultura') (Bern: Peter Lang, 2011).

20   Antonio Sáez Delgado and Luis Manuel Gaspar, eds, *Suroeste: relaciones literarias y artísticas entre Portugal y España (1890–1936)* (Madrid: MEIAC, 2010).

21   Helena Buffery, Stuart Davis, and Kirsty Hooper, eds, *Reading Iberia: Theory/History/Identity* (Oxford: Peter Lang, 2007).

22   Brad Epps and Luis Fernández Cifuentes, *Spain beyond Spain. Modernity, Literary History and National Identity* (Lewisburg, PA: Bucknell University Press, 2005).

New Spain, New Literatures,[23] although less 'Iberian' in spirit, also point out to the same questioning of established (national) discourses of identity from within and outside the Peninsula.

IV

This growing bibliographical record is promising, and shows that there is, in fact, a rich set of questions and problems yet to be resolved regarding Iberian literatures and cultures. However, as encouraging and extremely valuable as these contributions may be, they are still for the most part isolated and disconnected individual efforts with different cultural, academic and epistemological backgrounds. They therefore cannot be considered as having any kind of scientific unity. In the second part of my contribution, I would like to address a series of aspects which are, in fact, still open for debate on the field of Iberian Studies and which are the subject of discussion in other chapters by other colleagues in this same volume.

First of all, as stated above, the specificity of the field of Iberian Studies lies in its consideration of the Iberian Peninsula as a single but complex cultural and literary space. Needless to say, this definition of the Iberian Peninsula does not have any identitarian or political agenda, nor does it assume any essentialist definition of its object. It is not, in any way, a surreptitious reconfiguration of historical, mostly nineteenth-century, 'Iberism'. Iberian Studies is a scientific field which configures a scientific object, although it also considers historical or political 'Iberism' as a part of that same set of phenomena which it studies. In fact, a possible criticism to this new-born field is that it erodes or undermines some identities, in order to construct a wider one. In other words, it may be argued, as many nationalistic orators often do, that Iberian Studies exposes some identities

23   Luis Martín-Estudillo and Nicholas Spadaccini, eds, *New Spain, New Literatures* (Nashville: Vanderbilt University Press, 2010).

(like national ones) as being historically constructed and therefore arbitrary, while on the other hand it proposes a different – an Iberian – identity which is presented as essential and ahistorical. This criticism would be justified if we were, in fact, proposing a new 'Iberian' identity to substitute the previous ones, but this is not the case. This consideration of the Iberian Peninsula as a cultural and literary continuum is more methodological than ontological. It serves to question received historiographical traditions and to illuminate phenomena that usually lie in their margins or in their in-betweens. However, it does not invoke metaphysical or extra-historical entities to do so.

To put it another way, the Iberian perspective we adopt stems from the identification of a strong internal link and the cohesive literary historical background which, if not strictly common to all of its parts, are so inter-twined that it is almost impossible to dissociate them. Yet these links and this complex net of relations are considered to be historical and not essen-tialist. They are perceived after analysing the literary and cultural objects at hand, and not imposing on them *a priori*. They also do not exclude the possibility of the existence of other kinds of links or bigger or smaller cul-tural identities that challenge and question them.

V

As far as we know, the study of literature(s) within the Iberian Peninsula has been until now strongly mediated by the division of Literary Studies, with their respective canons and historiographical traditions in separate national and linguistic entities (in the case of Iberia, mainly Spain, Portugal, Catalonia, Galicia and the Basque Country). The idea that each nation, a concept that eludes definition but at the same time seems self-evident to most scholars, creates its own literature in accordance with its national character, and therefore merits its own specific literary criticism (often with its peculiar traditions and even methodologies) originated, expanded and triumphed during the nineteenth century, and is still considered valid by a great deal of contemporary Literary Studies.

This division, which may have been useful and productive in the past two centuries, is unable to respond to literary phenomena, which not only transgress boundaries, but also originate in the frontiers between different languages and 'nations'. In the context of multilingualism or multiculturalism, or in the context of identitarian or political articulations this cannot correspond to the divisions established in the nineteenth or twentieth centuries. The Iberian Peninsula, considered as a whole, is in fact inapprehensible by purely national and monolinguistic criteria, and offers plenty of examples of such dislocation: the Luso-Galician poetry of the Middle Ages; authors from Catalonia or Valencia who abandoned their mother tongue to write in Spanish; or bilingual writers between two Iberian languages like Luís de Camões, Boscán or Gil Vicente, among others.

However, Iberian Studies should not be limited to dealing with this type of phenomena. The consideration of the Iberian Peninsula as a multilingual cultural continuum, within a general and fundamental theoretical principle, can be applied to the study of many other texts, authors or events which manifest the inherent correlation of the different linguistic and cultural areas that constitute the Iberian Peninsula. We have, for instance, the use of Portuguese topics in Spanish Golden Age drama; the complex and varied network of affections and projects that link Portugal with Catalonia, Galicia or the Basque Country during the second half of the nineteenth century or the first half of the twentieth century; or the contemporary efforts of Basque, Galician and Catalonian writers to create a literary system apart from, or as a part of, the Spanish one. It could be argued then and quite paradoxically, that Iberian Studies are-and-are-not a part of Comparative Literature. They are, in the most traditional sense of the concept, 'Comparative Literature', whenever literatures in two or more languages are contrasted with each other. However, from an Iberian perspective, when they deal with matters of identity and representation, which may very well belong to 'just' one linguistic or literary system, they cannot be considered as Comparative, at least in the more traditional sense of the word.

This definition of the field is still tentative, nonetheless, one thing is clear: a conference, publication or department labelled as 'Iberian' should not consist in the juxtaposition of Spanish, Portuguese and (if that is the case) Galician, Basque or Catalonian Studies, but deal with interrelations among them, with affinities and differences, with attractions, mutual exclusions, influences and intertextualities; with their reciprocal translations and their effects in both literary systems. Iberian Studies could therefore encompass a wide range of works dealing with issues of identity, language, multiculturalism, and cultural or literary relations beyond linguistic or national boundaries within the Peninsula. For instance, the formation and representation of (national) identities in the Iberian Peninsula from the nineteenth to the twenty-first centuries has obvious interest for the constitution of this field since it is almost impossible to explain the formation and evolution of each of the identities of the Iberian Peninsula without understanding the way it relates to others, or at least to some of them.

From a historical and critical perspective, it is obvious that the geographical or linguistic boundaries imposed on any project of literary study are essentially questionable: the label 'Basque literature' is no less, and no more, equivocal than the labels of 'Spanish', 'European' or 'Western' literature, some of which are often used with the alleged univocity of all things that are self-evident as long as you do not think too much about them. The same can be said about the term 'Iberian Literature': while it defines its limits in what seems to be a fairly self-explanatory way, there are still many questions that need to be answered. For instance, how do these studies of Iberian literatures deal with its insularities, or with what in earlier times were Iberian colonies, including Latin America or the Lusophone world? Is this Iberian division strong enough to justify the exclusion of Basque literature written in Iparralde, the French part of the Basque Country? How about Latin, Arab or Hebrew writers in the Peninsula? Are writers from modern-day Gibraltar British, Iberian, or both?

So far, most of these questions have been avoided by scholars dealing with Iberian literary relations by focusing on unproblematic cases of modern and contemporary texts and authors (especially nineteenth- and twentieth-century literary relations between Portugal and other parts of the Peninsula). Of course, there are some extremely suggestive studies devoted to previous centuries (for instance, the aforementioned special issue by *Colóquio/Letras*, or the work by Maria Idalina Resina Rodrigues). However, I propose that it would be most fruitful to conduct research into this continuity of the Iberian Peninsula in times when no modern identity had yet been formed; periods in which the anachronism of national divisions in literature is more obvious.

In short, we need to be aware that any geographical or linguistic cut in the stream and turmoil of literary relations will be polemical and that the Iberian Peninsula, as we envisage it, is indeed a complex and relatively unitary system. It is not isolated, but should be considered in the light of wider constructions to which it belongs: the Romance continuum, from Lisbon to Constanța; the European and Western literary system, or the vast field of World Literature. The concept of 'South' applied to the Iberian Peninsula and other Southern Peninsulas reminds us that, even if Iberia is a specific and unique literary space, its conceptualization and ideological reconfiguration can and should be contrasted with that of other areas which may have followed similar paths.

Something must also be said on the type of cultural objects with which Iberian Studies deal: are they restricted to Literary Studies, or do they belong to the wider field of Cultural Studies or to the recently reformulated Area Studies? I think this is a key question at the present time that has yet to be resolved. It is one which will be addressed in the successive chapters of this volume. Even a cursory glance at the relevant bibliography cited above reveals an image of division around two poles: while most of the key publications[24] are strictly devoted to linguistic and literary aspects, others, such as Buffery, Davis and Hooper, Sáez Delgado or Martínez Gil, supersede the limits of Literary Studies to include wider historical, cultural and artistic elements. This volume, on the other hand, navigates these uncertain waters: while primarily focusing on literary texts and authors, some chapters will undertake the analysis of historical, artistic or cinematographic objects which would not be included in a more traditional approach to Literary Studies. This decision is crucial to our purpose: we are not just

---

24   Magalhães, *RELIPES*; Cabo *et al.*, *A Comparative History of Literatures*.

talking about including some topics and scholars and excluding others from this new field, but determining its epistemological location and filiations. If Iberian Studies are to have a future existence as a scientific field, there are three essential requirements: theoretical reflections on their specificity, their methodologies, and the specific set(s) of phenomena with which they work; networks of communication that allow scholars working in this area to communicate with each other; and some level of institutional or academic recognition. This publication aims at contributing to fulfil these requirements.

Works cited

Abreu, Maria Fernanda de, *Cervantes no Romantismo Português: cavaleiros andantes, manuscritos encontrados e gargalhadas moralíssimas* (Lisbon: Editorial Estampa, 1994).

Araújo, Teresa, *Portugal e Espanha: diálogos e reflexos literários* (Lisbon and Faro: Centro de Estudos Linguísticos e Literários da Universidade do Algarve/Instituto de Estudos sobre o Romanceiro Velho e Tradicional, 2004).

Besse, Maria Graciete, org., *Cultures lusophones et hispanophones: penser la relation* (Paris: Indigo & Côté-Femmes, 2010).

Buffery, Helena, Stuart Davis, and Kirsty Hooper, eds, *Reading Iberia: Theory/History/ Identity* (Oxford: Peter Lang, 2007).

Cabo Aseguinolaza, Fernando, Anxo Abuín, and César Domínguez, *A Comparative History of Literatures in the Iberian Peninsula*, 2 vols (Amsterdam and Philadelphia: John Benjamins, 2010).

Colóquio/Letras. Suplemento – Siglo de Oro: relações hispano-portuguesas no séc. XVII 178 (September–December 2011).

Damrosch, David, *What Is World Literature?* (Princeton: Princeton University Press, 2003).

Epps, Brad, and Luis Fernández Cifuentes, *Spain beyond Spain. Modernity, Literary History and National Identity* (Lewisburg, PA: Bucknell University Press, 2005).

Even-Zohar, Itamar, 'The Role of Literature in the Making of the Nations of Europe: A Socio-semiotic Study', *Applied Semiotics/Sémiotique appliquée* 1/1 (1996), 39–59.

Faber, Sebastiaan, 'Economies of Prestige: The Place of Iberian Studies in the American University', *Hispanic Research Journal* 9/1 (2008), 7–32.

Fernandes, Ângela *et al.*, eds, *Diálogos Ibéricos e Iberoamericanos: actas del VI congreso internacional de ALEPH* (Lisbon: Centro de Estudos Comparatistas da Universidade de Lisboa/Editorial Academia del Hispanismo, 2010).

Gallén, Enric, Francisco Lafarga, and Luis Pegenaute, eds, *Traducción y autotraducción en las literaturas ibéricas* (series 'Relaciones literarias en el ámbito hispánico: traducción, literatura y cultura') (Bern: Peter Lang, 2011).

Lafarga, Francisco, Luis Pegenaute, and Enric Gallén, eds, *Interacciones entre las literaturas ibéricas* (series 'Relaciones literarias en el ámbito hispánico: traducción, literatura y cultura') (Bern: Peter Lang, 2010).

Lotman, Yuri, 'On the Semiosphere', *Sign Systems Studies* 33/1 (2005), 205–29.

Lourenço, António Apolinário, *Estudos de Literatura Comparada Luso-Espanhola* (Coimbra: Centro de Literatura Portuguesa da Faculdade de Letras da Universidade de Coimbra, 2005).

Magalhães, Gabriel, *Garrett e Rivas. O Romantismo em Espanha e Portugal*, 2 vols (Lisbon: Imprensa Nacional–Casa da Moeda, 2009).

——, ed., *Actas do Congresso RELIPES III: 18, 19 e 20 de Abril de 2007* (Covilhã: Universidade da Beira Interior, 2007).

——, ed., *RELIPES. Relações Linguísticas e Literárias entre Portugal e Espanha desde os Inícios do Século XIX até à Actualidade* (Covilhã and Salamanca: Universidade da Beira Interior/Celya, 2007).

Martín-Estudillo, Luis, and Nicholas Spadaccini, eds, *New Spain, New Literatures* (Nashville: Vanderbilt University Press, 2010).

Martínez Gil, Víctor, *Portugal y Cataluña ante la modernidad: intercambios artísticos y literarios* (Badajoz: Sociedad Cultural de Conmemoraciones Culturales/MEIAC, 2010).

Pegenaute, Luis, Enric Gallén, and Francisco Lafarga, eds, *Relaciones entre las literaturas ibéricas y las literaturas extranjeras* (series 'Relaciones literarias en el ámbito hispánico: traducción, literatura y cultura') (Bern: Peter Lang, 2011).

Pérez Isasi, Santiago, 'Imágenes de la Península Ibérica en la historiografía literaria romántica', in Maria Jesús Fernández García and María Luísa Leal, coords, *Imagologías ibéricas: construyendo la imagen del otro peninsular* (Mérida: Gabinete de Iniciativas Transfronterizas del Gobierno de Extremadura, 2012), 181–98.

Resina, Joan Ramon, *Del hispanismo a los estudios ibéricos. Una propuesta federativa para el ámbito cultural* (Madrid: Biblioteca Nueva, 2009).

Revista de História das Ideias. Ibéria 31 (2010).

Ribera Llopis, Juan Miguel, and Antonio Arroyo Almaraz, eds, *Literaturas peninsulares en contacto: castellana, catalana, gallega y vasca* (Madrid: Universidad Complutense/Editorial Complutense, 2008).

Rodrigues, Maria Idalina Resina, *Estudos Ibéricos – Da Cultura à Literatura: pontos de encontro, séculos XIII a XVII* (Lisbon: Instituto de Cultura e Língua Portuguesa, 1987).

Sáez Delgado, Antonio, and Luis Manuel Gaspar, eds, *Suroeste: relaciones literarias y artísticas entre Portugal y España (1890–1936)* (Madrid: MEIAC, 2010).

Szanton, David, ed., *The Politics of Knowledge: Area Studies and the Disciplines* (Berkeley: University of California Press, 2004).

TERESA PINHEIRO

Iberian and European Studies – Archaeology of a New Epistemological Field

The present chapter aims at developing some preliminary and tentative thoughts on the potential shape of Iberian Studies as a part of a wider research field called European Studies. I will seek to establish connections between Iberian and European Studies using a cultural perspective as opposed to Literary Studies, and will analyse the example of Germany in order to support my reflection with empirical data. Germany is not an exception or an isolated case in Europe, so that the following reflections can be considered as a case study for a wider, European, context.

In the first section, I will go back in time to see how the Iberian Peninsula has been studied in Germany since the nineteenth century. This will bring us to two different traditions of study: Philology, on the one hand, and Area Studies, on the other. Since what is happening today to Iberian Studies is due in part to Area Studies, the second part of the chapter deals with the renewal of Area Studies in Germany today. Finally – in part three – I will sum up the potentials of Iberian Studies in its intersections with European Area Studies.

I. Iberian Studies in Germany

The origins of Iberian Studies in Germany go back to the study of foreign languages and literatures during the nineteenth century. In that period, Philology was established as a scientific field at German universities. The term 'Philology' attaches great importance to language and literature. One of the main concerns of traditional Philology was to translate major literary works from other national literatures into German. Another concern involved language study, especially by editing grammars of foreign languages. The publication of the first volume of Friedrich Dietz's grammar of Romance languages in 1836 became a myth of origin in Romance Philology. Nevertheless, in the decades immediately after Dietz's grammar, Romance Philology was still merged with the study of other philologies as in the *Jahrbuch für romanische und englische Literatur* [Yearbook for Romance and English Literature] (founded in 1859) and the *Archiv für das Studium der neueren Sprachen und Literaturen* [Archive for the Study of Modern Languages and Literatures] (founded in 1846). It was not until the end of the nineteenth century, however, that Romance Philology as a scientific field was institutionally recognized. In 1877, the *Zeitschrift für Romanische Philologie* [Journal for Romance Philology] was founded and this became a milestone for establishing Romance Philology independently from the study of other modern languages and literatures.[1]

Spanish and Portuguese Philology remained for a long time as an institutional part of Romance Philology. The main concern of Romance Philology in Germany with regard to Spanish and Portuguese literature was also the study of language and literature. In accordance with scientific orthodoxy during the nineteenth century, Linguistics was dominated by a historical approach. To study the Spanish and Portuguese languages meant classifying them within the history of Romance languages.[2] The study of literature was focused mainly on what was considered to be the most significant works of national literature, like Cervantes's *Don Quijote* and Camões's *Os Lusíadas*.[3]

1   Dietrich Briesemeister and Axel Schönberger, *Bestandsaufnahme und Zukunftsperspektiven der deutschsprachigen Lusitanistik. Standpunkte und Thesen* (Frankfurt a.M.: TFM, 1998).
2   Thomas Bräutigam, *Hispanistik im Dritten Reich: eine wissenschaftsgeschichtliche Studie* (Frankfurt a.M.: Vervuert, 1997), 18.
3   Matthias Perl and Gudrun Pfeiffer, 'Gedanken zur Entwicklung der lusitanistischen Lehre und Forschung an den deutschen Universitäten', in Axel Schönberger

World War I inaugurated a renewed interest in both the Portuguese-
and Spanish-speaking worlds. The study of Iberian languages and literatures merged with the political and economic interests of the German
governments in Portugal, Spain and Latin America, giving origin to an
epistemological field called *Kulturraumstudien*, which was concerned with
economic, political, and social issues relevant for the understanding of a
cultural area.[4] Bernhard Schädel founded in 1911 a section for Romance
languages and cultures within the Colonial Institute in Hamburg. This
section had a special focus on Portugal, Spain and – especially – Latin
America. Other than Classical Philology, the Romance Section was not
devoted to linguistics and literary criticism, but rather to more contemporary aspects of society and politics.[5] In 1912 a Deutsch-Südamerikanisches
Institut [German-South American Institute] was founded in Aachen, and
in 1917 the Ibero-Amerikanisches Institut [Ibero-American Institute] was
inaugurated in Hamburg. The Journal *Iberica* (published between 1924 and
1927) included contributions on Geography, Anthropology and Economics
and can be seen as a first step towards the establishment of a field of knowledge called Iberian Area Studies in Germany. Also the foundation of the
Ibero-Amerikanisches Institut in Berlin in 1930 contributed to this German
tradition of Area Studies, called *Landeskunde*.[6]

The end of World War II brought with it the end of the geopolitical
dimension of Iberian Studies and a return to the tradition of philology.
From the 1960s onwards, Romance Philologies became more and more
distinct as autonomous epistemological fields, established according to individual languages. The emancipation of Hispanic Philology from Romance
Philology occurred in 1977, as the Association for Hispanic Studies was
founded. This Association had, in fact, a focus not only on Spanish, but

and Michael Scotti-Rosin, eds, *Zur Wissenschaftsgeschichte der deutschsprachigen
Lusitanistik* (Frankfurt a.M.: TFM, 1990), 44.
4   Hans-Jürgen Lüsebrink, 'Kulturraumstudien und Interkulturelle Kommunikation', in
Ansgar Nünning and Vera Nünning, eds, *Konzepte der Kulturwissenschaft. Theoretische
Grundlagen – Ansätze – Perspektiven* (Stuttgart: Metzler, 2003), 308.
5   Bräutigam, *Hispanistik*, 22.
6   Perl and Pfeiffer, 'Gedanken zur Entwicklung', 46.

also on Portuguese and Catalan languages and literatures. It was not until 1987 that an Association for Catalan Studies was founded; the Association for Portuguese Studies was institutionalized even later, in 1993. All three associations hold a meeting every two years, in which sections traditionally devoted to linguistics and literature are organized.

II. Area Studies in Germany today

The epistemological field of Area Studies as an interdisciplinary field of research on a specific geopolitical region – which could be compared with the German *Kulturraumstudien* – goes back to the first half of the twentieth century in the USA. Area Studies have never been conceived as a discipline, but rather as a consortium of several disciplines – political and social sciences, economics, anthropology, history, linguistics, and so on. All of these disciplines have in common the promotion of research on the same region. As a consequence, we scarcely find Area Studies attached to departments, but rather to centres. This rather traditional form of Area Studies – as it emerged in the 1940s in the USA – has two main characteristics: first, the researchers did not usually focus their research interests on Europe; Africa, Latin America, Japan, China, South Asia, and the Soviet and post-Soviet world – these are the classical regions that American Area Studies are about. Europe was not traditionally a subject, with the exception of Eastern Europe. This is due to the geopolitical context of the Cold War. Western Europe has been seen as a part of the democratic world against communism, and, consequently, there has been no need to get to know this region better. As Comisso and Gutierrez stress: perhaps even more than Area Studies in other regions of the world, East European studies in the United States developed as an artefact of the

Cold War';[7] second, American Area Studies traditionally deal with Otherness. They were, at the beginning, concerned with regions outside the USA, consequently with different languages, different cultures and different political institutions. Moreover, it was precisely the fact that these regions were different that made it necessary to develop interdisciplinary areas for studying them.

Especially after the fall of the Iron Curtain, this concept of Area Studies became more and more criticized in the humanities and social sciences. They have been accused of being committed to American political concerns during the Cold War and of generating uncritical positivist knowledge of foreign cultures and societies, without considering theoretical frameworks from the social sciences. Finally, Area Studies were also criticized for ignoring the local context of social research, for not paying attention to what Chinese social scientists, for example, said on Chinese social phenomena.[8]

This criticism did not lead to the end of Area Studies, but rather to its re-evaluation. In fact, notwithstanding the end of the Cold War, the fact is that nowadays it is still necessary to generate knowledge about certain world regions, not in the narrow context of USA Cold War affairs, but in the wider realm of the current international politics that followed the dismantlement of the Soviet Union, the rise of economic powers in Asia, such as China, Japan and Southeast Asia, and in Latin America, and the rise of religious fundamentalist movements in the Islamic World.[9] Africa is an especially important partner in Europe, due to its historical and geographical proximity. This context stimulated a rethinking of the theoretical foundations of Area Studies. Some points of innovation are direct responses to the critiques:

---

7   Ellen Comisso and Brad Gutierrez, 'Eastern Europe or Central Europe? Exploring a Distinct Regional Identity', in David Szanton, ed., *The Politics of Knowledge. Area Studies and the Disciplines* (Berkeley: University of California Press, 2004), 262.

8   David Szanton, 'Introduction: The Origin, Nature, and Challenges of Area Studies in the United States', in David Szanton, ed., *The Politics of Knowledge. Area Studies and the Disciplines* (Berkeley: University of California Press, 2004), 19.

9   Lüsebrink, 'Kulturraumstudien', 308.

- A denial of essentialist concepts of culture. Cultures are no longer seen as homogeneous and holistic. They are rather conceived as blurred, in constant change, being steadily contested and recreated in communication processes.[10] The cultural turn in the humanities and social sciences introduced a semiotic concept of culture,[11] including all forms of meaning generation in society.
- An openness to cross-cultural processes. Area Studies tend to pay more attention to Diasporas, to the flow of populations within the area of study, but also from and to other world regions. Migration and exile, but also any other forms of mobility, therefore tend to become central themes of contemporary Area Studies.
- Cross-national collaboration, involving experts from the region to be studied as well as third-country researchers. This means that USA researchers working on Thailand collaborate with Thai researchers as insiders, but also with Canadian or Thailand experts from Africa. By these means, generating knowledge about a certain region becomes more deterritorialized due to the mutual influence of different perspectives, research agendas and theoretical traditions.[12]

As a consequence of this reassessment, a revival of Area Studies in the USA and in Europe takes place. The revival of Area Studies in Europe can easily be seen in the case of Germany. The Bundesministerium für Bildung und Forschung (BMBF) [German Ministry for Education and Research] initiated a programme aimed at increasing Area Studies in German research centres. The Ministry justifies the need for Area Studies in Germany with the context of globalization:

10   James Clifford, *The Predicament of Culture. Twentieth-Century Ethnography, Literature, and Art* (Cambridge, MA: Harvard University Press, 1988).
11   Clifford Geertz, *The Interpretation of Cultures. Selected Essays* (New York: Basic Books, 1973).
12   Szanton, 'Introduction', 29.

Der Bedarf an fundiertem Wissen über andere Regionen der Welt wächst stetig. Angesichts von Globalisierungsprozessen und Wanderungsbewegungen gewinnen Kenntnisse lokaler und regionaler sowie transnationaler und transkultureller Gegebenheiten und Beziehungen eine immer größere Bedeutung. Die Nachfrage nach geistes- und sozialwissenschaftlicher Expertise durch Politik, Kultur und Wirtschaft reicht dabei über die kurzfristige und punktuelle Behandlung von Themen, Regionen und Verflechtungen hinaus. Regierungen, Medien, Unternehmen, Verbände oder Organisationen der Entwicklungspolitik fragen Forschung und Beratung nach, um aktuelle Probleme und Konflikte lösen zu können.[13]

[The need for well-founded knowledge about other regions of the world is constantly growing. Globalization processes and migration movements make it necessary to generate the knowledge of local, regional, and transnational areas. The demand for expertise from the humanities and social sciences in politics and economics goes beyond the selective treatment of topics and regions and makes it necessary to develop systematic research capable of being applied in order to solve current problems and conflicts.][14]

Defining what should be understood under Area Studies in a German academic context, the BMBF stresses its interdisciplinarity as it argues that Area Studies analyse cultural, political, economic, religious, social, and juristic relations and exchanges in their global dimension.[15] The BMBF concedes that there exists authoritative research on world regions, cultures, and states, but criticizes the fact that this kind of expertise is dominated by philological disciplines. The aim of BMBF is thus to open Philologies to interdisciplinary research.

Also symptomatic of this renewal of Area Studies in Germany is the programmatic paper for the development of Area Studies in Germany published in 2006 by the Scientific Council of Germany, the Wissenschaftsrat. The paper is entitled *Recommendations for Area Studies in Universities and*

---

13 Angelika Willms-Herget, 'Bekanntmachung des Bundesministeriums für Bildung und Forschung von Förderrichtlinien zur Stärkung und Weiterentwicklung der Regionalstudien (Area Studies)', in *Bundesministerium für Bildung und Forschung* (2008) <http://bmbf.de/foerderungen/13101.php> accessed 2 September 2012.

14 Unless otherwise stated, all translations are my own.

15 Willms-Herget, 'Bekanntmachung des Bundesministeriums'.

other Research Institutions.[16] The paper aims at mapping existing research centres in Germany, which are already practising Area Studies. Taking this mapping as a starting point, it makes recommendations on how to increase the study of foreign regions of the world. The *Recommendations* encourage a modern understanding of what Area Studies should be nowadays. The authors of the paper stress that regional unities are not static, but rather constantly in change due to migration movements, globalization phenomena, or political upheavals.[17] The concept adopted by the Wissenschaftsrat[18] takes up the American tradition of Area Studies, meaning the generation of knowledge concerning a given region, without claiming to be a discipline. On the contrary, it stresses the need for interdisciplinary co-operation between the humanities and social sciences. But Area Studies as understood in the *Recommendations* is not a simple transfer of American Area Studies to the German context; it stands rather in the German tradition of research on overseas regions, starting with the interdisciplinary scientific work by Alexander von Humboldt on South America and culminating in the establishment of overseas institutes during the imperial age in the nineteenth and twentieth centuries.

From both the programme of the German Ministry for Education and Research and the Scientific Council of Germany we can infer which regions are currently important for Germany. The Wissenschaftsrat lists the following 'areas': Africa, North America, Asia (without Near East), Europe (without Eastern and Northern Europe), Latin America, Northern Europe, Eastern Europe, and Near East. This list shows that Area Studies in Europe are not only focused on 'Otherness', but they are also interested in Europe itself. So, it would appear that German Area Studies are not only concerned about getting to know distant regions outside Europe, but it is also about understanding Europe's diversity better.

16   Wissenschaftsrat, ed., *Empfehlungen zu den Regionalstudien (Area Studies) in den Hochschulen und außeruniversitären Forschungseinrichtungen* (Mainz: Wissenschaftsrat, 2006).
17   Wissenschaftsrat, *Empfehlungen*, 7–8.
18   The words 'Regionalstudien' and 'Area Studies' are used in the *Recommendations* synonymously.

In fact, by the end of the twentieth century, there were important changes, which contributed to the institutionalization of 'European Studies' as Area Studies in German universities. The emergence of this new field of academic studies is related to the process of European integration, especially after the fall of the Iron Curtain. In the last two decades, the European Union more than doubled the number of member states from twelve in 1986 to twenty-seven in 2007. It expanded more and more through the years, so that the small nucleus of countries from Central Europe began to include increasingly disparate regions, from South Western and South Eastern to Eastern Europe. There was a need to know these regions better, and this stimulated the emergence of European Studies as Area Studies in German universities and research centres. Most centres and institutes for European Studies in Germany combine the knowledge of European institutions with Area Studies from different regions of Europe, normally making a distinction between Western and Eastern Europe. What countries are included in these wider regions depends on the departmental strategy of each university.

III. Iberian and European Studies

What kind of epistemological field could Iberian Studies occupy within the framework of European Area Studies? Iberian Studies can learn much from Area Studies, especially from the more self-reflexive research of the last decades. In what follows, I would like to point out some of the possibilities of Iberian Studies in this context.

First, Iberian Studies can learn from Area Studies by overcoming national boundaries and studying more cross-cultural phenomena. Since Iberia can be defined as neither a state nor a nation, the risk of falling into national categories like Spain or Portugal can be reduced. This is distinct from traditional Philologies, which refer to the national domain, Spanish Philology or Portuguese Philology.

Secondly, and as a consequence of this, Iberian Studies open up the research horizon of cross-cultural relationships as a way of deterritorializing the Iberian Peninsula. I see three distinct possible directions for cross-cultural relationships:

- To look beyond Spain and Portugal as states, rather searching for relations among the different cultures of the Iberian Peninsula. Some examples of this kind of research could be the analysis of the relationship between Portugal and Catalonia during the Portuguese Restoration War and the Catalan Revolt in the seventeenth century; the relationship between Portugal and Galicia; the tension between political periphery and centralism in Spain but also the relation between the national peripheries, e.g. nation-discourses during the Galician *Rexurdimento* and the Catalan *Renaixença*; migration movements within the Peninsula.
- To look for intersections with other cultural areas outside the Peninsula. Research on migration and Diaspora is of huge importance for the study of cross-cultural relationships. Some examples are the Portuguese, Galician, Basque, Castilian or Catalan Diasporas in France, Germany or Latin America, but also migration in the opposite direction: German, Latin American or Eastern European immigration in Catalonia, Madrid, Lisbon or the Algarve. Migration flows change both the origin and the receiving societies, creating a third space of collective identity and offer the possibility of overcoming the analytical category of the nation-state in search of cross-cultural relationships.[19] For Iberian Studies, this means that the nation-state is but just one level of study, in concurrence with regions, nationalities and languages, within or outside the Iberian territory.
- Thirdly, to insert Iberian Studies as one among other Area Studies within European Studies offers the opportunity for comparative analysis especially with Eastern Europe or South-Eastern Europe. Migration, national and regional identities, former dictatorships, and

19   Szanton, 'Introduction', 28.

the politics of memory are some of the themes common to Eastern European and Iberian Studies. Bringing experts of both regions together should enrich the research on these areas. Some examples of this practice of comparative Area Studies show that this is already a reality. The International Society for Iberian and Slavonic Studies (CompaRes) was founded in 2007 and aims at promoting comparative research between Eastern Europe and the Iberian Peninsula. One example of this is given by the latest volume promoted by CompaRes devoted to a comparative analysis on the ways of coming to terms with the authoritarian regimes in Iberian and Eastern European countries.[20] Also the Geisteswissenschaftliches Zentrum Geschichte und Kultur Ostmitteleuropas an der Universität Leipzig (GWZO) [Research Institute for Eastern European Studies in Leipzig] has been editing books on Comparative Iberian and Eastern European Studies, especially on the politics of memory.[21] But it is not only Iberia in contrast with other European regions which can provide the framework for Iberian Studies. 'Genuine' comparative research on the Iberian Peninsula itself should be part of Iberian Studies, e.g. comparisons on the politics of memory at the level of the nation-state (Portugal, Spain), of the region (e.g. Madeira, Galicia), or at the more local level (Porto, Cáceres, Vic).

Finally, I would point out a fourth aspect, which Iberian Studies can benefit from the renewed Area Studies. As previously stressed, contemporary

---

20 Teresa Pinheiro, Beata Cieszynska, and Eduardo Franco, eds, *Peripheral Identities: Iberia and Eastern Europe Between the Dictatorial Past and the European Present* (Warschau u.a.: PearlBooks, 2011). See also Beata Elzbieta Cieszynska, ed., *Iberian and Slavonic Cultures: Contact and Comparison* (Lisbon and Warschau: CompaRes, 2007).

21 Krysztof Ruchniewicz and Stefan Troebst, eds, *Diktaturbewältigung und nationale Selbstvergewisserung. Geschichtskulturen in Polen und Spanien im Vergleich* (Wroclaw: Wydawnictwo Uniwersytetu Wrocławskiego, 2004); Stefan Troebst, ed., *Postdiktatorische Geschichtskulturen im Süden und Osten Europas* (Göttingen: Wallstein, 2010).

Area Studies overcome the unilateral practice of traditional Area Studies by means of connecting not only to local research but also to research centres in other regions. Iberian Studies could gain by expanding collaboration to other countries within or outside Europe. Each country has its own specific research agendas and specific scientific traditions that influence its approach to cultural and social phenomena. Exchange between them on common themes can enrich research. Two examples from the German–Iberian scientific exchange should illustrate this. The first example is the phenomenon of Nationalism. Due to Germany's own history, translating the cultural and social phenomenon of the Basque, Galician, or Catalan Nationalism to German researchers is likely to engender diverging reactions and interpretations. An important task of researchers as go-betweens in Area Studies should be precisely to promote dialogue and to identify sources of misunderstanding. Another example that concerns the study of Nationalism is the exhaustive and self-critical debate on the causes and consequences of Nazi Germany which put the deconstruction of Nationalism into the agenda of the cultural and social sciences in Germany. Portuguese and Spanish research has been profiting from this perspective especially in dealing with their recent history of dictatorship and war in the twentieth century.[22] Maintaining the scientific exchange is a way of avoiding 'the kind of isolated and parochial theorizing which is so much the subject of postmodernist critique.'[23]

These are just some of the examples of how Iberian Studies can learn from Area Studies. There is, however, a fundamental difference between Iberian and Area Studies. This is not an epistemological, but rather an

---

22   One example of this was the symposium *Kultur des Erinnerns. Vergangenheits-bewältigung in Spanien und Deutschland*, organized by the Instituto Cervantes in Berlin and the Goethe-Institut in Madrid on politics of memory in Spain and Germany today. Ignacio Olmos and Nikky Keilholz-Rühle, eds, *Kultur des Erinnerns. Vergangenheitsbewältigung in Spanien und Deutschland* (Frankfurt a.M.: Vervuert, 2009).

23   Paul W. Drake and Lisa Hilbink, 'Latin American Studies: Theory and Practice', in David Szanton, ed., *The Politics of Knowledge. Area Studies and the Disciplines* (Berkeley: University of California Press, 2004), 60.

institutional difference. As stressed before, Area Studies are not attached to departments, but rather to interdisciplinary research centres. Such centres integrate experts from several disciplines that share a common work area on a certain region. But this is not the case of Iberian Studies in Germany, first and foremost, because there are not only a few universities with Iberian Studies and, secondly, because Iberian Studies are integrated in departments with no more than one or two Full Professors of Iberian Studies at most. How can we integrate interdisciplinary perspectives of research as Area Studies do, without having a team of social scientists, historians, anthropologists, linguistics, and so on?

One way of combining both aspects could be through Iberian Cultural Studies. What I mean by this is the study of culture, and understanding culture from a semiotic point of view: 'Culture is the sum of all social meaning produced in communication processes in societies'.[24] The task of Iberian Studies would then be to study social discourses produced in Iberian societies. This being so, the Spanish Constitution of 1978 is as much a vehicle of social discourse as is the *Estatut d'Autonomia de Catalunya*, works by Castelao, the new monument in Lisbon in honour of the colonial war, press articles on the victory of La Roja in the World Cup, or the website of the Galician Immigrants' Association in Nuremberg. These are all examples of social discourses, which give insight into the way societies construct their own identity or contest hegemonic identities.

Adopting the perspective of Cultural Studies means looking below social discourses and asking why at a certain time certain assertions were made. Trying to understand social discourses brings with it the analysis of power relations in several fields of a society – from politics to economics and history – without falling into the temptation of generating naïve positivist knowledge on supposedly holistic nations made of homogeneous Spaniards or of homogeneous Portuguese.

24 Geertz, *The Interpretation*, 5.

Works cited

Bräutigam, Thomas, *Hispanistik im Dritten Reich: eine wissenschaftsgeschichtliche Studie* (Frankfurt a.m.: Vervuert, 1997).

Briesemeister, Dietrich, and Axel Schönberger, *Bestandsaufnahme und Zukunftsperspektiven der deutschsprachigen Lusitanistik. Standpunkte und Thesen* (Frankfurt a.m.: TFM, 1998).

Cieszynska, Beata Elzbieta, ed., *Iberian and Slavonic Cultures: Contact and Comparison* (Lisbon and Warschau: CompaRes, 2007).

Clifford, James, *The Predicament of Culture. Twentieth-Century Ethnography, Literature, and Art* (Cambridge, MA: Harvard University Press, 1988).

Comisso, Ellen, and Brad Gutierrez, 'Eastern Europe or Central Europe? Exploring a Distinct Regional Identity', in David Szanton, ed., *The Politics of Knowledge. Area Studies and the Disciplines* (Berkeley: University of California Press, 2004), 262–313.

Drake, Paul W., and Lisa Hilbink, 'Latin American Studies: Theory and Practice', in David Szanton, ed., *The Politics of Knowledge. Area Studies and the Disciplines* (Berkeley: University of California Press, 2004), 34–73.

Geertz, Clifford, *The Interpretation of Cultures. Selected Essays* (New York: Basic Books, 1973).

Lüsebrink, Hans-Jürgen, 'Kulturraumstudien und Interkulturelle Kommunikation', in Ansgar Nünning and Vera Nünning, eds, *Konzepte der Kulturwissenschaft. Theoretische Grundlagen – Ansätze – Perspektiven* (Stuttgart: Metzler, 2003), 307–28.

Olmos, Ignacio, and Nikky Keilholz-Rühle, eds, *Kultur des Erinnerns. Vergangenheitsbewältigung in Spanien und Deutschland* (Frankfurt a.M.: Vervuert, 2009).

Perl, Matthias, and Gudrun Pfeiffer, 'Gedanken zur Entwicklung der lusitanistischen Lehre und Forschung an den deutschen Universitäten', in Axel Schönberger and Michael Scotti-Rosin, eds, *Zur Wissenschaftsgeschichte der deutschsprachigen Lusitanistik* (Frankfurt a.M.: TFM, 1990), 41–53.

Pinheiro, Teresa, Beata Cieszynska, and Eduardo Franco, eds, *Peripheral Identities: Iberia and Eastern Europe Between the Dictatorial Past and the European Present* (Warschau u.a.: PearlBooks, 2011).

Ruchniewicz, Krysztof, and Stefan Troebst, eds, *Diktaturbewältigung und nationale Selbstvergewisserung. Geschichtskulturen in Polen und Spanien im Vergleich* (Wroclaw: Wydawnictwo Uniwersytetu Wrocławskiego, 2004).

Szanton, David, 'Introduction: The Origin, Nature, and Challenges of Area Studies in the United States', in David Szanton, ed., *The Politics of Knowledge. Area Studies and the Disciplines* (Berkeley: University of California Press, 2004), 1–33.

Troebst, Stefan, ed., *Postdiktatorische Geschichtskulturen im Süden und Osten Europas* (Göttingen: Wallstein, 2010).

Willms-Herget, Angelika, 'Bekanntmachung des Bundesministeriums für Bildung und Forschung von Förderrichtlinien zur Stärkung und Weiterentwicklung der Regionalstudien (Area Studies)', in *Bundesministerium für Bildung und Forschung* (2008) <http://bmbf.de/foerderungen/13101.php> accessed 2 September 2012.

Wissenschaftsrat, ed., *Empfehlungen zu den Regionalstudien (Area Studies) in den Hochschulen und außeruniversitären Forschungseinrichtungen* (Mainz: Wissenschaftsrat, 2006).

JOHN MACKLIN

Modernism and Modernity: Iberian Perspectives

Re-inscriptions of Iberia, Iberian culture, and Iberian national identity or identities, and the concomitant question of Iberian Studies, must be accompanied by an awareness of the preoccupations, prejudices and perceptions of those engaging in the re-inscription. While the notion of 'iberismo' assumed an importance in the minds of Antero de Quental and others in the nineteenth century, the emergence of Europe as an economic and increasingly political entity has again pushed the notion of Iberia to the forefront of critical and cultural debates. Hispanists in the United Kingdom, although their emphasis has been on Spain itself, have long been accustomed to seeing the Iberian Peninsula, and its former overseas Empire, as a complex whole. In Spain and Portugal, and to a large extent in the United States, a more fragmented approach is discernible, now being overcome through the work of comparatists, whose work transcends national boundaries and individual disciplines. The concept of Iberian Studies is a challenging one, requiring an interrogation of critical orthodoxies, an investigation into the epistemological foundations of the field from a comparative European and indeed global perspective, an exploration of the validity of the old paradigms together, with an analysis of the potentialities of new directions.[1] The locus of newer approaches is to be found in studies of cultural interaction, of the ways in which texts interact with broader cultural, historical, and social processes at a given moment and in a particular space. In order to contribute to the creation of a map of this emerging (in the Iberian Peninsula at least) area of research, and to offer a comparative European

---

1   Important work in this field has been undertaken already. See, for example, Helena Buffery, Stuart Davis, and Kirsty Hooper, eds, *Reading Iberia: Theory/History/Identity* (Oxford: Peter Lang, 2007).

approach to the relationship between collective identity formation and
the construction of literary narratives, I shall focus on a specific period of
Iberian literary history, always conscious that all these terms are inherently
unstable and provisional. In this chapter, I shall draw on my earlier work
on Modernism in Spain[2] in order to consider the predominance of perio-
dization, the concentration on great writers, and the delineation of a set
of aesthetic practices. The chapter will thus focus on an important literary
period, one which coincides with the great phase of nation-building, both
of which need to be viewed from a European comparative perspective.

The period from about 1870 to 1914, when Modernist writing is generally held to have replaced the aesthetics of Realism, is also the period when
many European nations as we conceive them today emerged. In the case
of the Iberian nations, the pattern is somewhat different. If the marriage
between nation and state is largely a nineteenth-century phenomenon, in
the case of the two nations that make up the Iberian Peninsula, we can trace
their existence to the Middle Ages. Portugal's national boundaries are the
same today as they were in the mid-thirteenth century, when the Portuguese
people rose up against a Castilian king in the name of national sovereignty.
In the case of Spain, today's national boundaries are more or less those
of kingdoms dating from at least the beginning of the sixteenth century.
Although in Spain many languages were spoken, two languages dominated
in Iberia, both of them being lexically very close. But the two nations, notwithstanding the fact that they exhibit great similarities in economic, social
and political development, have experienced two very different routes to
national identity. In some respects, we could say that Portuguese identity
has been forged in relation to Spain, and has been uncontested internally.

---

2   See in particular John Macklin, *The Window and the Garden: The Modernist Fictions
     of Ramón Pérez de Ayala* (Boulder, CO: Society of Spanish and Spanish-American
     Studies, 1988). Also 'Competing Voices: Unamuno's *Niebla* and the Discourse of
     Modernism', in J. J. Macklin, ed., *After Cervantes: A Celebration of 75 Years of Iberian
     Studies at Leeds* (Leeds Iberian Papers) (Leeds: Trinity and All Saints College, 1993),
     167–93, and 'Modernismo, postmodernismo y la novela española de principios de
     siglo: Unamuno y Pérez de Ayala', *Cuadernos para la investigación de la literatura
     hispánica* 20 (1995), 365–74.

Spain's nationalist, essentially Castilian, discourse has, in contrast, been energetically contested from within, and Spain's nation-building in the nineteenth century was fraught with conflict and failure, and its struggle towards modernity was slow and faltering.[3] In both cases, key factors were imperial decline, rural predominance, the gap between economic change and political development, and the conflict between liberalism and reaction, usually identified with traditional Catholicism. If we are to look at Modernism in the Iberian literary space from a comparative European perspective, we need to take this factor into account. One reason for this is that 1898, which marks the ending of the Spanish Empire, is used to define literary history largely in terms of the debate about nationhood. The subsequent *crise de conscience*, the need for regeneration, conceived more as a return to traditional values, corroded by the Renaissance, the Reformation, and the French Revolution, rather than an embracing of modernity, and more introspective forms of writing, are all taken to signal a shift in cultural sensibility. This largely Spanish reading of the period in turn affected the ways in which British configured the Iberian literary space until comparatively recently. Iberian Studies implies a reconsideration of the construction of the discipline in the United Kingdom and its impact on the writing of literary history.

Hispanists, like Lusists, Iberianists, or Catalanists, are scholars from outside the Peninsula who are dedicated to studying its languages and cultures. Curiously, interdisciplinary approaches have in recent decades been complemented by a countertendency to study ever smaller units, a tendency intensified by the creation of institutions such as the Instituto Cervantes (though it is now committed to promoting languages other than Castilian), the Instituto Camões in Portugal, and the Institut Ramón Llull in Catalonia. For many decades in the twentieth century, the discipline of Hispanism in the United Kingdom drew on philological study and focused its scholarship on historical linguistics and medieval texts. In fact, given the initial importance of philological study, arguably it was not until well into

---

3   See Clare Mar-Molinero and Angel Smith, *Nationalism and the Nation in the Iberian Peninsula: Competing and Conflicting Identities* (Oxford: Berg, 1996).

the 1980s that British Hispanism ceased to be dominated by medievalists. Interesting too is the fact the leading early twentieth-century historians of Spain in Spain were philologists, Ramón Menéndez Pidal and Américo Castro being prime examples. Whereas French and German Schools of History had been in existence since the nineteenth century, the Centro de Estudios Históricos [Centre for Historical Studies] was only founded in Spain in 1910, and its Sección de Filología [Philology Section] was its strongest.

This can obscure the fact that Hispanism in the United Kingdom had significantly more practical origins than is often thought to be the case. Several of the earliest Chairs of Spanish – in Liverpool, London, Glasgow, Belfast, for example – were founded, and funded, in universities by wealthy entrepreneurs who feared the country's lack of competitiveness in the markets of Latin America. Indeed, the Stevenson Professor of Spanish at Glasgow was also appointed to the city's College of Commerce with a contractual requirement to teach commercial Spanish there. This general commercial impulse was further stimulated by a Government desire to build its diplomatic expertise in the Spanish-speaking world in the face of increased competition from the United States. The Academy, mainly in the form of the provincial universities, and the first Professors, however, notwithstanding the commercial ethos of the founders, gave the subject the academic orientation and character it developed throughout most of the twentieth century. The point is that the way we configure Iberia is inseparable, in the first instance, from the ethos and demands of the University. And this, in turn, is not divorced from modernity: the United Kingdom Government Committee set up in 1916 to look at these matters was called the Committee on Modern Studies, and modern languages was the focus of their concerns. Due to institutional pressures and the search for economies of scale, small individual language departments merged into larger Schools, some of which included English, thereby preparing the way for a more intercultural approach. In the United Kingdom, Portuguese and Catalan had been included from the outset in 'Spanish' syllabi, more recent additions being Galician and Basque. Thus for British Hispanists, Iberian Studies is hardly a new concept, a fact usually obscured by the ubiquitous use of Hispanic Studies.

Another aspect of the outside configuration of Iberia, which also had a significant impact on the development of the discipline, is the so-called 'myth of the south'.[4] Some of this originates in social Darwinism, and gave rise to the idea that the northern Aryan races are superior to southern Mediterranean ones. Nineteenth-century, and indeed earlier, travellers were attracted to Spain's and Portugal's 'difference', their exotic nature, precisely because they were backward, pre-capitalist, exotic, and therefore dissonant with modernity. They provided a welcome antidote to industrialization and the new capitalism. Spain's strangeness, and the alienation from it of English sensibility, can be appreciated in the uproar when the National Gallery bought a Zurbarán in 1853. *The Times* referred to a 'small, black, repulsive picture'. On the other hand, the Alhambra, declared a national monument in 1874, inspired Victorian fabrics and wallpaper, becoming part of the nineteenth century's Oriental obsession. Much of the fascination Spain held for the British drew inevitably on the legacy of Islam, of which an example is the architect James Murphy's *The Arabian Antiquities of Spain* (1815). To this we can add photography, where the leading exponent is undoubtedly Charles Clifford, who opened a shop in Madrid, which he called the *Daguerrotipo inglés*, and the writings of later travellers such as Gerald Brenan and the Bloomsbury group. Thus, for early Hispanists, the discipline was arguably based upon this idea of a world lost and subsequently romanticized. This is highly relevant to the period – the late nineteenth and early twentieth centuries – on which I wish to concentrate in this chapter. I shall focus on Spain, but it should be remembered that there was a Catalan modernism, known as *modernisme* or *decadentisme*, which marked a kind of return to Romanticism after the hegemony of Naturalism, associated with the poetry of Joan Maragall. These Catalan modernists show their European affinities by drawing on the influences of Carlyle, Ruskin, Nietzsche, and others. Portuguese

4   Key works detailing the attraction of an exotic Spain are Richard Ford's *A Handbook for Travellers in Spain and Readers at Home* (1845), William Maxwell Stirling's *Annals of the Artists of Spain* (1845), and the famous work by George Borrow, *The Bible in Spain: Journeys, Aventures and Imprisonments of an Englishman* (1845).

modernism, similarly influenced by European writing and ideas, appears a little later and is associated with the magazine *Orpheu*, which appeared in 1915, and with writers such as Fernando Pessoa and Mário de Sá-Carneiro. Any wider focus on Iberian Studies would need to embrace the totality of Modernism in Iberia in a way that the traditional Spanish reading has consciously avoided, as I outline below.

Traditionally, Spanish literary history has divided late nineteenth- and early twentieth-century literature into two movements, *modernismo*, originating in Latin America from Symbolist influences and being mainly poetic, and the Generation of 1898, a group of mainly prose writers taking their name from Spain's defeat in 1898 and the loss of the final vestige of its Empire.[5] In this respect, writers in Spain again appear unique in construing a period in literary history in terms of two distinct, and even opposing, movements. In fact, in Spain the notion of the *fin-de-siglo* acquires a kind of fixity, a rootedness, whereas in other countries the same period is often viewed as an age of transition.[6] In historical and literary terms, then, 1898 has been seen as a key date by Hispanists and became inextricably linked to the idea of a literary generation. Based on the ideas of Julius Petersen, the concept of the literary generation was used, for example, by Hans Jeschke, José Martínez Ruiz ('Azorín'), José Ortega y Gasset, and Pedro Salinas in forging their influential and long-lasting configuration of the period.[7] The

---

5   See Guillermo Díaz-Plaja, *Modernismo frente a 98* (Madrid: Espasa–Calpe, 1959), Donald L. Shaw, *The Generation of 1898 in Spain* (London: Ernest Benn, 1975), which, though contested by myself and others, is still the best account of the Generation in English. The most influential work in Spanish was Pedro Laín Entralgo's *La Generación de 1898* (Madrid: Espasa–Calpe, 1945).

6   See Malcolm Bradbury and James McFarlane, eds, *Modernism 1890–1930* (Harmondsworth: Penguin, 1976), for a good overview of the period. The bibliography on Modernism is copious and cannot be listed in this short chapter.

7   Hans Jeschke, *La Generación de 1898 en España* (Santiago de Chile: Ed. de la Universidad de Chile, 1954; originally published in German in 1934); Azorín José Martínez Ruiz, 'La generación de 1898', in *Obras completas*, vol. II (Madrid: Aguilar, 1947 [1913]), 896–914, and 'Dos generaciones', in *Obras completas*, vol. IX (Madrid: Aguilar, 1954 [1910]), 1136–40; Pedro Salinas, *Literatura española del siglo XX* (Madrid: Alianza Editorial, 2001; first published in Mexico, 1949).

Generation became established as a group of writers who, broadly speaking, sought the essence of 'casticismo', the 'soul of Spain', often in the Middle Ages, prior to the Protestant Reformation, in contrast to Europeanization and modernity. While of course such writers were influenced by European thinkers, such as Schopenhauer, and Max Nordau, and specifically by German cultural nationalism with its emphasis on race, spirit, culture and language, the construction of the Generation has been essentially Spanish, perpetuating the myth of Spanish difference, of otherness, a myth which was particularly potent in the years of the Dictatorship. It effectively reinforced ideas of Spain's traditional values, which were deemed to be essentially Castilian and Catholic. British Hispanists, in their majority hardly steeped in the tenets of Counter-Reformation Catholicism, both accepted and promulgated it. The fact is that the Generation of 1898 as constructed offered a Castilian perspective on Spanish identity, while at the same time the emphasis on making *lo castellano* synonymous with *lo español* made it highly attractive to Francoist intellectuals. Azorín's *Castilla*, and his ideas of the *eterno retorno*, Unamuno's notion of *intrahistoria*, Baroja's less palatable thoughts on the Semitic and the Iberian, all hark back to a pre-modern age of racial essence, which in the 1980s seemed ripe for reassessment in the light of new ideas on modernism and modernity. When my own work appeared in the wake of the Dictatorship situating Spain's early twentieth-century writers within a framework constituted by European Modernism, it was described in Spain, to my surprise, as highly innovative and indeed paradigm-shifting. Others asking similar questions, though in a different way, were Alex Longhurst and John Butt.[8]

This work, which derived from topographies of narrative influenced by Formalism, and ultimately Structuralism, attempted to break the traditional paradigm and account in a different way for the turn of the novel in Spain without reference to external historical factors. The emphasis was less on the spiritual crises of individual writers, and on the peculiarly Spanish

8   C. A. Longhurst, 'Coming in from the Cold: Spain, Modernism and the Novel', *Bulletin of Spanish Studies* LXXIX/2–3 (2002), 263–83; John Butt, 'The Generation of 1898: A Critical Fallacy', *Forum for Modern Language Studies* 16 (1980), 136–53.

circumstances which both caused and reflected these crises, than on the
anti-realist tendencies which characterized many European and North-
American novelists of the period, such as André Gide, Thomas Mann,
Virginia Woolf, Henry James, Marcel Proust. The turn of the novel away
from naïve mimeticism to a concern with consciousness and its forms is a
commonplace of writing in and on the period. By tracing a trajectory from
Cervantes onwards, however, whose *Don Quijote* on one reading can be
said to question the truth of the external world, and then which could be
traced in the work of Benito Pérez Galdós and in the Spanish notion of
'naturalismo espiritual' [spiritual naturalism], associated with Emilia Pardo
Bazán, it was possible to construct a narrative which modified the idea of
complete artistic and philosophical rupture from the nineteenth to the
twentieth century. Therefore, in essence, my work at the time sought to
demonstrate that a literary historiography which stressed Spain's uniqueness in the early twentieth century distorted both its own literary tradition
and its cultural affinities with developments in other countries. It could
accommodate both uniqueness and difference. Moreover, the rejection of
a purely nationalist, generational approach and the new emphasis placed
on Spain's European character and significance had a particular resonance
within Spain at the time of its appearance – some years after the end of
the Dictatorship and a few years before the entry of Spain into the then
European Community. One is reminded of Peter Widdison who, in his
work on D. H. Lawrence, observed that 'every historical moment "writes"
the literature it wishes to read'.[9] This insight applies to writers and critics
alike. While my approach may have had significant impact in changing
the traditional paradigm, and had a certain explanatory power, it in turn
now deserves revaluation from the vantage-point of today. For one thing,
it rested on the notion of the existence of a Modernist movement and of
a literary period and, for another, it conceived of Modernism as essentially a set of literary practices, which were to be found in the giants of
Modernism. In a way, the mode of enquiry conditioned the outcome in a

9   Peter Widdison, ed., *D. H. Lawrence* (London: Longman, 1992), 11.

kind of self-sustaining circle. Reflection of Iberian Studies necessitates a reflection on one's own critical positions.

My approach, as I indicated, also drew heavily on the structuralist or, more accurately, Saussurean notion that all forms of culture are structured like language and that signs communicate through difference.[10] Rather than search for meaning in a text, the emphasis was on what a text is though, since I was concerned with narrative and its relation to the world as commonly perceived, I did of course focus on the relationship between text and reality. I was able to demonstrate a number of commonly accepted features of the Modernist novel – anti-realism, anti-representationalism, use of myth, experimentation, absence of causality and plot, absence of character, introversion in the sense both of artistic self-consciousness a concern with the workings of consciousness, the use of myth, and so on – and link them to the work of Modernists such as Joyce, Proust, Virginia Woolf, Gide, Mann. A particular theme was the notion of synchronicity, which could stand as the defining feature of Modernism. On one level, this could refer to simultaneous narration in an attempt to overcome chronology and linearity, but it could also mean linking past and present (as in Proust), and contemporary literature with older literature and myth (as in Joyce), in which narratives are constructed as a kind of literary palimpsest. Literature, on this view, does not imitate reality, but imitates other literature, other ways of writing about reality. This approach offered a new model for understanding the writers of early twentieth-century Spain, and the intercultural aspects of their writing, without seeking explanations in the external events in the contemporary political world. If we are to think further about the Iberian literary space, such a conception surely requires further development, both in the context of the Iberian Peninsula and of Modernism itself, and the peripheral factors which nuance the perhaps over-tidy nature of the structuralist paradigm. I still think, however, that

---

10   An important book at the time was David Lodge's *The Modes of Modern Writing: Metaphor, Metonymy, and the Typology of Modern Literature* (London: Edward Arnold, 1977), which engages fruitfully with structuralism while paying detailed attention to specific texts.

the central notion of synchronicity, which underlay my argument, has much
to offer us when thinking about Iberia. Synchronicity, as I indicated above,
refers to attempts at simultaneous narration, to the use of previous literature
in a new text, and to the atemporal aspects of psychological experience.
It thus offered a way of understanding texts and contexts across borders,
across boundaries, and across time, as well as across genres and cultural
forms. It militates against small-scale discrete analysis and offers a model
for dealing with complexity in an understandable way.

   Enough therefore has changed in thirty years to suggest that further
reflection and scholarship need to be undertaken. Firstly, we can now talk
of new modernist studies in which Modernism in the singular has been
replaced by modernisms in the plural. Critical work is no longer concentrated on the consecrated figures of Proust, Joyce, Eliot, Mann, and so
on, as the field has increasingly encompassed the whole range of cultural
production. No longer conceived of as a period or geographical monolith,
Modernism is seen as manifold and diverse, existing in many guises, places
and times. We now think less of forms and paradigms and more on intersections, networks, and dialogues. This points away from the limitations
Spanish and Portuguese Studies and towards Iberian Studies, and which
connects with European, Global and Comparative Studies. Theory, arguably of a piece with the critical spirit of Modernism, has played a major role
in this shift, for if Modernism saw itself as the repudiation of modernity,
theory in turn has offered an incisive critique of modernism as expressive,
indeed as emblematic, of modernity.[11] In its more recent manifestations,
it has espoused the role of challenging canon formation. It has, moreover,
drawn on a whole range of new ideas, on postcolonial theory, feminism,
race, interest in the marginal, in popular culture and so on, to strike at the
foundations of the traditional study of modernism, while still remaining
part of the modernist enterprise. In fact, even newer approaches to modernism have eschewed theory as being in a continuum with the spirit of

---

11   Although concerned with English literature, *Modernism and Theory: A Critical
     Debate*, edited by Stephe Ross (Abington: Routledge, 2009), offers an interesting
     perspective on this question.

modernism, seeing it as sharing the elitism of high modernism, arguing instead in favour of the archival, the socio-historical, the rooted. John Ruskin wrote in 1877, in his *St Mark's Rest. The History of Venice*: 'Great nations write their autobiographies in three manuscripts – the book of their deeds, the book of their words and the book of their art. No one of these books can be understood unless we read the other two'.[12] This obvious point, with its insistence on the plurality of cultural forms and its perhaps unintended emphasis on interdisciplinarity, is relevant to the question of Iberian national identities.

Reflecting on this 'new' construction has, to my mind, implications for our thinking on the Iberian literary space. Frederic Jameson reminds us that 'modernity is not a concept [...] but a narrative category'.[13] The same is true in the case of Iberia. In constructing Iberia, we narrativize it by constantly reinventing Iberia, making it modern. And, as Paul de Man observes, 'although it is the nature of modernity to be without precedent [...] "modern" movements occur again and again, and become the very articulations of history'.[14] I would still maintain that the proposition that Modernism is defined by a spirit of critique allied to formal experimentation is uncontestable. At the same time, the modern misrepresents the old to authenticate its own representation, its claim to 'Make it new', in the words of Ezra Pound. This kind of thinking has implications for our reconfiguration of Iberia. We live, I would argue, for our academic and ideological purposes, with distortions of Iberia, with the tensions created by competing versions.

These competing versions, based not on objective truth but on discourses of power, are examples of how history and memory interpenetrate through what Maurice Halbwachs called 'the social frameworks of

---

12 John Ruskin, *St Mark's Rest. The History of Venice* (New York: J. Wiley & Sons, 1877), 1.

13 Frederic Jameson, *A Singular Modernity: Essays on the Ontology of the Present* (New York: Verso, 2002), 40.

14 Paul de Man, 'What is Modern? (1965)', in Lindsay Waters, ed., *Critical Writings 1953–1978* (Theory and History of Literature, vol. 66) (Minneapolis: University of Minnesota Press, 1989), 137.

memory',[15] and memory has a history of its own. It is worth introducing memory at this point because the late nineteenth and early twentieth centuries in Spain were the period in which, arguably, memory divorced from history informs writing of all kinds. In pursuing a notion of what Spain is, the writers of the time evoked a remembered Spain, even a timeless Spain, and memory in this sense is not individual, but communal and collective. The apparent 1898 preoccupation with Spain, *hispanidad*, and nationhood go together, as evidenced by works like Ramiro de Maeztu's *Hacia otra España* (1899), Ricardo Macías Picavea's *El problema nacional* (1899), and Luis Morote's *La moral de la derrota*. Recent interdisciplinary scholarship, however, has shown less interest in the dynamics of nationalism and more and more on language and symbolism in creating collective identities. Cultural historians inquire into texts as the means by which communities are imagined or narrated. All study in the Humanities is about the past. As we think about national identities in so many places, be it Ireland, or Italy, or Iberia, we inevitably refer to tradition, but of course we are increasingly aware of the fact that tradition does not objectively exist: it is invented. As we observed earlier, Unamuno was concerned with *intrahistoria*, Azorín with the *eterno retorno*, just as Pérez de Ayala sought *los valores eternos*, all of which imply a kind of stasis of ideality. Contemporary communities may be said to simulate a pre-modern past – for the 1898 it was medieval Spain, pure, unsullied and authentic, before the Reformation and the French Revolution. It is worth reiterating at this point that medieval studies were prestigious in Spain in the twentieth century and that there existed a close connection between historians of Spain and philologists.

A useful stimulus to thinking in this way is to be found in the impressive collection of essays by Pierre Nora, *Lieux de mémoire* (1992),[16] which, greatly simplified, shows how French traditions were created or recreated in the nineteenth century as part of a general argument about the relationship

15   Maurice Hawlbachs, *On Collective Memory*, ed. and trans. Lewis A. Coser (Chicago: The University of Chicago Press, 1992), 36.

16   Pierre Nora, *Realms of Memory*, 3 vols, ed. Lawrence D. Kritzman, trans. Arthur Goldhammer (New York: Columbia University Press, 1996).

between history, memory and national identity. Nora surveys the 'schools' of history in France from Michelet's work on the French Revolution as a manifestation of the 'national soul', a phrase redolent of the *Alma española* of the Generation of 1898, through the Germanic phase of archival research, the creation the *Annales* school and the movement towards the study of *mentalités*, to the present-day concern with the packaging of history. For Nora, '[m]emory is life [...]. History is the reconstruction of what is no longer'.[17] Conceived in this way, there is no duality of past and present, and Modernist synchronicity returns to centre stage. All cultural memories are simultaneous, itself a very Modernist notion, and any reconfiguration of Iberia, or Iberian Studies, needs to eschew our obsession with the modern, and with the easy categorizations of period. Memory and identity are caught in a two-way dialectic, and our task in reconfiguring Iberia is not so much historical reconstruction, but understanding the motivations, mostly of power of course, in all its diverse manifestations, underlying those myriad reconstructions.

What does that mean for our notion of the Iberian literary space? We might say that we have set ourselves an agenda of challenge and disruption, and which is temporal as well as spatial. For Iberian Studies to develop, we need new configurations, institutional as well as intellectual, and we should think in terms of new insights and perspectives rather than an attempt to reach any final truth. Because of the persistence of the 98 mentality, we see nation and identity as inseparable. Ernest Renan, in his essay of 1882 'What is Nation?' wrote that the principle of nationality is undeniably founded upon the desire to live together, but also, and very significantly, on the 'possession in common of a rich legacy of memories'.[18] In other words, familiar criteria of racial origins, language, religious affiliation, natural frontiers, do not in themselves adequately explain the nation states of Europe. So how do we explain Iberia in a way that justifies

---

17   Nora, 'General Introduction: Between Memory and History', in *Realms of Memory*, vol. 1, 3.

18   Ernest Renan, 'What is Nation?', in Homi K. Bhabha, ed., *Nation and Narration*, trans. Martin Thom (London: Taylor & Francis, 1990), 19. The original lecture was delivered at the Sorbonne on 11 March 1882.

Iberian Studies? The difficulty, in my view, is that, because of the impact of postmodernism on Cultural Studies, some are inclined to believe in a simplistic manner that since all is construction in language, there is only language. There is, however, a real challenge as we attempt to reconfigure Iberia, and Iberian Studies. It is how to avoid a position of total relativity in our desire to avoid fixity. Perhaps we should simply accept that we do not seek truth, but only express ideology, as have writers and critics before us. The issue is not the pursuit of the real, but the exposure of relations of power and ideology, in politics, in social relations, in the Academy, where institutional and even disciplinary power are crucial definers of critical perspectives, active agents as we create, impose, or reconfigure our own versions of Iberian identity. The intellectual challenge of Iberian Studies is the process, not the product.

Works cited

Bradbury, Malcolm, and James McFarlane, eds, *Modernism 1890–1930* (Harmondsworth: Penguin, 1976).

Buffery, Helena, Stuart Davis, and Kirsty Hooper, eds, *Reading Iberia: Theory/History/ Identity* (Oxford: Peter Lang, 2007).

Butt, John, 'The Generation of 1898: A Critical Fallacy', *Forum for Modern Language Studies* 16 (1980), 136–53.

Díaz-Plaja, Guillermo, *Modernismo frente a 98* (Madrid: Espasa–Calpe, 1959).

Hawlbachs, Maurice, *On Collective Memory*, ed. and trans. Lewis A. Coser (Chicago: The University of Chicago Press, 1992).

Jameson, Frederic, *A Singular Modernity: Essays on the Ontology of the Present* (New York: Verso, 2002).

Jeschke, Hans, *La Generación de 1898 en España* (Santiago de Chile: Ed. de la Universidad de Chile, 1954).

Laín Entralgo, Pedro, *La Generación de 1898* (Madrid: Espasa–Calpe, 1945).

Lodge, David, *The Modes of Modern Writing: Metaphor, Metonymy, and the Typology of Modern Literature* (London: Edward Arnold, 1977).

Longhurst, C. A., 'Coming in from the Cold: Spain, Modernism and the Novel', *Bulletin of Spanish Studies* LXXIX/2–3 (2002), 263–83.

Macklin, John, 'Competing Voices: Unamuno's *Niebla* and the Discourse of Modernism', in J. J. Macklin, ed., *After Cervantes: A Celebration of 75 Years of Iberian Studies at Leeds* (Leeds Iberian Papers) (Leeds: Trinity and All Saints College, 1993), 167–93.

——, 'Modernismo, postmodernismo y la novela española de principios de siglo: Unamuno y Pérez de Ayala', *Cuadernos para la investigación de la literatura hispánica* 20 (1995), 365–74.

——, *The Window and the Garden: The Modernist Fictions of Ramón Pérez de Ayala* (Boulder, CO: Society of Spanish and Spanish-American Studies, 1988).

Man, Paul de, 'What is Modern? (1965)', in Lindsay Waters, ed., *Critical Writings 1953–1978* (Theory and History of Literature, vol. 66) (Minneapolis: University of Minnesota Press, 1989), 137–44.

Mar-Molinero, Clare, and Angel Smith, *Nationalism and the Nation in the Iberian Peninsula: Competing and Conflicting Identities* (Oxford: Berg, 1996).

Martínez Ruiz, Azorín José, 'Dos generaciones', in *Obras completas*, vol. IX (Madrid: Aguilar, 1954), 1136–40.

——, 'La generación de 1898', in *Obras completas*, vol. II (Madrid: Aguilar, 1947), 896–914.

Nora, Pierre, *Realms of Memory*, 3 vols, ed. Lawrence D. Kritzman, trans. Arthur Goldhammer (New York: Columbia University Press, 1996).

Renan, Ernest, 'What is Nation?', in Homi K. Bhabha, ed., *Nation and Narration*, trans. Martin Thom (London: Taylor & Francis, 1990).

Ross, Stephe, ed., *Modernism and Theory: A Critical Debate* (Abington: Routledge, 2009).

Ruskin, John, *St Mark's Rest. The History of Venice* (New York: J. Wiley & Sons, 1877).

Salinas, Pedro, *Literatura española del siglo XX* (Madrid: Alianza Editorial, 2001).

Shaw, Donald L., *The Generation of 1898 in Spain* (London: Ernest Benn, 1975).

Widdison, Peter, ed., *D. H. Lawrence* (London: Longman, 1992).

GABRIEL MAGALHÃES

Europe: The Letter of Numbers. From the Alpha of Peninsular Comparative Literature to the Omega of European Comparative Literature*

The expansion of knowledge areas goes through an accumulation of cardinal sins. Look at the case of scientific knowledge, for example, which has been promoted to an authentic theology of the present time. Science prevails as it adheres to a political power that believes in the pragmatic advantages of scientific research. All knowledge has to be knowledge for something in order for it to spread socially. Nonetheless, this 'be for' of knowledge constitutes an instrumentalization that is at times very dangerous. Take the case of a person who fluctuates in the research of theoretical Physics and suddenly finds himself designing an atomic bomb.

And so, what were the sins of Literary Studies from the nineteenth century onwards? First of all – and quite clearly – there is nationalism. In a European world that was vested with a secular nature, nationality has become a new religion whose believer responds to the call of 'citizen'. Thus, the literature of each culture has profiled itself as a series of sacred texts that constitute the *Bible* of each country. Each nation would therefore choose their Moses, which could be Shakespeare, in the case of England, Goethe, for Germany, or Cervantes and Camões, if we think about Spain and Portugal.

Thus, the philologists constituted a strange Levitical tribe whose task consisted in preserving the sacred letters of a country. In a sense, the faculties of letters became neo-monasteries in charge of preserving this textual tradition. We all feel as monks at a certain point in our careers, no matter

*   This essay was translated from Portuguese by Rui Vitorino Azevedo.

how secular we may be. And the literary production of the European continent classified itself entirely, and quite surprisingly, with little country
flags: the exact same flags that so many people marked the map of Europe
with as they accompanied the incidents of World War II on the radio.

As an initiative of the States, secondary schools were filled with language and literature teachers whose ultimate mission was the transmission
of this nationalism which was propagated through literary texts. It was a
nationalism that frequently achieved an undeniable spiritual dignity, when
such works as *Os Lusíadas, Mensagem, Viagens na Minha Terra* or *A Ilustre
Casa de Ramires* were studied to the bone. However, we also found ourselves
assuming a frontier, the construction of a castle and the possibility of a war.

Did this make sense? In reality the only sense it made was our agreement that it was all non-sense. If we intend to study literature without
flags, without the background music of national hymns, perhaps we will
understand it even better. Realities such as the Galician-Portuguese lyric,
the work of Gil Vicente, or the world of Camões become clearer with the
telescope of Comparative Literature than with the microscope of national
literature.

And this is also true for authors who are typically more national or
more closed in the cultural pub of each country, or for works whose theme
is markedly Portuguese. For instance, anyone wanting to understand *Os
Maias* should especially look through *L'Éducation sentimentale* by Gustave
Flaubert: the great novel by Queirós is a variation inspired by the French
writer's narrative. Despite the fact that they were loaded by national boundaries, we can contrast Eça and Camilo who played a game of village rivalries.
However, we must also understand that the work of the 'poor man from
Póvoa de Varzim' is mainly a challenge of titans with the prodigious author
of *Madame Bovary*.

A nationalist perspective is a way to misconceive works in order to be
able to invent the fiction of a country. And the philology courses themselves
usually come with a national passport. But if we think a bit we see that
reading the texts on a patriotic basis means getting to know and interpret
them with one eye only. *Os Lusíadas* constitutes a fact that is, to say the
least, European and yet it is much more than a Portuguese event. Pessoa is
a prophet of globalization, the first virtual poet, the creator who knew how

to turn his work into a ludic derision, a literary PlayStation, where changing heteronyms is equivalent to choosing a new player for the next match in a disquieting attempt to always move on to the next level. We cannot see him only as a Portuguese vagabond, a mysterious radiation from the mirrors of the cafés in downtown Lisbon. Literary nationalism was and is a sin that we have become accustomed to and we do not recognize how it amputates the texts of everything that breathes out from them.

Later on, in the twentieth century, philology commits a second cardinal sin: it kneels before science when the sciences triumph. This brought about the apogee of the formalists and structuralists: more and more diagrams projected into texts that often imprisoned literary words. In so doing Literary Studies abdicated their specific personality and, if they survived, it was only because the education systems still needed teachers who were actually destined to the nationalist mission mentioned beforehand.

However, this alchemy of being attentive to the arithmetic of words sometimes leads us to the equation that serves as the basis of a text. And in those blessed moments the critic feels he was capable of tracing the score of a tune present in the literary words. Our head beats to the rhythm of an enigmatic cadence when we read a masterpiece. There is a hidden number in the best literature, a mysterious Pythagorean key that is at times acceded by wielding the magnifying glass of science, the calculating machine of rigorous analysis.

There has been such beautiful work in the literary field achieved with the ruler of formalism and the square of structuralism. But with time, science has basically transformed itself into an official rhetoric: a kind of military service of works consulted. Deep down, the scientific frame of an academic study allows you to give the appearance of geniality to the most absolute lack of talent. It was the empire of science that gave Literary Studies the grey tone it possesses today, a dead colour that has made the reading of these works a quite dreadful experience.

While this was going on, while Literary Studies was amusing itself with nations and science, there was a noticeable acceleration from the eighteenth century onwards of that which we can call civilizational speed. The world was starting to gain momentum to arrive at a day where it would hover over itself, thus giving rise to today's globalization which is a universal fluctuation. Transnationality lived side by side with nationalism – as we can see in Eça de Queirós's *A Cidade e as Serras* – and it is in this context that there is a particular growth in Comparative Literature. It intended to blur the boundaries laid down by the usual philological studies.

The aims of the comparatist project are presented at times in a particularly dreamlike fashion, as if the scholars from this field were Botticelli's angels. In reality, Comparative Literature represents a manner of thinking about transnationality that is outlined from institutions such as the European Union, the past Society of Nations and the current United Nations. And if comparatism lives in a perpetual indefiniteness, remaining in that which is called its crisis, these political institutions also hover over their own uncertainty. That is to say: comparatism did not need to have its own terms because internationalism also resides in a kind of sketch of itself.

In the case of the Peninsula, the increase of Portuguese and Spanish Comparative Literary Studies throughout the nineteenth century coincided with the vibrant blossoming of Iberist feelings. That is: comparativism and Iberism shook hands, mutually contemplated each other, and together reflected about the possibility of a unified Peninsula. The way Oliveira Martins[1] tried to find a common Iberian spirit is almost touching, just as we cannot help but be moved by the way in which Ribera i Rovira[2] defends a certain nostalgia that belongs to both Portugal and Catalonia.

We all choose our homeland in the secret of our heart. But our life, especially today, always has a balcony that faces another national sensitivity. Actually, Portugal is a nation with its windows facing Spain, much more so than what is usually thought, and it has a magnificent terrace made with mosaics from the ocean. It therefore becomes easy for a Portuguese person to have two countries in its soul, as was the case of Pessoa or Eça, who was Lusitanian in a Gaulish manner. Nowadays, for instance, we want to be European within our Portuguese being.

---

1   Joaquim Pedro de Oliveira Martins, *História da Civilização Ibérica* (Lisbon: Guimarães Editores, 1973 [1879]); *Vida de Nun'Álvares* (Lisbon: Guimarães Editores, 2009 [1893]).
2   Ignasi Ribera i Rovira, *Iberisme* (Barcelona: Biblioteca Popular de 'L'Avenç', 1907).

That is perhaps why Comparative Literature hesitates between stressing and erasing frontiers. You will find that hesitation at the core of its most intimate personality. When one watches the borrowings from one culture to another, one acts as a literary tax and customs officer and at times one notices a curious tendency in measuring forces between literatures. But, in other occasions, comparatism is capable of an open-minded spiritual porosity that is, perhaps, the best portrait of itself. And that would be a good definition for Comparative Literature: transnationalism in the shape of indecision just as the current world searches for a fusion that it cannot find, or that is not quite satisfactory once found – the same way comparatism is kept at the threshold of itself and surely advances but without definitely consolidating itself.

The right time for the Iberian project was the nineteenth century – but there was no unified Peninsula at that time. To a certain extent, Peninsular Comparative Literature failed its broader goal. However, that defeat left an extensive cartography of relations between Portugal and Spain and a much wider understanding between the two countries. What remained then was the union of a disunion – and not the disunited disunion that would become, in fact, a tragedy. If comparatism does not bring frontiers to an end, it can at least put an end to wars.

The game we play today in Comparative Studies is no longer that of Iberia, but of Europe since Iberia lost or found itself in the nineteenth century. Nowadays, a peninsular political project would only be justifiable in the scenario of a European catastrophe: Europe's collapse would demand that we unite here, and prepare for a raft of pure survival. And all of Europe would be a chaos of several rafts, adrift in the tempestuous oceans of globalization. What is at stake in the coming years is the destiny of the European continent, which oscillates between a shipwreck in a degraded Greek condition and a flight which was always our best destiny.

One of the biggest mistakes from recent times was the economic mirror in which we, Europeans, wanted to see ourselves in. It is true that Europe began with coal and steel, but that was a way to stop with the cannons. It had to do with a materiality that was falsely material: a spiritual materiality. In recent years, however, we entered a material materiality – and the Euro appears more and more as a pact with the worst demons of globalization.

We put aside a possible European national feeling, based on a European matrix, and stuck ourselves into a pirate's chest. It was and is a big, enormous mistake. In fact, it would be much better to have a cathedral or a verse on our flag than a dollar sign – and the acute profile of Don Quixote would always symbolize us in a more effective way than an employee from some bank branch.

For that reason, while the Euro was being forged, exactly as if you melted a golden calf destined to be adored by our entire continent, the creation of a constitution where we could see ourselves in was shattering. In the end, it is up to Comparative Literature to informally – because everything in comparatism is informal – design that constitution which we are not able to reach. In my opinion, just as Iberism was the great challenge of peninsular comparatism during the 1800s, Europeanism will be the great battle of European comparatism of our time.

Deriving towards Cultural Studies or Interart Studies has without a doubt all the interest in recovering the margins towards the centre of knowledge. But, to be capable of inventing European literature – because we are dealing with invention, even when it has to do with discovering – constitutes perhaps the noblest task of comparatism currently under practice in our continent. I must confess that I am in love with a Europe that I am not really sure about, just like you never really know what love is throughout the act of loving. I just conceive a space of culture, spirit, adventure and liberty that may be a counterpoint to new tyrannies.

What is Europe? This is a big question, one that is particularly sonorous in the echoes of an academic amphitheatre as it leaves us in the situation of Saint Augustine when he came upon the problem of time. We all know what the European spirit is until this question is thrown at us, and then doubts invade our thoughts in an interrogative mode. We are European and feel European, but we mix up the several heteronyms and pseudonyms implicit in this cultural fact. It is not easy at all to move from being European to being of Europe.

Otherwise, our frontiers are chaotic and they function as a lottery of history, a game of checkers in which the pieces jump over each other: Galicia should be Portuguese, or Portugal should be Galician, and Catalonia has French hemoglobin, and even a fossil through time like the Basque people has achieved the prodigy of dividing themselves into two nationalities. And we would not even talk about the Irish labyrinth, the central European puzzles, or go through the shattered world of the Balkan space.

The Europe that can be made will not be a geometrical union, but rather a puzzle solved without all its pieces. Parts will be left out in order for there to be an ample interior space. Europe will not be the Europe of an integral platonic idea, but of a possible organism that is intensely amphibian and is born of the mutation of various countries. It is likely that the British look at us from afar, from the distance of being an island. What will happen to Greece, lost in the paradox of itself, and transformed into a ruin of ruins?

It would be excellent if the Greeks stayed: it would be a gesture of liberty, a choice of cultural DNA over financial logic. However, we should be conscious of our principal cultural frontiers which are similar to the immaterial walls of Berlin within the European space: they are very difficult to overcome. First of all, we come across a dividing line between the Protestant universe, which adapted itself quickly to the current foxtrot for money because it possesses a good cultural capitalist memory, and the world of the south which is Catholic and does not get along very well with the present globalization. Actually, this is the main abyss from which we have to jump: something far from easy.

The bridge for such will come especially from our love for freedom, and the way in which that triumphed over our past dictatorships. There is also our multiple spiritual tree, which includes Catholic, Protestant and Orthodox branches. But let us not forget the political faith in the left-wing revolution, 'the Christianity of the modern world' that Antero[3] spoke about, as well as the adventure of science, with its divine particles, and the love for art. All of this comprises the glue of our identity.

It may not be a coincidence that the European continent has been targeted by the new universal financial oligarchy which wants an enslaved

---

3 Antero de Quental, 'Causas da decadência dos povos peninsulares [1871]', in Joel Serrão, ed., *Prosas Sócio-Políticas* (Lisbon: Imprensa Nacional–Casa da Moeda, 1982), 255–96.

world through the cruel logic of money. Inventing Europe through Comparative Literature will also be a way to defend ourselves: to protect our culture and liberty with the shield of fantasy. A Comparative Literature that is capable of becoming a solid European literature, at the same time open to the rest of the world, would be a worthwhile capital sin, no matter what the theoretical problems of these concepts may be.

I assume that this project could give a new sense of direction to culture, and especially to the study of literature. Large part of the lack of vigour of Literary Studies, the endless anemia from the faculties of letters, comes from its social ineffectiveness. It is therefore necessary to find a new project for reading and studying literary works. It would not be science or nationalism that justifies us, but the capacity to invent Europe could be a task that makes libraries become an event with practical interest. It will be in our culture, and particularly in literature, that we will find our flag.

Europe has already been invented in Camões and in Cervantes, in Shakespeare and in Dante, in Goethe and in Hugo. What happens is that until now we have x-rayed the books of these authors in search of a national bone, without wanting to know about their European skeleton. But that European cartilage exists in the works of these and other writers and if we had the courage to turn national philological studies upside down we would confirm that Europe always knew about itself, at the same time that it forgot about itself. Can books give us that which a currency denies us?

We need the letter of our so often disconnected numbers. Let us make a shield out of our books and an original union from our divisions. Let us be immensely Greek in being European. Europe is the only Greece that can survive in a world of barbarians that are preparing themselves for the invasion of the Roman empire of the United States of America. This is the big issue of our time as Iberism and Peninsular Comparative Literature were the greatest struggle of the nineteenth century. If we are defeated, just as Iberism was, we, Europeans, will get to know ourselves so much better that we will actually be incapable of truly hating our European neighbours. If we triumph, we will once again become one of the biggest horizons of mankind.

Works cited

Martins, Joaquim Pedro de Oliveira, *História da Civilização Ibérica* (Lisbon: Guimarães Editores, 1973 [1879]).

——, *Vida de Nun'Álvares* (Lisbon: Guimarães Editores, 2009 [1893]).

Quental, Antero de, 'Causas da decadência dos povos peninsulares [1871]', in Joel Serrão, ed., *Prosas Sócio-Políticas* (Lisbon: Imprensa Nacional–Casa da Moeda, 1982), 255–96.

Ribera i Rovira, Ignasi, *Iberisme* (Barcelona: Biblioteca Popular de 'L'Avenç', 1907).

ROBERTO VECCHI

Thinking from Europe about an Iberian 'South': Portugal as a Case Study

It may sound obvious that when we talk about Iberia or Iberian Studies we first deal with an ontological problem. What exactly is Iberism and where do we inscribe Iberian Studies in the academic and cultural cartography? And in this context, we have a sort of double tension: on the one hand, we have a sliding object that is a peninsula that has been historically configuring itself as a moving border (see, e.g., Camões' *Os Lusíadas* [The Lusiads] for an exemplar poetical arrangement of the topic: '—"Os Portugueses somos do Ocidente,/Imos buscando as terras do Oriente"'[1] ['—"We are Portuguese from the Occident;/We seek the passage to the Orient"']²), that becomes extremely complex as it inscribes in a definite and static circle, without warning about the irreducible differences ('European, but not only', 'Atlantic, but European', 'a pier of Europe to new worlds', etc.). On the other hand, and by highlighting differences, we produce a sort of specificity that might itself become dangerous, because through the shadow of ideology (Iberism?) we contribute towards the founding of a sort of regressive mythology on that difference (an essentialism actually, feeding old nationalisms, regionalisms and particularisms). Then, as an effect of ideology[3] this 'specificity' naturalizes itself. So, in a provoking act, I would rather think about Iberism(s) in the plural and always in an intersubjective or relational way that uses Iberism as part of a bigger compound or

---

1   Luís de Camões, *Os Lusíadas*, 3rd edn (Lisbon: Ministério da Educação/Instituto Camões, 1992), canto I, stanza 50, v. 13.
2   Luís de Camões, *The Lusiads*, trans. Landeg White (New York: Oxford University Press, 2008), canto I, stanza 50, v. 13.
3   See Louis Althusser, *Sull'ideologia*, trans. M. Gallerani (Bari: Dedalo libri, 1976), 37.

circle. I mean using a relational *dispositif* as a way to understand forces and powers that insist on an object whose nature is eminently cultural, but with strong political consequences. Thus, I would like to discuss the concept of South,[4] which I think is crucial in order to define a relational framework for Iberian Studies. In particular, I tackle such a perspective from a particular point of view, Portugal, which is only a 'side' of a wider 'problem' (Iberia as a problem) – even if I would like to avoid other adjectives such us exceptional, or extraordinary, to define the case, in order to ward off, as has been said, the risks of an ideological manipulation of singularities – but, at the same time, with a theoretical force, which I hope could extend the consequences of the case to the entire Peninsula.

The concept of the South concerns a relationship between space and power. Therefore, it is, in some way, topographic, in the sense that it gives a space to time. Above all, the South is a relational concept and a relationship is essential for its configuration. If the East arises from a cultural relationship with the West (and Orientalism is created from an image of the East in the West) then the South comes from its relation with the North, that is, the connection mainly deals with power and its inscription in a space.

Nevertheless, an alternative reconstruction outside an intersubjective framework would also be possible: in this perspective, Franco Cassano's proposal about approaching the South through a 'meridian thought' is based on the effort to emancipate the Southern condition from any relational subalternity. Such a reconfiguration of the South as a subject and not an object of thought takes to a reconsideration of modernization processes, which are not imperfect or insufficient, but characterized by a real consistence producing a proper Southern modernity.[5] Even if not endorsed in the present reflection, which focuses more on some visible or latent links between Iberia (Portugal) and Europe, it would be interesting in future occasions to carry out a critical movement that assumes difference as an

---

4   I will use in this article the term 'South' (capitalized, as in a proper noun) in order to express the relational concept implied by the Southern condition, while I will adopt the term 'south' when it refers simply to the spatial dimension.

5   See Franco Cassano, *Il pensiero meridiano* (Bari: Laterza, 2003), 5.

alternative modernity, without any relational and contrastive perspective, through an innovative investment of theoretical sources in order to redefine the South (and its modernity) or to find out its 'proper noun'.

In an attempt to open the relational perspective, Gramsci actually contrasts the geometric logic with another logic inscribed in the history of spatial concepts:

> Cosa significherebbe Nord-Sud, Est-Ovest senza l'uomo? Essi sono rapporti reali, e tuttavia non esisterebbero senza l'uomo e senza lo sviluppo della civiltà. È evidente che Est e Ovest sono costruzioni arbitrarie, convenzionali, cioè storiche, poiché fuori dalla storia reale ogni punto della terra è Est e Ovest nello stesso tempo. Ciò si può vedere chiaramente dal fatto che questi termini si sono cristallizzati non dal punto di vista di un ipotetico e malinconico uomo in generale ma dal punto di vista delle classi colte europee che attraverso la loro egemonia mondiale li hanno fatti accettare ovunque.[6]

> [What would North-South or East-West mean without man? They are real relationships and yet they would not exist without man and without the development of civilization. Obviously East and West are arbitrary and conventional, that is historical, constructions, since outside of real history every point on the earth is East and West at the same time. This can be seen more clearly from the fact that these terms have crystallized not from the point of view of a hypothetical melancholic man in general but from the point of view of the European cultured classes who, as a result of their world-wide hegemony, have caused them to be accepted everywhere.][7]

Iberia therefore always provokes a reconfiguration of the idea of the (European) south in relation with other 'South(s)' (in a plural, conceptual sense), such as the Italian 'Meridione', which is defined in an extremely sharp and seminal way by Antonio Gramsci. In 1929, Gramsci wrote about the so-called 'Mistero di Napoli' [Mystery of Naples] in accordance with which, moving from a previous impression by Goethe, he wondered why such an industrious and active city like Naples was not productive and

---

6 Antonio Gramsci, *Quaderni del carcere*, ed. Valentino Gerratana, vol. II (Roma: Editori Riuniti, 1991), 1419.

7 Antonio Gramsci, *Selections from Prison Notebooks*, ed. and trans. Quintin Hoare and Geoffrey Nowell Smith (New York: International Publishers, 1971), 447.

focused on satisfying the needs of the productive classes. The intimate *dispositif* that the Italian philosopher caught in Naples allows us to interpret the Mystery through the relations of force and power in particular with what he defined as the 'Quistione merdionale' [Southern Question].

What is impressive in the conceptual reflection about the South is its operating analogy with another key category of Gramsci's thought, which is the subaltern. First of all because Subalternity, like the South, is intersubjective too (starting from the proper Latin etymology), besides the fact that it arises from a relationship. Therefore, South and Subaltern, but not only in Gramsci's thought, are defined in the context of an organic reflection on power and its spatial projections. In this sense, the case of the Italian Mezzogiorno may become, as Subaltern Studies still do, a minimum field to deconstruct more complex and global apparatuses such as empire or colonialism.

The text of the *Quaderno* number 1 (1929) about the 'Mystery of Naples' captures the importance of the connection that is always implied by the South. Most of its interpretative power should be a consequence of an apparently invisible fold that, on the contrary, reveals itself as quite substantial. Significatively, the note is referred to as 'Americanism', which is a radical view, with lights and shadows, of the American modernization process, especially the importance of the deep cultural effects determined by the industrial growth in North America and the peculiarity of the forms that it assumes. Much of the content of the 'Mystery of Naples', which the philosopher rewrites in *Quaderno* number 22 (1934) was already present in a more ambitious project entitled 'Alcuni temi della quistione meridionale' [Some Themes of the Southern Question] (later interrupted and left incomplete, because of his time in prison). It was written in 1926 and elaborated on previous articles on the topic: this is the work he was reviewing when he was arrested, and which was later found and first published in 1930, in Paris. Gramsci rewrote, in some regards, on the decay of some parasite classes in opposition to the social change induced by Americanism. As he observes in 1934:

La 'tradizione', la 'civiltà' europea è invece proprio caratterizzata dalla esistenza di classi simili, create dalla 'ricchezza' e 'complessità' della storia passata che ha lasciato un mucchio di sedimentazioni passive attraverso i fenomeni di saturazione e fossilizzazione del personale statale e degli intellettuali, del clero e della proprietà terriera, del commercio di rapina e dell'esercito prima professionale, poi di leva poi, ma professionale per la ufficialità. Si può anzi dire che quanto più è vetusta la storia di un paese, e tanto più numerose e gravose sono queste sedimentazioni di masse fannullone e inutili, che vivono del 'patrimonio' degli 'avi', di questi pensionati della storia economica. Una statistica di questi elementi economicamente passivi (un senso sociale) è difficilissima, perché è impossibile trovare la 'voce' che li possa definire ai fini di una ricerca diretta; indicazioni illuminanti si posso ricavare indirettamente, per esempio dall'esistenza di determinate forme di vita nazionale.[8]

[European 'tradition', European 'civilization', is, conversely, characterized precisely by the existence of such classes, created by the 'richness' and 'complexity' of past history. This past history has left behind a heap of passive sedimentations produced by the phenomenon of the saturation and fossilization of civil-service personnel and intellectuals, of clergy and landowners, piratical commerce and the professional (and later conscript, but for the officers always professional) army. One could even say that the more historic a nation the more numerous and burdensome are these sedimentations of idle and useless masses living on 'heir ancestral patrimony', pensioners of economic history. Statistics of these economically passive elements (in a social sense) are very hard to work out because it is impossible to find a 'heading' under which they can be defined for the purposes of immediate research. But useful indications can be derived indirectly, for example, from the existence of specific forms of national life.][9]

Endorsing Gramsci's reflection on the South, Edward Said (*Culture and Imperialism*) defines the relationship between Naples and Turin, north and south. It is what he calls the 'Gobbetti factor',[10] which is the possibility of establishing an axis between the Northern proletariat and the Southern peasants. As a matter of fact, Said assumes Gramsci's sharp analysis on the South as one of the most relevant points of a geographic and territorial reflection on culture. In *Culture and Imperialism* actually, the famous musical metaphor of the counterpoint for the cultural archive resulting

---

8   Gramsci, *Quaderni del carcere*, vol. III, 2141.
9   Gramsci, *Selections*, 281.
10 Edward W. Said, *Culture and Imperialism* (London: Vintage, 1994), 58.

from the combination of the metropolitan archive with colonial archives thus forming alternative and polyphonic narrations[11] is tributary to the Gramscian reflection. In Said's vision, the *Quistione meridionale* indicates the incorporation of space and territory into a social cultural analysis. He proposes a sharp comparison between Lukács and Gramsci, putting in contrast the two philosophers: what emerges is that if Lukács refers to the Hegelian and Marxist tradition and assumes time as his principle concern, Gramsci refers to an alternative, endogenous (national) tradition, that is the constellation composed with Vico and Croce dismounting the social frame and the reality from a geographical perspective.[12] Gramsci's metaphorology directly communicates with the space, based on a lexicon such as 'ground', 'terrain', 'blocks', or 'regions', which define a particular topography of the South characterized by a strong contrast between the vast anonymous masses of peasants and the presence of big landowners.

In this context, the situation of intellectuals is emblematic: as in Croce's case, thinkers are committed to interpreting the great European decadence or the great philosophical systems much more than the degradation of the context in which they live. Here, Said defines the 'Gobbetti factor' or the possibility of creating a relationship, as opposed to Croce's and Fortunato's point of view on the Meridione, to establish an axis between the Northern proletariat and the Southern peasants, as two sides of the same 'issue', in a strict combination or counterpoint. In all actuality, Piero Gobbetti represented a deep and organic rift within the culture characterized by a long duration, as it is conceived *sub specie aeternitatis*. The extrapolation of the 'Gobetti factor' allows Said to consider that a common linkage exists between the development of Comparative Literature and the affirmation of an imperial geography. In this frame, he raises the possibility of rein-terpreting the archive of Western culture from Gramsci's spatial dimen-sion in association with the *Quistione meridionale*. Such a vision induces a review of the imperial narrative through the musical metaphor of the

11   Said, *Culture*, 59.
12   Said, *Culture*, 57.

'counterpoint' intersecting, as we have mentioned, metropolitan history with alternative, Southern narrations.

The South configured in this way is very close to other crucial categories of Gramsci's thought. First of all, it must be remembered that the 'Mystery of Naples' is central to a reflection on Americanism. Americanism and Fordism are the two keys through which Gramsci interprets modernization as a wide and complex process with deep material and immaterial consequences. They are responsible for building what he calls the 'mass man' who is a new kind of man that puts serious problems of cultural issues. This original analysis of Americanism from a radical point of view, distinguishing positive and negative aspects of the same process, inscribes itself far beyond any ideological controversy or prejudice in front of the impetuous of American modernization. Besides Americanism, other categories can be thought in conjunction with the South in the Gramscian perspective: Subalternity as we saw (and it is not a coincidence that Said wrote a famous introduction to the first Subaltern Studies anthology, precisely starting from Gramsci's position) and popular culture and folklore which is not at all a degraded cultural value in this perspective, but quite the contrary it merges all cultural issues.[13]

Inside the general frame that has been outlined here, would it be possible to determine a time when Portugal became aware of its Southern condition? It would be necessary to think of a Foucaultian genealogy to handle such fragmented and dispersed objects like the concept of South. The consciousness of the South is somehow associated to a radical revision of Portuguese ontology, in its complex dialectics between the Atlantic and Europe. This occurs at a time when Europe emerges as prevailing over the sea and Portugal regains its marginal, extreme status of a European country turned out of a weak and vulnerable Atlantic dispersion (in a certain way, this resembles the dualism depicted by Eduardo Lourenço when he refers

---

13   See Giorgio Baratta, 'Gramsci e i subalterni', in Sergia Adamo, ed., *Culture planetarie. Prospettive e limiti della teoria e della critica culturale* (Roma: Meltemi, 2007), 91–3.

to the conflict, in the case of Portugal, between an ontological strength
and an ontic weakness that characterizes Portuguese history as a whole).[14]

So if the South comes out of a relationship or an articulation with the
North, as we previously saw, more than a spatial location, which is situated
in the geographic and historical case of Portugal, it is configured – not
in a theoretical but in a practical and historical way – as a clash of power
intensities resulting from a complex dialectics or, it would be better to
say, a tension between north and south (generating the 'South' from their
conflict). Therefore, it is an intellectual process that first 'produces' the
South. That is, the consciousness of the South comes before the definition
of its socio-historic conditions. It can be explained given the complexity
of the location of Portugal, within a double geography, at least.

The awareness that Portugal's reterritorialization was a not deferrable
urgency occurs with the emergence of Europe. It does not strictly deal
with events (even if the 1890 Ultimatum could probably be mentioned as
an epiphenomenon of this condition) but more with a process in transit
between the nineteenth and the twentieth century.

In the folds of a 'particular' modernity – and someone might say,
with some risks, 'specific' – representations of Portugal are fed by a fantasy
of the centre which is anyway inadequate to hide all the evidences of an
imminent peripheral co-presence. Modern European colonial topographies
are based on more tortuous, eccentric figures in the Portuguese case. For
this reason, the triad modernization, modernities and Modernism has a
proper function in twentieth-century Portugal, at least until the fracture
of the full European inscription and the end of any imperial temptation
(after the Carnations Revolution in 1974 and the decolonization in 1975).

The turning point of such a process may be located still in the twentieth
century when the discussion on modernities localizes the country and the
national culture in what sociologically can be defined as a semi-periphery
(it is interesting, here, to evoke Maria Irene Ramalho's reflection on poetry,
in particular Fernando Pessoa's poetic project and practice, as the first field

---

14   Eduardo Lourenço, *Nós e a Europa ou as Duas Razões*, 3rd edn (Lisbon: Imprensa
      Nacional–Casa da Moeda, 1990).

where the semi-peripheral consciousness is focalized).[15] For this reason, it might be worthwhile to begin a brief recovery of a Portuguese Southern genealogy by quoting some points and presuming the problematic potential of the South as a theoretical topic, from the point of view of a Portuguese modernity experience.

It is a fragment of the best known poem by Mário de Sá-Carneiro ('Dispersão' [Dispersion]), a lyric that permits a post-colonial reading as well as the reconfiguration of the dispersed 'body' of the nation ('Perdi-me dentro de mim/Porque eu era labirinto,/E hoje, quando me sinto,/É com saudades de mim'[16] [I lost myself inside of me/ For I was a maze,/And now, when I feel myself,/I miss me][17]):

> As minhas grandes saudades
> São do que nunca enlacei.
> Ai, como eu tenho saudades
> Dos sonhos que não sonhei!...
> E sinto que a minha morte –
> Minha dispersão total –
> *Existe lá longe, ao norte,*
> *Numa grande capital.*[18]

> [I miss the most
> What I never seized.
> Oh, how I do miss
> The dreams I never dreamt!...
> And I feel that my death –
> My total dispersion –
> *Is there, far away in the north,*
> *In a great capital.*][19]

15   Maria Irene Ramalho, 'A poesia e o sistema mundial', in Boaventura de Sousa Santos, ed., *Portugal: um retrato singular* (Porto: Afrontamento, 1993), 125.
16   Mário de Sá-Carneiro, 'Dispersão', in *Poesias* (Lisbon: Edições Ática, 1973), 61.
17   My translation.
18   Sá-Carneiro, *Poesias*, 64; emphasis added.
19   Translated by Amândio Reis.

Somehow, *Orpheu* is the culmination of a process of the 'inscription' of Portugal as South with much deeper roots. They may be detected in several reflexes of the Southern condition (see the emblematic journal entitled *SW South West* in 1935). These roots are strictly intertwined with the lines of what we can call critical Portuguese thought (that is a critical thinking about Portugal) whose beginnings are much less definable. It is curious that this thought finds its most relevant figures in the literary archive of prose but particularly in poetry, a less obvious circumstance that will deeply reverse its effects on twentieth-century literary imagination.

Rather than simply locating itself, as we have seen, the South is constituted as a clash of powers, a concentration of force and social violence that always keeps the continent in its background. In this brief reconstruction, the beginnings of such genealogy (very far from defining its proper and idealistic origins without activating an ideological operation) may be referred to Almeida Garrett's works as a conscious initiation of a specific stream of Portuguese self-critical thought. There is much evidence of his awareness, but it is in *Portugal na Balança da Europa* (even though it was published in 1830, it contains a collection of articles written in the previous decade, since 1825) that Portugal settles its image as South (with all the corresponding dimensions):

> Estava reservado ao pequeno Portugal, situado no ângulo mais ocidental da Europa, o dar à Europa e ao universo-mundo o espectáculo maior, mais tremendo e mais extraordinário de que há lembrança [...], o espectáculo de uma nação imolada, assassinada por defender seu legítimo soberano, perseguida por todos os reis da Terra por ser fiel ao seu rei – é exemplo novo e terrível, cujos resultados funestos, todavia mais o serão aos reis do que aos povos, e virão a ter sobre os destinos da Europa uma influência tremenda.[20]

> [It was meant for little Portugal, located in the westernmost corner of Europe, to give Europe and the world-universe the greatest, the most terrific and extraordinary spectacle there is in living memory [...], the spectacle of a nation slain, murdered

---

20   João Baptista da Silva Leitão Almeida Garrett, *Portugal na Balança da Europa. Do que tem sido e do que ora lhe convém ser na nova ordem de coisas do mundo civilizado* (Lisbon: Livros Horizonte, 2005), 63.

for defending its legitimate sovereign, chased by all the kings of the Earth for being loyal to its own king – this is a new and terrible example, whose dismal results will be even worse to the kings than to the people, and have on the fates of Europe a tremendous influence.][21]

Nevertheless, if Garrett relocalizes Portugal as a country where 'somos poucos e pequenos'[22] [we are few and small], it is the Geração de 70 [Generation of 1870] that created a new mythology of Europe (and consequently a reconfiguration of Iberia) restoring Portugal to its Southern position in a radical discussion on its delay in comparison with European modernity. In this case, the key text is certainly Antero's lecture from 1871, which provides a remapping of Portugal. In *Causas da Decadência dos Povos Peninsulares* [Causes of the Decline of the Peninsular Peoples], 'peninsular' stands for Southern in Antero's modern concept of geography.[23]

For its seminal value, it is worthwhile quoting, even if extensive, some crucial passages from Antero's lecture:

> Ora esses fenómenos capitais são três, e de três espécies: um moral, outro político, outro económico. O primeiro é a transformação do catolicismo, pelo Concílio de Trento. O segundo, o estabelecimento do absolutismo, pela ruína das liberdades locais. O terceiro, o desenvolvimento das conquistas longínquas. Estes fenómenos assim agrupados, compreendendo os três grandes aspectos da vida social, o pensamento, a política e o trabalho, indicam-nos claramente que uma profunda e universal revolução se operou, durante o século XVI, nas sociedades peninsulares. Essa revolução foi funesta, funestíssima. Se fosse necessária uma contraprova, bastava considerarmos um facto contemporâneo muito simples: esses três fenómenos eram exactamente o oposto dos três factos capitais, que se davam nas nações que lá fora cresciam, se moralizavam, se faziam inteligentes, ricas, poderosas, e tomavam a dianteira da civilização. Aqueles três factos civilizadores foram a liberdade moral, conquistada pela Reforma ou pela filosofia: a elevação da classe média, instrumento

---

21   Translated by Amândio Reis.

22   Garrett, *Portugal na Balança da Europa*, 12.

23   Other authors of the Geração de 70 are involved in a very similar and radical European reconfiguration. One of the most important is certainly Oliveira Martins, especially in *História da Civilização Ibérica* [History of the Iberian Civilization] (1879). I take the opportunity to thank Gabriel Magalhães for the reference in his reading of the present text.

do progresso nas sociedades modernas, e directora dos reis, até ao dia em que os destronou: a indústria, finalmente, verdadeiro fundamento do mundo actual, que veio dar às nações uma concepção nova do Direito, substituindo o trabalho à força, e o comércio à guerra de conquista. Ora, a liberdade moral, apelando para o exame e a consciência individual, é rigorosamente o oposto do catolicismo do Concílio de Trento, para quem a razão humana e o pensamento livre são um crime contra Deus: a classe média, impondo aos reis os seus interesses, e muitas vezes o seu espírito, é o oposto do absolutismo, esteado na aristocracia e só em proveito dela governando: a indústria, finalmente, é o oposto do espírito de conquista, antipático ao trabalho e ao comércio. Assim, enquanto as outras nações subiam, nós baixávamos. Subiam elas pelas virtudes modernas; nós descíamos pelos vícios antigos, concentrados, levados ao sumo grau de desenvolvimento e aplicação. Baixávamos pela indústria, pela política. Baixávamos, sobretudo, pela religião. [...] Somos uma raça decaída por ter rejeitado o espírito moderno: regenerar-nos-emos abraçando francamente esse espírito. O seu nome é Revolução: revolução não quer dizer guerra, mas sim paz: não quer dizer licença, mas sim ordem, ordem verdadeira pela verdadeira liberdade. Longe de apelar para a insurreição, pretende preveni-la, torná-la impossível: só os seus inimigos, desesperando-a, a podem obrigar a lançar mãos das armas. Em si, é um verbo de paz, porque é o verbo humano por excelência.[24]

[Now then, there were three principal phenomena, and of three kinds: one moral, another political, and the last economic. The first is the transformation of Catholicism, by the Council of Trent. The second is the establishment of Absolutism, through the destruction of local liberties. The third is the advance of the distant Conquests. These three phenomena thus brought together, taking in the three main aspects of social life, thought, public affairs, and production, clearly show us that a profound and universal revolution took place, during the sixteenth century, in Peninsular societies. That revolution was ruinous, quite ruinous. If a counter-proof were necessary, it would be sufficient to consider a very simple parallel fact: these three phenomena were the exact opposite of the three main features seen in other nations which grew, elevated themselves morally, that made themselves intelligent, rich and powerful, and carried civilization forward. Those three civilizing features were moral autonomy, won by the Reformation or by philosophy; the raising of the middle class, the instrument of progress in modern society, and the governor of kings, until the day it deposed them; and finally industry, the true basis of contemporary society, which gave nations a new conception of Justice, substituting trade for violence, and commerce for the war of conquest. Now moral autonomy, appealing to enquiry and individual conscience,

24   Antero de Quental, *Causas da Decadência dos Povos Peninsulares*, 3rd edn (Lisbon: Ulmeiro, 1979), 55–64.

is completely the opposite of the Catholicism of the Council of Trent, for which human reason and free thought are a crime against God; the middle class, imposing on kings its interests, and very often its values, is the opposite of Absolutism, based on the aristocracy and governing only for its benefit; and industry, finally, is the opposite of the spirit of conquest, hostile to trade and commerce. So while other nations rose, we sank. They rose on account of the modern virtues; we sank on account of the old vices, concentrated, taken to the highest degree of development and application. We sank in our industry, and our public affairs. And we sank, above all, in our religion. [...] We lag behind as a race because we rejected the modern spirit; we shall renew ourselves by freely embracing that spirit. Its name is Revolution. Revolution does not mean war, it means peace. It does not mean wantonness, but order, true order through true liberty. Far from seeking insurrection it aims to avoid it, to make it impossible; only its enemies, by frustrating it, could force it to take up arms. It is in itself the essence of peace because it is the human essence, par excellence.][25]

Effectively, his 1871 lecture is a treatise on the South, on the production of the South by various factors that the author sharply radiographed. Antero's topography of Peninsular – or Southern – decadence is due to the idea of Modernity, through a translation or comparative exercise, that can be detected between Europe and south. What is at stake is a rereading of the history of the nation, stripped off of any mythological aura and, in this sense, deepening the deconstructive mission initiated by Garrett.

Beyond Antero's critical threshold, referring to the definition of a thought about the South (of Europe), an ironic mythology of the South is built and finds its privileged space in poetry. In some way, poetry with a considerable mythopoetic exercise feeds an early imagination of the South that has an even more persistent force (a 'mythology', actually) to be projected on the one hand in many contemporary literary figures, and on the other in the form of the interpretative essay devoted to the (literally) very complex and opaque link between Portugal and Europe.

In such a perspective, poetry is probably the prominent field responsible for a critical re-elaboration of the imagination of the South.

25　Antero de Quental, 'Causes of the Decline of the Peninsular Peoples in the Last Three Centuries', trans. Richard Correll, *Portuguese Studies* 24/1 (2008), 76.

Among a lot of possible examples, we can quote some fragments connected with a redefinition of modern lyricism deriving from a Baudelairian matrix. The first case is the blague concocted by the 'first' Carlos Fradique Mendes, a 'philosopher of the boulevard', which in 1869 is defined as a poet who

> pertence a uma grande escola que por toda Europa veio substituir em parte, e em parte opor-se à escola romântica. Sabemos que essa escola tem uma estética sua, uma poética, tudo enfim quanto caracteriza um verdadeiro movimento no mundo do espírito, e conta à sua frente chefes do maior talento, dos mais variados recursos. Baudelaire é hoje um nome Europeu: crítico e poeta, legislou e pôs em obra as doutrinas da nova pléiade. Van Hole, Hulurugh, Schatchlig em Alemanha, em França Leconte de Lisle e Barrilot, seguiram exagerando-o ainda, o princípio do autor das *Flores do Mal*. O satanismo é hoje um facto literário europeu, um grande movimento.[26]

> [belongs to a great school that came partly to replace and partly to oppose the Romantic school all over Europe. We know this school has an aesthetic of its own, a poetics, ultimately, everything that characterizes a true movement in the world of spirit, and ahead of it are leaders with the greatest talent and the most varied resources. Baudelaire is now a European name: a critic and a poet, he legislated and put to work the doctrines of the new Pleiade. Van Hole, Hulurugh, Schatchlig in Germany, Leconte de Lisle and Barrillot in France, followed it, overdoing it still, the principle of the author of *Fleurs du mal* [Flowers of Evil]. Satanism is nowadays a European literary fact, a great movement.][27]

It sounds clear from the ironic mood of the description that, in such a context, Europe is synonymous to North, therefore the modern southern geography is fully unfolded.

Strengthening a Southern mythology for Portugal, another poet, Cesário Verde, elaborates a sort of counter topography of Portugal (e.g., 'Sentimento de um ocidental' [Feeling of a Western]) highlighting the 'luz meridional' [southern light] ('Nós' [Us]) and significantly entitling a quite famous poem 'Meridional' [Southern]. In this case too, beyond the presumable Parnassian tribute, Cesário extends the geographical figuration of

---

26   Joel Serrão, *O Primeiro Fradique Mendes* (Lisbon: Livros Horizonte, 1985), 266.
27   Translated by Amândio Reis.

Portugal and 'Meridional' becomes an aesthetic, Mediterranean, religious dimension of South.[28] A feeling that we can catch even in later times, when a strong poetic consciousness of South takes poetic (and political, through Antero's contemporary lesson, as mentioned beforehand) shape in verses composed by Gomes Leal (*Claridades do Sul* [Southern Clarities], 1874) where a fluctuation between typical and topical, political and poetical, becomes sensible ('A tortura das quimeras' [The Torture of Chimeras]):

> Sim, nestes climas lúcidos do Sul,
> Tão propenso às visões sentimentais
> E às quimeras – quem não terá jamais
> Tido a cruel melancolia azul?[29]

> [Yes, in these lucid climates of the South,
> So prone to sentimental visions
> And chimeras – who will never have
> Had the cruel blue melancholy?][30]

The mythology arising from such poetical production has the (vicarious) role of demythologizing the symbolic accumulation of Portugal's history, configuring a Southern condition of the country towards Europe. In this way, it is important to emphasize, considering other prominent poets such as António Nobre (in whose lyrics, south and north work as cardinal points for regimes of sea and wind, in this way associated to the memory of Portugal, in a spatial/temporal distance from Paris) and who induces us to rethink the relationship with other poetic movements such as Symbolism or *Saudosismo*, the idea of an opaque poetic veil always implied by the South, where a residue of a peripheral, Southern condition never dilutes, thus establishing permanent links with the other Peninsular – i.e. Southern – European nations. In a certain way the Ultimatum was

28 For example, Cesário Verde, *O Livro de Cesário Verde: 1873–1886*, ed. António Barahona (Lisbon: Assírio & Alvim, 2004).

29 Gomes Leal, *Claridades do Sul*, ed. José Carlos Seabra Pereira (Lisbon: Assírio & Alvim, 1998), 135.

30 Translated by Amândio Reis.

a compensatory residue of historical losses, a remnant that resists to a symbolization of the trauma-synthesis. Eventually, the South becomes a poetic sign that crosses a large part of twentieth-century poetry through different aesthetic movements.

Therefore, is it possible to compare the construction of Portugal as a South with other historical and symbolic processes concerning other Iberian contexts? Would it be feasible to find an ontological, latent connection for the Peninsula in this movement of loss, decadence, or drift from European centres? It deals with an alternative perspective, external to ideological risks of re-use of the past or obsolete identities, to re-read the Iberian narratives with a radical decentralization of the most sensitive issues, and in particular outside of any mythological aura.

Among the principal projections of this tendency, it is worthwhile to mention Eduardo Lourenço's work, which consists in one more topography of Iberia as South. According to him, 'vivemos real e simbolicamente numa Europa *diferente* da que fora marcada pela Reforma'[31] [we have been living really and symbolically in a *different* Europe] since the sixteenth century as a consequence of religious and political issues.

Such a re-inscription of Iberia as South carries out, first and foremost, the task of blocking any mythological drift in order to isolate differences whose value for the articulation of an ideological peninsular identity is quite negative. It would be useful, and the South as a concept shows it in a persuasive way, that a new translational approach may be defined, if we move not from the achievements or glories (of a time completely passed) but through a melancholic recognition of losses, vacuums, or remnants that call for open and sharable narratives that might redeem them.

For all these reasons Iberian Studies still has a very dense object to decipher and discuss and a titanic interpretative mission still has to be accomplished.

31   Lourenço, *Nós e a Europa*, 148; emphasis added.

Works cited

Althusser, Louis, *Sull'ideologia*, trans. M Gallerani (Bari: Dedalo libri, 1976).

Baratta, Giorgio, 'Gramsci e i subalterni', in Sergia Adamo, ed., *Culture planetarie. Prospettive e limiti della teoria e della critica culturale* (Roma: Meltemi, 2007), 91–3.

Camões, Luís de, *Os Lusíadas* (Lisbon: Ministério da Educação/Instituto Camões, 1992).

——, *The Lusíads*, trans. Landeg White (New York: Oxford University Press, 2008).

Cassano, Franco, *Il pensiero meridiano* (Bari: Laterza, 2003).

Garrett, João Baptista da Silva Leitão Almeida, *Portugal na Balança da Europa. Do que tem sido e do que ora lhe convém ser na nova ordem de coisas do mundo civilizado* (Lisbon: Livros Horizonte, 2005).

Gramsci, Antonio, *Quaderni del carcere*, ed. Valentino Gerratana, vols I–IV (Roma: Editori Riuniti, 1991).

——, *Selections from Prison Notebooks*, ed. and trans. Quintin Hoare and Geoffrey Nowell Smith (New York: International Publishers, 1971).

Leal, Gomes, *Claridades do Sul*, ed. José Carlos Seabra Pereira (Lisbon: Assírio & Alvim, 1998).

Lourenço, Eduardo, *Nós e a Europa ou as Duas Razões*, 3rd edn (Lisbon: Imprensa Nacional–Casa da Moeda, 1990).

Quental, Antero de, *Causas da Decadência dos Povos Peninsulares*, 3rd edn (Lisbon: Ulmeiro, 1979).

——, 'Causes of the Decline of the Peninsular Peoples in the Last Three Centuries', trans. Richard Correll, *Portuguese Studies* 24/1 (2008), 67–94.

Ramalho, Maria Irene, 'A poesia e o sistema mundial', in Boaventura de Sousa Santos, ed., *Portugal: um retrato singular* (Porto: Afrontamento, 1993), 93–128.

Sá-Carneiro, Mário de, *Poesias* (Lisbon: Edições Ática, 1973).

Said, Edward W., *Culture and Imperialism* (London: Vintage, 1994).

Serrão, Joel, *O Primeiro Fradique Mendes* (Lisbon: Livros Horizonte, 1985).

JÜRI TALVET

How to Research Iberian Literatures from a European Perspective? Premises and Contexts

There is hardly any need to imagine that while Comparative Literary Studies have prospered in the past, in the present time they are in a directly opposite state of a decline or a crisis. The situation in this field has never been ideal, stable or homogeneous. It would be misleading to imagine that a kind of uniform platform for a permanently balanced research of literatures of big and small nations, centres and peripheries, major and minor language areas would ever be established.

Yet it also remains a fact that during the times of Romanticism and along the nineteenth century a tentative canon of world literature, whatever its claws and gaps, indeed was taking shape, while those personalities in the vanguards of introducing the notion of world literature, the German romantic writers Johann Gottfried Herder, Johann Wolfgang Goethe, Friedrich and August Wilhelm Schlegel in the first place, not only recognized the greatness of literary achievements of the English (Shakespeare, Milton), the Italians (Dante, Boccaccio, Petrarch), the French (*Chançon de Roland*, Villon, Rabelais), Spaniards (*Cantar de mío Cid*, Cervantes, Calderón), and Portuguese (Camões), but also tried to be open to the vast periphery of world literature and, whenever possible, make the West conscious of great literary works beyond the Western-centric area.

Indeed, it happened simultaneously with a great 'leap' or 'explosion' – to use Yuri Lotman's terms[1] – within German culture itself in the late eighteenth century and the first half of the nineteenth century. While German culture after its long medieval period had clearly fallen into the

---

1   Юрий М. Лотман, *Культура и взрыв* (Москва: Радуга, 1992).

shadow of other great Western nations, becoming during the Renaissance and following Neoclassicism (the sixteenth and seventeenth centuries) a kind of a European semi-periphery, in Romanticism it acquired a new self-consciousness, backed by renewed criteria of aesthetic-philosophic judgement of literature and arts. It was in a strong opposition to rationally orientated neoclassical criteria. On that basis, Herder could claim the equality of the spiritual legacy of all nations, great and small, centres and peripheries. Poetry and poetic language were perceived as the nucleus of all literary creation. In the discourse of these German writers and philosophers, poetry permanently occupied the foreground. In his young days, while working as a pastor in the Latvian capital Riga, Herder manifested a keen interest in the traditional poetic creation of the three East-Baltic nations, Estonia, Latvia and Lithuania, gathering samples of their folksongs in his collection *Stimmen der Völker in Liedern* (1778–9), where he also included examples from the rich medieval lyrical tradition of Iberian nations. In his older days, inspired by Spanish medieval romances and the epic, Herder wrote himself a poem with the title 'Cid' (1805). As inspired above all by Oriental poetry and, more concretely, by the Iranian poet Nizami (Shah Name), Goethe created a cycle of poems called *West-östlicher Diwan* (1819).

Now I ask: where are the philosophically minded writers and literary-cultural scholars of our days, capable of transcending a limited national perspective and trying to establish a dialogue between 'own' and 'other'? Frankly, I cannot see such examples among the major Western cultural philosophers of the last part of the twentieth century. They have been either self-centred or their theoretical universalism has not descended to the level of concrete literary creation. Perhaps one of the few happy exceptions was Yuri M. Lotman who especially in his late cultural-semiotic philosophy was fascinated by the processes taking place on the border between 'own' and 'other' and the possibility of a dialogue in which the individuality of any culture would not only be conserved, but would also become enriched and expanded.[2]

---

2   Юрий М. Лотман, 'О семиосфере', *Труды по знакоым системам* 17 (1984), 5–23.

Thus the most essential condition for researching any national literature in the context of a broader area, transcending national frontiers, means to accept and adapt a perspective of comparative literary research. In a more detailed way, I have dwelt on the issue in my essay '*Edaphos* and *Episteme* of Comparative Literature'.[3]

One of the factors strongly restricting the possibilities of comparative research in our days has been language. Its role has been grotesquely exaggerated by postmodern cultural criticism. Realities beyond language have been denied or made exclusively dependent on the use of language. There has been a general scepticism as regards transcending one's own language. Also, there has been an obvious tendency to favour extreme positions in translation theories: you either adapt the 'other' in your own language and create a new literary work in its own rights, the 'other' being swallowed and neutralized (the Brazilian theory of anthropophagy), or you translate the 'other' into your language as intact as possible, including the grammatical constructions of the 'other's' language.

Little if anything has been learned from the past. The poets of the French Pléiade in the Renaissance days tried to adapt Latin grammar to the French language, but failed. French writers of Neoclassicism (Corneille, Lesage) were extremely active in adapting works of Spanish literature into French. Even in our days, the German writer Hans Magnus Enzensberger has published an adaptation of Calderón's drama *La hija del aire* (*Die Tochter der Luft*, 1992) under his own name, as its author (though in smaller letters, Calderón's name is also printed on the book cover). However, the copyright laws approved in most European countries along the twentieth century contradict such practices of literary 'cannibalism'.[4]

Some well-known American comparative scholars of our days (for instance, Gerald E. Gillespie, Dorothy Figueira) have voiced their strong opposition to the tendency at USA universities to replace Comparative

3   Jüri Talvet, '*Edaphos* and *Episteme* of Comparative Literature', *Interlitteraria* 10 (2005), 46–56.

4   Jüri Talvet, 'Contemporary Translation Philosophy: Cannibalism or Symbiosis?', *Interlitteraria* 12 (2007), 268–86.

Literature with 'World Literature'. Such a trend, as they claim, in reality means a monopolization of the research field by Departments of English Literature: 'World Literature' has come to mean first and foremost the creation of literature and literary criticism in English in the entire world. Vast areas of literature and criticism written outside the domain of English are being either ignored or paid little attention to.[5]

These are the main difficulties of comparative literary research in our days. Theory has been torn apart from the real processes taking place in literary creation. It does not favour literary practices or creating a dialogue between cultures and realities. Ego- and ethnocentric, monologic and solipsistic tendencies clearly contradict the spiritual needs of humanity.

In this background, I would add some remarks about international Spanish and Portuguese Studies as well as the phenomenon of *hispanismo*. There are Departments of Spanish and Portuguese at many universities throughout the world. There is no need to doubt that scholars of a number of nations, above all bigger nations beyond Spain and Portugal, have made important contributions to the study of Spanish and Portuguese literature.

However, it also remains a fact that a great part of international scholars specializing in Iberian cultures and literatures have become members of the same guild: there is hardly any difference between international scholars, on the one hand, and Spanish and Portuguese scholars of Spanish and Portuguese literature, on the other. Once again, a 'self' has formed, with little if any transcendence to the 'other' or to genuine comparative literary research.

It has become fashionable to include interdisciplinary elements in literary research. However, once fragmentation remains in the aesthetic-philosophic ground (*edaphos*) of literature, as an object of research, an interdisciplinary approach can hardly hope to contribute to overcoming the gulf separating 'self' from 'other', or 'centre' from 'periphery'.

5   Dorothy Figueira, 'Comparative Literature and the Origins of World Literature in National Literatures', *Interlitteraria* 17 (2012), 10–17.

What about the position of Iberian literatures in the canon of European and world literature, in the past and our days? Have they been sufficiently present in the European cultural scene, and if not, what are the reasons?

At the start of the eighteenth century, one of the first great French Enlightenment thinkers, the writer, philosopher and jurist Montesquieu mentioned that in Spanish literature there was only one great work, Cervantes's *Don Quixote*, against the background of the rest of Spanish literature which in the opinion of the Frenchman was lacking any value. Montesquieu's ideas about Spain, Portugal and Spanish literature appeared as playfully camouflaged in his epistolary novel *Lettres persanes* (1721).

Without any camouflage, approximately similar ideas have been voiced in our days by the dean of the USA literary scholarship, Harold Bloom. While receiving the Spanish Príncipe de Asturias Prize Bloom claimed that Cervantes's masterpiece *Don Quixote* was in a strong contrast with the weakness of his plays.[6]

Thus, there exists an amazing superficiality in the outside view at Iberian literatures. I have mentioned only the case of two top intellectuals, belonging to different epochs, but their views may well reflect the feelings of a layman who reads books as such, but has no special knowledge of literature. It could be even worse. Many nice young people of our days, including university students enjoying the advantages of the EU exchange scheme within the Erasmus programme, have surely never heard who Erasmus was and what his merits were. Even if they have heard of Don Quixote, as a kind of grotesque idealist, one may be fairly sure that a great part of highly educated people of our days have really never read Cervantes' novel. Though it could seem a flagrant injustice to those who have read more of Spanish or Portuguese literature than Montesquieu or Bloom, we have to accept the reality. By the way, such a generalized biased opinion can be explained by some reasons which are a part of objective reality, as regards intercultural and inter-literary processes.

As is well known, the international reception of any national literary work depends strongly on translation, in the first place, and secondly, on

6   Harold Bloom, 'Entrevista con Harold Bloom', *El País/Babelia* (4 May 2002).

the reception of the work in criticism beyond the national space (though the case of some of the most powerful cultural-linguistic areas, like Anglo-American and French literature, obviously stands apart). Last but not least, it depends on the reading public, which can hardly be reduced to the abstract term of 'reader', more than often employed by literary scholarship. Readers not only vary by individual people reading books, but also by nationalities and gender, as well as by generations and entire epochs. On the one hand, literary-comparative research cannot ignore these factors. In most cases, it directly depends on them. Thus there are fashionable trends, 'key theoreticians', mainstream authors, etc., whom a university professor obviously cannot neglect entirely. On the other hand, any serious literary scholarship should still try to resist the temptations and commands of fashionable trends and attempt to illuminate literary phenomena which unjustly have been moved away from the centre of research either by commercial, political or ideological factors.

As compared with other vast ethnic areas, linguistic access to Iberian literatures can hardly be seen as a problem, because Spanish and Portuguese are taught all over the world. As the result, at least literary works of prose fiction created in Spanish and Portuguese are quite actively being translated into other languages. They surely cannot rival Anglo-American mass literature, but at least some of the examples of the best-known achievements of prose fiction created originally in Spanish have long ago transcended the frontiers of the Iberian Peninsula, reaching other nations. Thus for instance, if an Estonian university professor would like to carry out a comparative course on the poetics and philosophy of Western existentialist and neo-realistic prose fiction, he/she can provide the students a reading list of translations in Estonian not only including the novels or short stories by Albert Camus, Jean-Paul Sartre, Ernest Hemingway or Günter Grass, but also by Camilo José Cela, Juan García Hortelano, Juan Goytisolo, Ana María Matute or some other Spanish authors. As for prose fiction created in Portuguese, indeed, we have to admit that at least our Estonian literary *edaphos* in this area still appears as insufficient.[7]

Looking at the past, one probably has to accept the fact that no other Iberian prose fiction work of the classical period can rival the originality of Cervantes's *Don Quixote* in its aesthetic-philosophic dimension. But I very much doubt if teaching *Don Quixote* at an average European university goes beyond what is being done at the seminars and lectures of Departments of Spanish. Are there many university courses at which Cervantes's *Don Quixote* is treated in a general context of the formation of Western novel, or as an arch-text of meta-narrative in Western prose fiction?

The 'Golden Age' of Spanish literature has important works in the picaresque genre. Their grasp of reality as well as their philosophy remains to some extent narrower, as compared with Cervantes's masterpiece. Yet from a general viewpoint of the development and modification of auto-biographical first-person narrative in Western prose fiction, the arch-text of *Lazarillo de Tormes*, as well as the novels by Mateo Alemán, Francisco de Quevedo and other Spanish authors have a fundamental role. As in a number of twentieth-century existential novels, the exposition of their philosophy depends directly on the narrative form chosen by their authors. I am not sure that people who deal with detailed analysis of narrative techniques at Western universities today have heard much of these early Spanish narratives. It is an obvious consequence of the separation and fragmentation of Literary Studies which characterize most Western universities. Comparative Literary Studies genuinely miss, or they have been replaced by a fragmentary dedication to some narrow aspect of comparison.

Baltasar Gracián's *El criticón* is a fascinating allegory, but its *conceptismo* and puns make it an extremely difficult task for translation. In fact, its translations exist only in some major languages. At the same time, even if perfection in translation could be achieved, there still remains a doubt, whether *El criticón's* accentuated culturological and intellectual dimension would favour its wider reception among international readers.

---

7   Mele Pesti, 'The Reception of Portuguese-language Literatures in Estonia', *Interlitteraria* 16/2 (2011), 607–27.

Despite some sporadic success after modern translations in English, it would be by far overoptimistic to expect that the world could acclaim as openly as *Don Quixote* the Catalan masterpiece by Joanot Martorell and Martí de Galba, *Tirant lo Blanc*. These generic limitations are obvious. The same conditions have restricted the outside reception of Cervantes's own last novel, *Los trabajos de Persiles y Sigismunda*.

Yet in my opinion Montesquieu and Bloom are deeply mistaken, when imagining *Don Quixote* to be fated to tower in loneliness amid the supposed literary mediocrity of the Spanish *Siglo de Oro*. As is known, the vast majority of literary works of the period were written in verse form, including Spanish Golden Age drama. In my opinion, that is where we will find the most extensive gaps and blank spaces in international reception, including translation, criticism and research.

Among the internationally renowned writers and intellectuals who have appreciated Francisco de Quevedo's poetic work, the Argentine Jorge Luis Borges stands out. However, even Borges's statue and prestige would be inadequate for stimulating a wider international reception of Quevedo's existential poetry, if talented (new) translations are missing. Influential criticism and scholarship should go hand in hand with skilful poetic translations, preferably made by capable poets or at least translators possessing poetic sensibility. An exemplary case from the past is August Wilhelm Schlegel who not only made talented poetic translations of Petrarch's poetry, but also provided philosophically shaded commentaries on those writers whose work he conveyed to German readers.

The greatness of Pedro Calderón de la Barca's dramatic work can hardly be disputed. Yet it remains a fact that while Shakespeare's plays have been and are still being staged all over the world, Calderón is almost an unknown writer for the overwhelming international cultural community. Among the few influential modern writers who have paid attention to Calderón's work, Albert Camus and Pier Paolo Pasolini stand out. Yet, once again: talented new translations of Calderón's most important works are lacking. Germany and Russia are perhaps among the few happy exceptions, but even there Calderón has never rivalled Shakespeare in popularity.

Naturally, there are ideological reasons, like Calderón's religious-Catholic accents. It could have had the effect of a certain prejudice regarding his work since the radical turn to hard sciences and positivistic philosophy at the end of the nineteenth century. However, much more serious reception problems are those connected with specific translation difficulties. I do not suppose a return to the early practices of translating Spanish Golden Age drama in accordance with the original Spanish metric and rhyme patterns would provide a perspective for stimulating international reception. Instead, talented free or blank verse translations made by capable writers and poets could offer a solution.

For myself, there is little doubt that Tirso de Molina's verse play *El burlador de Sevilla y convidado de piedra*, the source text of Don Juan's myth in world culture, is poetically as well as philosophically superior to Molière's prose comedy *Don Juan*. Yet even in today's Spain many educated people do not know much about Tirso de Molina's drama, while in the wider world of literature and arts Don Juan's myth has been represented in the first place as inspired by Molière's comedy.

Once the canon has been established, it is a really hard task to change it radically for posterity. However, an opposite process can also take place in the canon. Some works which seem to have become part of the canon of world or European literature may fall out of it.

I will conclude my essay with a brief observation about the Spanish-language twentieth-century novel. Almost simultaneously, the Spanish neo-realistic novel and the Spanish-American 'new novel' emerged in the 1950s and 1960s. Spanish neo-realism was strongly supported in its international repercussion by its prevailing opposition to Franco's dictatorship. It was a predominantly socio-critical narrative that also had points of contact with European existentialism. It was quite widely translated abroad.

By today, not only the Spanish neo-realistic novel but also the Latin-American magic-realistic novel has been exhausted as a living phenomenon. We can look at both in retrospect and compare the position of both from a certain time distance. I hope I am not wrong in concluding that the Spanish neo-realistic novel has by today ceased to be an object of international discussion in literary criticism. From an active canon it has fallen into a passive one. If situated in a general context of Western post-war novel, the originality and novelty of the Spanish novel will fade in comparison with the neo-realistic and existentialist narrative produced in France, Italy and Germany.

By contrast, Latin-American authors of the *nueva novela* managed to create a new narrative paradigm in their work. Even though there are sporadic magic-realistic elements in the work of some Western and European novelists before World War II (such as Kafka, Bulgakov, and also Faulkner), it is a generally accepted fact that only since the Latin-American 'new novel' has the magic-realistic narrative as a phenomenon started to be a clearly perceived autonomous object of international discussion in criticism and scholarship. Its novel features were not limited to social criticism, but had first and foremost to do with philosophy and aesthetics. Even though the apex of Latin-American magic-realistic narrative is past, the subsequent international discussion on modern narrative, including its postmodern phase, can hardly ignore the experience of the Latin-American novel.

When researching and teaching Iberian literatures in the wider European context, we probably cannot leave these aspects unnoticed. A comparative study should first feel its ground beyond a national culture. If national works appear in a comparative context as imitative or lacking originality, one can naturally research them. But then the question arises: what is the purpose of such research? Would it really expand the existing understanding of world literature?

Maybe in some aspect, it could. However, I think a by far more important task within our limited human resources would be to attempt to locate and discuss in international contexts those original national works that most unjustly have been left out of the canon of world literature or (mainly thanks to the respective contributions by national scholars) exist only in the passive canon of international dictionaries. They are not few.

To recapitulate my answer to the question in the title of my essay, the most urgent and important task in researching Iberian literatures in the context of European literatures would be to expand the comparative basis of Literary Studies at all European universities, with the main aim of relating 'own' to 'other'. Generic comparative courses on the history of European and Western literatures, including the literary phenomena of both 'centres' and 'peripheries' in their historical dynamics should have an essential position in future university curricula. Europe should be able to (re)discover the valuable part of its literature beyond fashionable mainstream phenomena. It should definitely transcend a limited national perspective and perceive as its 'own' literature that of the whole continent and, whenever possible, establish a dialogue with the 'other' beyond the existing Western canon.

Works cited

Bloom, Harold, 'Entrevista con Harold Bloom', *El País/Babelia* (4 May 2002).

Figueira, Dorothy, 'Comparative Literature and the Origins of World Literature in National Literatures', *Interlitteraria* 17 (2012), 10–17.

Лотман, Юрий М., *Культура и взрыв* (Москва: Радуга, 1992).

——, 'О семиосфере', *Труды по знакоым системам* 17 (1984), 5–23.

Pesti, Mele, 'The Reception of Portuguese-language Literatures in Estonia', *Interlitteraria* 16/2 (2011), 607–27.

Talvet, Jüri, 'Contemporary Translation Philosophy: Cannibalism or Symbiosis?', *Interlitteraria* 12 (2007), 268–86.

——, '*Edaphos* and *Episteme* of Comparative Literature', *Interlitteraria* 10 (2005), 46–56.

.

CÉSAR DOMÍNGUEZ

Literatures in Spain: European Literature, World-Literature, World Literature?*

According to the short description of key objectives, the European Science
Foundation workshop *Looking at Iberia from a Comparative European
Perspective*, which was at the origin of this volume, aimed at exploring
the scientific accuracy and validity of the concept 'Iberia' as a starting
point for academic work and, therefore, the discipline of what one may
call 'Iberian Studies'. My contribution to the discussion of these conceptual
and epistemological issues is, on the one hand, based upon a specific perspective, namely meta-geography, and, on the other hand, framed within
what has been called the new inflections of Hispanism. After providing
basic information on both perspective and discipline history, I will present
three case studies which may help to question the use of the plural for the
term 'literature' in my title and, consequentially, explore three different
settings – European literature, world-literature, world literature – wherein
'literatures in Spain' may convey different but not altogether contradictory
meanings. I have tried to ensure that these three case studies be as diverse
as possible in order to highlight the several nuances of the move from a
national paradigm to a geo-literary paradigm, as advocated by what it is
being called in this volume 'the field of Iberian Studies'.

It is my contention that it would make sense to advocate a paradigm
shift, which may include several aspects, from an updating of methodology
to interdisciplinary collaboration, only if a requirement is met. Namely, that

*   This essay is part of the research project 'Europe, in Comparison: European Union,
    Identity and the Idea of European Literature,' funded by the Spanish government
    (FFI2010-16165). It is also related to th research activities of the Jean Monnet Chair
    'The Culture of European Integration' (n° 528689).

specific problems which previous methods and/or paradigms neither consider being problems *per se*, nor can adequately address, are identified. The
feasibility of a field of discipline called 'Iberian Studies' depends, therefore,
on the central position that Claudio Guillén accorded to Spain for being
'metodológicamente crucial porque en él se destaca visiblemente que la
historia consta no de una serie de períodos dispares sino de la coexistencia
y confrontación de procesos y duraciones'[1] [methodologically crucial
because in it we see that history is not a series of disparate periods but
rather, the coexistence and confrontation of processes and timespans].[2]
This matches his definition of Comparative Literature as a discipline which
is 'characterized by the posing of certain problems that only comparative
literature is in a position to confront.'[3]

What sort of object is Iberia?
What sort of discipline is Iberian Studies?

During recent years, the emergence in Literary Studies of spatial categories
such as Iberia/Iberian Peninsula, Sub-Saharan Africa, East-Central Europe,
Scandinavia, the Pacific rim, to name but a few, is directly linked to what
one may call a 'cartographical anxiety', which is the result of the inadequacy
of the maps used or which are, much of the time, taken for granted, that is,
political maps. In 1991 the Belgian comparatist José Lambert, in an article
titled 'In Quest of Literary World Maps', argued that 'the relationship
between literature and socio-political structures is not a self-evident matter

1   Claudio Guillén, 'Sobre el objeto del cambio literario', in *Teorías de la historia literaria (ensayos de teoría)* (Madrid: Espasa–Calpe, 1989), 203.
2   Unless otherwise stated, all translations are my own.
3   Claudio Guillén, *The Challenge of Comparative Literature*, trans. Cola Frenzen (Cambridge, MA: Harvard University Press, 1993), 104.

but *needs to be investigated*[4] and, therefore, he advocated the need for maps in order to overcome our 'indistinct, even medieval image of the literary world'.[5] Twenty years later, whereas spatial concepts have been overused in a rather vague and metaphorical way, works such as, for instance, Gian Mario Anselmi's *Mappe della letteratura europea e mediterranea* may not contain a single map; thereby demonstrating that literary mapping is still in its infancy. The only exceptions are Franco Moretti's *Atlas of the European Novel, 1800–1900*, and Eric Bulson's *Novels, Maps, Modernity*.

Lambert was well aware of the difficulties posed by literary mapping even though his maps were still framed by politics rather than by literary data. '[L]iterary scientists *do not yet have a model of their own*, and [...] literature is not their real subject', Lambert states, however, he suggests that 'we speak about "literature *in* France", "literature *in* Germany" or "literature *in* Italy", instead of "German literature", "French literature", "Italian literature" and so on'.[6] But if one advocates a discipline field called 'Iberian Studies', the object of study is not exclusively the political map of Spain and Portugal and its history, but rather Iberia or the Iberian Peninsula. Either concept is of a geographical nature, which may lead to the wrong conclusion about its greater degree of objectivity and neutrality for the mapping of those literatures produced within this area, in contrast to the predicament of political categories. Here it is worth applying the meta-geographical perspective, for Iberia may indeed highlight problems which can be overlooked when seen with a national-literary lens, and yet Iberia is as much a construction as Spain and Portugal are constructed polities in the Anderson-like sense of 'imagined communities'.[7]

I have extensively dealt with this issue elsewhere. For the sake of my argument, let me only recall that, according to Martin W. Lewis and Kären

---

4 José Lambert, 'In Quest of World Literary Maps', in Dirk Delabatista, Lieven D'hulst, and Reyne Meylaerts, eds, *Functional Approaches to Culture and Translation. Selected Papers by José Lambert* (Amsterdam: John Benjamins, 2006), 72.

5 Lambert, 'In Quest', 64.

6 Lambert, 'In Quest', 72; italics in the original.

7 Benedict Anderson, *Imagined Communities. Reflections on the Origin and Spread of Nationalism* (London: Verso, 1998).

E. Wiggen, meta-geography is 'the set of spatial structures through which people order their knowledge of the world'.[8] The slightest familiarity with the basic notions of meta-geography – North/South, East/West, First/Second/Third World, continents, orientalism and Eurocentrism are just a few examples – leads us to realize that it is a code based on oppositions; that it operates on a large scale, over a long period of time and long after the disappearance of the entities to which it refers (in the post-Berlin-Wall era, the ternary politico-economic division of the world has not been reformulated.) Meta-geographies are, therefore, meta-narrations that tend to be all encompassing and exclusionary; spaces of power and strategies of assimilation/exclusion. And despite the explicit difference signalled by Lewis and Wigen between their concept of meta-geography and Hayden White's notion of meta-history, in the sense that their 'concerns are far more prosaic; we are largely interested in the primary spatial structures around which we habitually conceptualize global geography',[9] I believe that meta-geography ends up being another level in the deep structure through which we select and emplot material with the aim of making it comprehensible.

In the case of Iberian Studies, Iberia/the Iberian peninsula is, therefore, a meta-geographical object whereby one may select and emplot literary material in a different way to the selection and emplotment provided by national literary objects such as Spanish literature and Portuguese literature. Both the alternative selection and emplotment may pose questions regarding the literary material, which have either not been asked or not been considered 'problems' so far in the disciplinary sense used by Claudio Guillén. What one should not neglect, however, is that the meta-geographical perspective is intertwined with the rationale of those disciplines wherein the meta-geographical objects have been formulated. And most meta-geographical categories have been formulated by Area Studies, which is a discipline of regional organization whose impetus was the entry of the USA into World War II and whose growth paralleled the expansion

---

8   Martin W. Lewis and Kären E. Wigen, *The Myth of Continents. A Critique of Metageography* (Berkeley: University of California Press, 1997), ix.
9   Lewis and Wigen, *The Myth*, 207 n. 2.

of American universities. Iberia and Iberian Studies are not exceptions as far as the disciplinary rationale is concerned; for Iberian Studies, like other Area Studies, is interdisciplinary and history-oriented.[10] However, its distinctiveness derives from having been subsumed within a larger area – Latin America – which, for the regional organization advocated by Area Studies, is characterized by being a coherent regional entity. It is important to remember, however, that Latin America is a designation coined by French scholars in the mid-nineteenth century in their desire to include the Spanish-, Portuguese- and French-speaking portions of America[11] within the framework of Napoleon III's imperial project. (A similar enterprise was the creation of the Near and Middle East by the British Empire.) The supposed conceptual cohesion of the delimitation must be questioned, since its final result is the emphasis on religious, linguistic, historic and political affinities through an adjective (Latin) which specifically denies the indigenous and African-American elements.

In its literary counterpart, Iberian Studies in the USA fosters an image of Iberia as a province of Latin America, a phenomenon that Joseba Gabilondo has cleverly identified as the 'Antonio Banderas effect'. 'A *heterosexual, Spanish* actor, out of the movies of a gay Spanish director, Pedro Almodóvar', Gabilondo argues, 'comes to represent Latin American, Latino, or gay characters in every [Hollywood] mainstream film portraying such identities.'[12] I rewrite here the Antonio Banderas effect in its institutional dimension as the conception that understands 'Hispanic' Studies as the analysis of Latin American literature (but not in Portuguese/Brazilian,

---

10   Patrick Manning, *Navigating World History. Historians Create a Global Past* (New York: Palgrave Macmillan, 2003), 145.

11   Fernand Braudel, *A History of Civilizations*, trans. Richard Mayne (New York: Penguin, 1994), 247; Simon Collier, Harold Blakemore, and Thomas E. Skidmore, eds, *The Cambridge Encyclopedia of Latin America and the Caribbean* (Cambridge: Cambridge University Press, 1985), 9.

12   Joseba Gabilondo, 'One-Way Theory: On the Hispanic-Atlantic Intersection of Postcoloniality and Postnationalism and Its Globalizing Effects', *Arachne: Journal of Iberian and Latin American Literary and Cultural Studies* 1/1 (2001) <http://arachne.rutgers.edu/vol11gabilondo.htm> accessed 1 October 2011; italics in the original.

much less in indigenous languages) and, only secondly, of Peninsular (in Castilian) literature. Paradoxically, with the homogenization of the Iberian Peninsula as a Latino region by the Area Studies of the Cold War, one has erased not only internal difference (Catalan, Galician, Portuguese, Basque), but also historical difference. The philological reactionarism evidenced by the loss of ground by medieval Spanish literature as a taught subject testifies to this fact.

The emergence of Iberian Studies may mean, therefore, both a reaction to the way in which Iberia has been provincialized within Latin America and an attempt to disclose the literary richness of those cultures which have been either regionalized or erased from the Iberian Peninsula. A recent example of this tendency is Gary W. McDonogh's book *Iberian Worlds*, in which Iberia is described as a region that 'now comprises three European nationstates (Spain, Portugal and Andorra) and a British Overseas Territory (Gibraltar). These territories also incorporate multiple distinctive nationalities and cultures that are not states, while many immigrants, postcolonial and global, have contributed to a population of more than 51 million people'.[13] McDonogh advocates naming this region Iberia, because '"Iberian" would scarcely be a primary identity among madrileños (citizens of Madrid), Gypsies, Catalans, Andalusian Muslims or Europeans. Yet, the term's very "neutrality" allows us to use it to look at history, culture and power in new and important ways'.[14]

The assumed neutrality of the concept of Iberia and, hence, its use as a non-identitarian category, which is in line with other recently created regional categories across Europe – such as East-Central Europe, in contrast to *Mitteleuropa* or Central Europe, the effacement of any meta-geographical element and the oblivion of the nineteenth- and early twentieth-century indigenous movement of Iberism in McDonogh's proposal are key issues worth discussing. It is here that a confrontation between Lambert's world mapping, whose neutrality as an activity matches McDonogh's position,

13   Gary W. McDonogh, *Iberian Worlds* (New York: Routledge, 2009), 3.
14   McDonogh, *Iberian*, 3.

and Djelal Kadir's[15] caveat about the location of the person who maps provides insight about the plurality of the object (Iberia/s) and, consequentially, of the discipline. It is important then to contextualize McDonogh's stance about Iberia/Iberian Studies within recent inflections of Hispanism in the USA academia. Joan Ramon Resina has identified the German, Spanish and American traditions as central areas of the development of Hispanism. As for the American tradition, Resina highlights a new move within Hispanism, a new consciousness that emerges as 'meta-Hispanism' and which studies '[t]he cultural system of the Iberian Peninsula, hitherto conceived as a relatively unproblematic continuum of the "Spanish" tradition, [...] as a process of differentiation of cultures which constitute the system's internal environment'.[16] Resina himself likens this inflection to the postnational paradigm[17] and Catalonia, whose literature 'represents the *largest* vacuum in the incomplete, dismembered Peninsular picture that Hispanic studies presents'.[18]

A case in point about Hispanism's new inflections is the book co-edited in 2010 by Luis Martín-Estudillo and Nicholas Spadaccini, whose basic assumption is that '[i]t is common knowledge that Spain's transformation during the last several decades from an authoritarian, centralist State with a homogeneous population into a democratic, plurinational, and multicultural society has also been marked by a thriving cultural production, which highlights "difference" as a major asset'.[19] This 'difference' is stressed by the use in the plural of the term 'literature', both in the book title (*New Literatures*) and in the title of the editors' introduction ('Spanish Literatures').

15   Djelal Kadir, 'To World, to Globalize – Comparative Literature's Crossroads', *Comparative Literature Studies* 41/1 (2004), 1–9.
16   Joan Ramon Resina, 'Hispanism and Its Discontents', *Siglo XX/20th Century* 14/1–2 (1996), 89.
17   Resina, 'Hispanism', 114.
18   Resina, 'Hispanism', 120; italics added.
19   Luis Martín-Estudillo and Nicholas Spadaccini, eds, *New Spain, New Literatures* (Nashville: Vanderbilt University Press, 2010), ix.

Whereas in the USA academia this move towards meta-Hispanism is paralleled by a decreasing institutional weight of Comparative Literature in favour of world literature; in the Spanish academia, a shift within Hispanic Studies and not Iberian Studies is paralleled by an increasing institutionalization of Comparative Literature. Antonio Monegal, for instance, advocates a stronger position for Comparative Literature as a way of overcoming national-oriented models that 'draw a map that separates the domestic from the alien, the inside from the outside'.[20] Comparative Literature, as an 'appreciation of the interconnections between literary systems', seems thus to provide a 'fitting framework'[21] for addressing what Monegal terms 'Peninsular multiculturalism'. This is still, however, a multiculturalism defined along national lines, as proven by the fact that literary interconnections are restricted to those between the 'central' literary system (in Spanish) and each of the 'peripheral' literary systems (in Basque, Catalan and Galician). Not to mention the peculiar use of the adjective 'Peninsular', which seems to implicitly endorse a long-established tradition regarding the minor role of Portuguese culture and literature, as seen from Spain.

This is, in my opinion, the general picture within which any future reflection about Iberian Studies should be located. Namely, between an Anglophone tradition wherein Iberian Studies is the result of the regional categorization of Cold War Area Studies, which sees Iberia in its cultural and literary dimension as a paradigm of multiculturalism, and an 'indigenous' tradition wherein Hispanism tries to overcome its imperial implications by way of comparison. In what follows, I will present three case studies which may shed light on the kinds of problems that could define Iberian Studies as a discipline.

20   Antonio Monegal, 'A Landscape of Relations: Peninsular Multiculturalism and the Avatars of Comparative Literature', in Brad Epps and Luis Fernández Cifuentes, eds, *Spain beyond Spain. Modernity, Literary History, and National Identity* (Lewisburg: Bucknell University Press, 2005), 246.
21   Monegal, 'A Landscape', 245.

Case study 1: towards European literature

That the location of Iberian literatures within European literature has worked through their peripherality, minorization and orientalization is well known. In fact domestic literary history was born as an act of vindication of the role played by Spanish literature in Europe. In one of the few textbooks available to aid the teaching of European literature nowadays, Iberian literatures – restricted to Spanish and Portuguese literature – are still dealt with in terms of exceptionality. 'La définition de l'originalité ibérique' [the definition of Iberian originality], Daniel-Henri Pageaux says, 'passe donc par l'affirmation ou la reconnaissance de la "différence" radicale, de l'Altérité absolue, tantôt avancée par les "Ibériques" eux-mêmes, tantôt reprise par les Européens'[22] [stems from the affirmation or the acknowledgement of a radical 'difference', of an absolute Otherness, sometimes claimed by the 'Iberian' themselves, and other times employed by the Europeans].[23] And as for Iberian 'regional' literatures, the domestic erasure results in teleology of non-existence, as proven by recent research on the European canon, wherein not a single Basque, Catalan or Galician writer is included.[24]

But this is not the kind of relationship between Iberian and European literature I want to discuss here. I am interested in a new dimension of Europeanism of Iberian literatures, namely, the fact that Iberian literatures are working as host-literatures for migrant writers. This is the case for the Moroccan migrant writer Laila Karrouch, whose book in Spanish *Laila* may be found at bookstores in the latest edition of July 2010 by Oxford, a leading publishing house in the Spanish education system at the moment. Although the edition is linked to 2010, the copyright year is given as 2004.

---

22   Daniel-Henri Pageaux, 'La Péninsule Ibérique et l'Europe', in Béatrice Didier, ed.,
        Précis de littérature européenne (Paris: Presses Universitaires de France, 1998), 166.
23   Unless otherwise stated, all translations into English are my own.
24   Roberto Antonelli, 'Il canone europeo' <http://w3.uniroma1.it/studieuropei/ilcan-
        one/index.htm> accessed 1 October 2011.

If one checks the ISBN database, one will find that there are eight entries under the name of Laila Karrouch, and that the first edition of *Laila* was printed in February 2005 by Planeta & Oxford. This does not solve the issue of the 2004 copyright, except if one realizes that the ISBN database includes a 2004 book in Catalan titled *De Nador a Vic*. Once the Spanish *Laila* and the Catalan *De Nador a Vic* – which was published in 2004 by the publishing house Columna after the manuscript was awarded the prize Columna Jove 2004 – are compared, one notices that we are dealing with the 'same work'.

From a translation theory perspective, one wonders whether *Laila* is an original or a 'pseudo-original'. If an original, it would mean that Karrouch is a bilingual writer who may write both in Catalan and in Spanish, and therefore her novel works within two literary systems at the same time. If a 'pseudo-original', a term which I coin drawing on pseudotranslation, *Laila* is a mimetic work addressed to a target-audience who reads as an original, what is, in fact, a translated text. Whereas the ISBN database presents *Laila* as a work written originally in Spanish, it is a pseudo-original, a Spanish translation of the 2004 Catalan original. But who is the translator of *Laila*? One possibility is that Karrouch herself had translated her work from Catalan into Spanish, which favoured its presentation as pseudo-original and the concealment of any information regarding the translator. Another possibility is that the translation had been made by a translator proper. In either case, the question remains valid: why has information about the translator been concealed?

Both Columna and Oxford refused to provide me with this information. It is important to note that Columna is one of the companies of Grup 62, which, in its turn, is one of the companies of the Grupo Planeta, which published jointly with Oxford in 2005 the Spanish pseudo-original. In a personal communication on 17 January 2001, Karrouch confirmed me that she also does not know who translated her book and that, in any case, it was Oxford that commissioned the translation. This issue is most important, for a comparison between the Catalan work and the Spanish translation shows the high degree of changes experienced by the former, as summarized in the title change from *De Nador a Vic* to *Laila*. Whereas the original in Catalan presents Laila's migrant experience from Nador to

Vic and her adaptation to the bilingual reality of Catalonia, the translation into Spanish erases any trace of Catalonia in order to restrict the migrant experience as an adaptation process to a monolingual, Castilian-centric society. It is, therefore, most telling that, while for the *Cuaderno para el desarrollo lector* of Oxford Educación, reading *Laila* makes possible an understanding of 'los choques culturales que vive alguien que se muda de ciudad o país'[25] [the cultural clashes suffered by someone who moves to a different city or country], a comparison between the original in Catalan and the pseudo-original in Spanish shows that this aim depends on both exoticizing the alien Other and eradicating the domestic Other; operations which the average reader of the Spanish version cannot discern.

Case study 2: Iberian literatures as world-literature

World-literature is a concept coined upon Immanuel Wallerstein's theory of world-systems. 'World-systems analysis', Wallerstein argues, 'makes the unit of analysis a subject of debate. [...] It substitutes for the term "society" the term "historical system"'.[26] Drawing on Fernand Braudel's concept of *économie-monde*, Wallerstein has tentatively distinguished three varieties of historical systems, namely, mini-systems, world-empires and world-economies. Wallerstein himself has made possible its application to culture and literature through the notion of 'geoculture', which he defines as the superstructure of the world-economy.[27] To my knowledge, there exist only two such applications.

25   Oxford Educación, *Cuaderno para el desarrollo lector: Laila* (Madrid: Oxford University Press, 2010), 2.
26   Immanuel Wallerstein, 'World-Systems Analysis', in *The Essential Wallerstein* (New York: The New Press, 2000), 139.
27   Immanuel Wallerstein, *Geopolitics and Geoculture. Essays on the Changing World-System* (Cambridge: Cambridge University Press, 2001), 11.

The most comprehensive one is due Alexander Beecroft, who, paradoxically, deprecates the concept of world-literature on the grounds that it 'has the perhaps unintended effect of re-inscribing a hegemonic cultural centre'.[28] Although I agree with Beecroft that this negative effect is most conspicuous in Pascale Casanova's[29] and (to a lesser extent) Franco Moretti's[30] models of world literature, I think the non-intentionality Beecroft himself acknowledges is an important reason to not dismiss a concept which does not convey a 'mono-centric' meaning *per se*. Actually, Beecroft's 'panchoric literature', which he defines as 'literary texts and systems of circulation operating across a range of epichoric communities, united to some degree in language and culture',[31] seems to me to be very much indebted, not only to the concept of the 'Panhellenic', as this author claims, but also to world-literature itself when it is defined as 'a world-system within which literature is produced and circulates'.[32]

The second application may be considered a French reply to the Anglophone theories about world literature. I refer to the concept *littérature-monde*, which has been articulated in order to overcome the imperial overtones of *Francophonie*. 'Fin aussi d'une conception impérialiste de la langue' [end, also, of an imperialist conception of the language], Michel Le Bris states. 'Ou bien en effet l'on postule un lien "charnel" entre la nation et la langue qui en exprimerait le génie singulier et dans ce cas, en toute rigueur, la francophonie s'avoue comme le dernier avatar du colonialisme, ou bien l'on délie le pacte langue-nation, de sorte que la langue, libérée, devienne l'affaire de tous'[33] [either we indeed postulate a 'carnal' link between the nation and the language which supposedly expresses

28   Alexander Beecroft, 'World Literature without a Hyphen: Towards a Typology of Literary Systems', *New Left Review* 54 (2008), 88.
29   Pascale Casanova, *The World Republic of Letters*, trans. M. B. Debevoise (Cambridge, MA: Harvard University Press, 2004).
30   Franco Moretti, *Atlas of the European Novel, 1800–1900* (London: Verso, 1998).
31   Beecroft, 'World Literature', 93.
32   Beecroft, 'World Literature', 88.
33   Michel Le Bris, 'Pour une littérature-monde en français', in Michel Le Bris and Jean Rouaud, eds, *Pour une littérature-monde* (Paris: Gallimard, 2007), 45 and 45–6.

its singular spirit and, in that case, strictly speaking, the 'Francophonie' manifests itself as the last reincarnation of colonialism, or we undo the pact between language and nation, so that the language, now freed, becomes everybody's matter].

In the case of the Iberian Peninsula, either application might be translated into the issue of *exophonie*, that is, what in Portuguese is traditionally called *Lusofonia*; whereas in Spanish there exists no concept to name this phenomenon. However, Spanish is the third most spoken language in the world, the third most used language on the Internet, the fifth most spoken language of the European Union; and in addition Spain occupies the ninth position of global presence according to the 2010 Índice Elcano.[34] Spain's ranking in cultural diffusion (the seventh worldwide) has contributed greatly to its degree of global presence and, consequently, one would expect a deep reflection on the role of Spanish culture and literature on a world scale to take place. Actually, Spanish is the sixth most translated language in the world according to the database *Index Translationum*. This database provides a challenging picture of 'Spanish literature' in a world-literature context, for its top nine most translated fiction writers are Gabriel García Márquez, Isabel Allende, Mario Vargas Llosa, Cervantes, Borges, Neruda, Lorca, Cortázar, and Manuel Vázquez Montalbán.

When it comes to addressing the reasons for the absence of a reflection on the exophonic dimension of Spanish literature/s, some distinctions need to be made in the case of Spain between 'central' and 'peripheral' cultures. The latter are starting to interact with some theories on world literature,[35] especially – and paradoxically so – those of Pascale Casanova. Furthermore, some distinctions also need to be made in the case of Latin America specifically: are Latin Americanists working in the USA academia[36] those who are engaging in discussions on a world-literature in Spanish? Finally,

34   Ignacio Molina and Iliana Olivié, 'IEPG: un índice para medir la globalización', *Política exterior* 141 (2011), 95.

35   Carlos Lema, ed., 'Da literatura nacional á literatura mundial', *Grial: Revista Galega de Cultura* 167 (2005), 12–53.

36   Ignacio Sánchez-Prado, ed., *América Latina en la 'literatura mundial'* (Pittsburgh: Universidad de Pittsburgh, 2006).

in contrast to the French academia, the Spanish academia cannot partici-pate in these discussions on the basis of its equivalent concept *hispanidad*, for this is a loaded term which even today echoes its heritage of extreme-right Catholic, anti-democratic ideology on both sides of the Atlantic. I cannot address all of these issues now, except to say that it is evident that any future involvement of Iberian Studies in world-literature discussions requires an address to what one might call the 'post-imperial conundrum' and to deconstruct the underlying composite character of *hispanidad* as a combination of, on the one hand, linguistic and cultural bonds and, on the other, a postcolonial, telluric celebration of atavistic unity.

Case study 3: the world connection

World literature became a global critical object in 2003–4, when Norton, Bedford and Longman simultaneously published three anthologies of world literature in the USA. If world literature is defined, as David Damrosch puts it, as 'literary works that circulate beyond their culture of origin, either in translation or in their original language'[37] and, therefore, as 'an elliptical refraction of national literatures',[38] one has to conclude that for Iberian Studies the analysis of such a refraction is an important endeavour. I cannot analyse here all of the data on Iberian literatures in a world context provided by these anthologies. For the purpose of my argu-ment and with the aim of avoiding the danger of presentism in Iberian Studies, I will stick to the data related to literary works in medieval Iberia, as shown in Table 1.

37   David Damrosch, *What Is World Literature?* (Princeton: Princeton University Press, 2003), 4.
38   Damrosch, *What Is World Literature*, 281.

Authors/Works	Norton	Longman	Bedford	Language
Poema de Mio Cid		•		Castilian
Castilian ballads		•		Castilian
Kharjas		•		Mozarabic
Martin Codax		•		Galician/Portuguese
Don Dinis		•		Galician/Portuguese
Juan Ruiz, *Libro de buen amor*		•		Castilian
Ibn Rushd (Averroes)		•		Arabic
Ibn al-Arabi		•		Arabic
Ramon Llull, *Blanquerna*		•		Catalan
Solomon Ibn Gabirol		•		Hebrew
Ibn Hazm	•	•		Arabic
Yehuda Ha-Levi	•	•	•	Hebrew
Ibn Zaydun			•	Arabic
Wallada			•	Arabic
Ibn Faraj			•	Arabic
Ibn al-Labbana			•	Arabic
Ibn Quzman			•	Arabic
Alfonso X	•			Galician/Portuguese
Ibn Arfa' ra'Suh	•			Arabic
Abu-l-Hasan ibn al-Qabturnuh	•			Arabic
Meir Halevi Abulafia	•			Hebrew

Table 1 shows the texts selected by either of the anthologies and the languages taken into consideration. The result is enlightening and informative for at least two reasons. Firstly, there is surprisingly very little overlap when comparing their content in this area. Secondly, were overlap a criterion for worldliness, only two authors, the Hispano-Arab Ibn Hazm and the Hispano-Jewish Yehuda Ha-Levi, would obtain such recognition, which previously had been accorded to the latter by the *Norton Anthology of World Masterpieces* within the framework of, paradoxically, a 'Western tradition'. The world Iberian canon advocated by the Norton, Bedford and Longman anthologies is completely different from the Iberian canon advocated until recently by histories and anthologies with a more limited regional scope. The aim of expanding the canon to represent the world has resulted in Castilian- and Lusocentrism having been replaced by an Arabo- and Judeocentrism. The role played in the creation of this anticanon by the myth of the Iberian Peninsula as a (Western) intercultural contact point of tolerance does not seem minor; not to mention two further important facts. First, the selection may offer a satisfactory library of world literature for a USA audience captivated by orientalism. Second, as far as publishing factors are concerned, most of the selected texts have already been published in English translation. Therefore, the relation between the Arabo- and Judeocentrism of these three anthologies and a real influence of world literature as a critical object of study is subject to discussion.

The refraction analysed by Iberian Studies may be implemented by taking into consideration anthologies with a more restricted, regional scope, such as *Locus amoenus: antología de la lírica medieval de la Península Ibérica*,[39] published in 2009, and the still widely used *Medieval Literature in Translation*, edited by Charles W. Jones.[40] Except for the ballads, the *Poema de Mio Cid* and the excerpts from *Blanquerna*, which are not included due to either their oral or narrative character, *Locus amoenus* includes a

---

39   Carlos Alvar and Jenaro Talens, eds, *Locus amoenus: antología de la lírica medieval de la Península Ibérica* (Barcelona: Galaxia Gutenberg/Círculo de Lectores, 2009).

40   Charles W. Jones, ed., *Medieval Literature in Translation* (Mineola, NY: Dover, 2001 [1950]).

few of the works selected by the Norton, Bedford and Longman anthologies, along with many works in Arabic, Hebrew, Mozarabic, Castilian, Galician-Portuguese and Catalan not included by the USA anthologies. Besides, *Locus amoenus* also pays attention to the Latin and Provençal lyric traditions in Iberia. In the case of Jones's anthology, the 'Europeanness' of Iberian works is strictly restricted to the *Poema de Mio Cid*. Further key differences arise when the selection of Arab and Hebrew poets in either anthology is compared, as shown in Table 2.

Authors/Works	Norton/ Longman/ Bedford	Locus amoenus	Medieval Literature in Translation
Poema de Mio Cid	•	(different genre option)	•
Castilian ballads	•	(different genre option)	
Kharjas	•	•	
Martin Codax	•	•	
Don Dinis	•	•	
Juan Ruiz, *Libro de buen amor*	•	•	
Ibn Rushd (Averroes)	•		
Ibn al-Arabi	•		
Ramon Llull, *Blanquerna*	•	(different genre option)	
Solomon Ibn Gabirol	•	•	
Ibn Hazm	•		
Yehuda Ha-Levi	•	•	
Ibn Zaydun	•		
Wallada	•		
Ibn Faraj	•		

Authors/Works	Norton/ Longman/ Bedford	Locus amoenus	Medieval Literature in Translation
Ibn al-Labbana	•		
Ibn Quzman	•		
Alfonso X	•	•	
Ibn Arfa' ra'Suh	•		
Abu-l Hasan ibn al-Qabturnuh	•		
Meir Halevi Abulafia	•		

For *Locus amoenus*, most of the Arab and Hebrew poets selected by Longman, Bedford and Norton as 'world authors' are not considered to represent an Iberian literary tradition. Correspondingly, most of the Arab and Hebrew poets selected by *Locus amoenus* as 'Iberian authors' do not deserve a 'world recognition' by Longman, Bedford and Norton. In the case of *Medieval Literature in Translation*, the absence of any Arab/Hebrew poet whatsoever is justified by Jones on the grounds that he has 'chosen what worked best with [...] [his] students, with whom [...] [he has] been reading medieval literature for some years.'[41]

Claudio Guillén pointed out several times how the practice of Comparative Literature in Spain 'en cualquier momento amenaza con tropezar frontalmente, como en un accidente de carretera, con el inexorable "hispanocentrismo español"'[42] [is at all times in danger of crashing, as in a road accident, against the inflexible 'Spanish Hispano-centrism']. Today the situation of Comparative Literature is rather different when it comes to comparing an Iberian with a non-Iberian literature. A reflection

---

41 Jones, *Medieval Literature*, vi.
42 Claudio Guillén, 'La Literatura Comparada y la crisis de las humanidades', in *Entre lo uno y lo diverso. Introducción a la Literatura Comparada (ayer y hoy)* (Barcelona: Tusquets, 2005), 16.

as the one fostered by the European Science Foundation workshop on Iberian Studies from within the Iberian Peninsula may announce another disciplinary change, one in which a comparison on an equal footing of the Iberian literatures poses specific questions which only Iberian Studies is in a position to confront. In my opinion, for Guillén such a field, defined by the comparatist among the several possibilities offered by literature, would only make sense provided that, on the one hand, the comparatist does not rely on 'unas realidades dadas y visiblemente delimitadas' [given realities with obvious limits] and, on the other hand, the object of research, its definition and its demarcation be a 'proyecto' [project].[43]

Works cited

Alvar, Carlos, and Jenaro Talens, eds, *Locus amoenus: antología de la lírica medieval de la Península Ibérica* (Barcelona: Galaxia Gutenberg/Círculo de Lectores, 2009).

Anderson, Benedict, *Imagined Communities. Reflections on the Origin and Spread of Nationalism* (London: Verso, 1998).

Anselmi, Gian Mario, ed., *Mapas de la literatura europea y mediterránea. De los orígenes al Renacimiento*, trans. María Pons Irazazábal (Barcelona: Crítica, 2002).

Antonelli, Roberto, 'Il canone europeo' <http://w3.uniroma1.it/studieuropei/ilcanone/index.htm> accessed 1 October 2011.

Beecroft, Alexander, 'World Literature without a Hyphen: Towards a Typology of Literary Systems', *New Left Review* 54 (2008), 87–100.

Braudel, Fernand, *A History of Civilizations*, trans. Richard Mayne (New York: Penguin, 1994).

Bulson, Eric, *Novels, Maps, Modernity. The Spatial Imagination, 1850–2000* (New York: Routledge, 2007).

Casanova, Pascale, *The World Republic of Letters*, trans. M. B. Debevoise (Cambridge, MA: Harvard University Press, 2004).

---

43 Claudio Guillén, *Entre el saber y el conocer. Moradas del estudio literario* (Valladolid: Universidad de Valladolid/Cátedra Jorge Guillén, 2001), 103.

Collier, Simon, Harold Blakemore, and Thomas E. Skidmore, eds, *The Cambridge Encyclopedia of Latin America and the Caribbean* (Cambridge: Cambridge University Press, 1985).

Damrosch, David, *What Is World Literature?* (Princeton: Princeton University Press, 2003).

——, and David L. Pike, eds, *The Longman Anthology of World Literature: The Medieval Era*, 2nd edn (New York: Longman, 2009).

Davis, Paul *et al.*, eds, *The Bedford Anthology of World Literature. The Middle Period, 100 C.E. 1450* (Boston: Bedford/St Martin's, 2004).

Gabilondo, Joseba, 'One-Way Theory: On the Hispanic-Atlantic Intersection of Postcoloniality and Postnationalism and Its Globalizing Effects', *Arachne: Journal of Iberian and Latin American Literary and Cultural Studies* 1/1 (2001) <http://arachne.rutgers.edu/vol11gabilondo.htm> accessed 1 October 2011.

Guillén, Claudio, *Entre el saber y el conocer. Moradas del estudio literario* (Valladolid: Universidad de Valladolid/Cátedra Jorge Guillén, 2001).

——, 'La Literatura Comparada y la crisis de las humanidades', in *Entre lo uno y lo diverso. Introducción a la Literatura Comparada (ayer y hoy)* (Barcelona: Tusquets, 2005), 11–24.

——, 'Sobre el objeto del cambio literario', in *Teorías de la historia literaria (ensayos de teoría)* (Madrid: Espasa–Calpe, 1989), 199–248.

——, *The Challenge of Comparative Literature*, trans. Cola Frenzen (Cambridge, MA: Harvard University Press, 1993).

Kadir, Djelal, 'To World, to Globalize – Comparative Literature's Crossroads', *Comparative Literature Studies* 41/1 (2004), 1–9.

Karrouch, Laila, *De Nador a Vic* (Barcelona: Columna, 2009).

——, *Laila* (Madrid: Oxford, 2010).

Jones, Charles W., ed., *Medieval Literature in Translation* (Mineola, NY: Dover, 2001 [1950]).

Lambert, José, 'In Quest of World Literary Maps', in Dirk Delabatista, Lieven D'hulst, and Reyne Meylaerts, eds, *Functional Approaches to Culture and Translation. Selected Papers by José Lambert* (Amsterdam: John Benjamins, 2006), 63–74.

Lawall, Sarah, ed., *The Norton Anthology of World Literature. Beginnings to A.D. 100*, 2nd edn (New York: W. W. Norton, [2003]).

——, ed., *The Norton Anthology of World Masterpieces. The Western Tradition*, vol. 1., 7th edn (New York: W. W. Norton, [1999]).

Le Bris, Michel, 'Pour une littérature-monde en français', in Michel Le Bris and Jean Rouaud, eds, *Pour une littérature-monde* (Paris: Gallimard, 2007), 23–53.

Lema, Carlos, ed., 'Da literatura nacional á literatura mundial', *Grial: Revista Galega de Cultura* 167 (2005), 12–53.

Lewis, Martin W., and Kären E. Wigen, *The Myth of Continents. A Critique of Metageography* (Berkeley: University of California Press, 1997).

Manning, Patrick, *Navigating World History. Historians Create a Global Past* (New York: Palgrave Macmillan, 2003).

Martín-Estudillo, Luis, and Nicholas Spadaccini, eds, *New Spain, New Literatures* (Nashville: Vanderbilt University Press, 2010).

McDonogh, Gary W., *Iberian Worlds* (New York: Routledge, 2009).

Molina, Ignacio, and Iliana Olivié, 'IEPG: un índice para medir la globalización', *Política exterior* 141 (2011), 90–100.

Monegal, Antonio, 'A Landscape of Relations: Peninsular Multiculturalism and the Avatars of Comparative Literature', in Brad Epps and Luis Fernández Cifuentes, eds, *Spain beyond Spain. Modernity, Literary History, and National Identity* (Lewisburg: Bucknell University Press, 2005), 231–49.

Moretti, Franco, *Atlas of the European Novel, 1800–1900* (London: Verso, 1998).

Oxford Educación, *Cuaderno para el desarrollo lector: Laila* (Madrid: Oxford University Press, 2010).

Pageaux, Daniel-Henri, 'La Péninsule Ibérique et l'Europe', in Béatrice Didier, ed., *Précis de littérature européenne* (Paris: Presses Universitaires de France, 1998), 161–6.

Resina, Joan Ramon, 'Hispanism and Its Discontents', *Siglo XX/20th Century* 14/1–2 (1996), 85–135.

Sánchez-Prado, Ignacio, ed., *América Latina en la 'literatura mundial'* (Pittsburgh: Universidad de Pittsburgh, 2006).

Wallerstein, Immanuel, *Geopolitics and Geoculture. Essays on the Changing World-System* (Cambridge: Cambridge University Press, 2001).

——, 'World-Systems Analysis', in *The Essential Wallerstein* (New York: The New Press, 2000), 129–48.

PART II

Images of Iberia:
Historical Perspectives on a Geographical, Political and Cultural Space

MARIA FERNANDA DE ABREU

Iberia in Search for a Literary Identity: A Stone Raft?

> Diversos són els homes i diverses les parles, i han convingut molts noms
> a un sol amor.
>
> — SALVADOR ESPRIU, *La pell de brau*

Taking as starting points: i) a geocultural Iberian space, ii) an Iberian singularity, in contrast with other identitarian clusters, in cultural or literary fields, and iii) a pan-regional, multinational and multilinguistic identity within the European context, the Iberian Peninsula has come to be considered as an identitarian mega-frame, between the most restricted national identities which form it and the wider European one. I propose, therefore, to scan some of the 'foundations' – anthropological, geographical or any other – along with clusters that have been used in the 'narration' of Iberian literary and cultural history, in order to create that singularity.

In this sense, I think that a project such as *A Comparative History of Literatures in the Iberian Peninsula*, directed by scholars of the University of Santiago de Compostela,[1] establishes 'scientific accuracy and its validity as a starting point for scientific and academic work'.[2] According to the main goals of this collective study, and in the premise that a Literary Iberian

---

1   See Fernando Cabo Aseguinolaza, Anxo Abuín, and César Domínguez, *A Comparative History of Literatures in the Iberian Peninsula*, vol. I (Amsterdam and Philadelphia: John Benjamins, 2010).

2   From the 'Objectives' of the ESF Exploratory Workshop from which this volume derives: 'More precisely, this Workshop focuses on the concept of Iberia itself: its scientific accuracy; its validity as a starting point for scientific and academic work' <http://lookingatiberia.wikispaces.com/Objectives> accessed 6 February 2012.

Identity is the result of literary, cultural and historiographical discourses, and of the narration of diverse literatures, this reflection focuses on the following key objectives: the concept of Iberia itself, its scientific accuracy, its validity as a starting point for scientific and academic work, its relation to other, more established concepts and identities, namely the European one, its relation to historiographical literary discourses and literary narratives constructed to 'support' (or perhaps, better stated, to create or invent) such a collective identity, that is, the Iberian one, within the European context.

For that purpose, I examine here some contributions from Portuguese scholars (distinguished experts in different areas of Iberian Studies: geography, anthropology, history, culture, literature). This includes a set of documents from different areas and nature that were produced in different contexts and by very different personalities.

I propose a reflection upon premises and arguments that we can find in the following theoretical and essayistic *corpus*: in chronological order, 'Causas da decadência dos povos peninsulares' [Causes of the Decline of the Peninsular Peoples] (1871), a lecture by Antero de Quental; *História da Civilização Ibérica* [History of the Iberian Civilization] (1879), by J. P. de Oliveira Martins; *Pyrene* (1935), by Fidelino de Figueiredo; *Portugal, o Mediterrâneo e o Atlântico Atlântico* [Portugal, the Mediterranean and the Atlantic] (1945), by Orlando Ribeiro; *Originalidade da Literatura Portuguesa* [Originality of Portuguese Literature] (1977), by Jacinto do Prado Coelho; 'Hispanismo: archipiélago de glorias y vanidades en el mar-océano de la ignorancia universal' [Hispanism: archipelago of glories and vanities in the ocean of universal ignorance] (1977), by Jorge de Sena; and *Nós e a Europa ou as Duas Razões* Razões [We and Europe or the Two Reasons] (1988), by Eduardo Lourenço. It is my belief that these titles, on their own, and their respective times of publication, are meaningful enough.

In the study of literary relationships between Portugal and Spain, I asked myself in another occasion:

Quem, ao longo dos séculos, e obedecendo a que programas ou planificações nos tem inventado a identidade, ou originalidade, ou diferença – como quiserem – na oposição, quase sempre redutora e simplista, tantas vezes esquizofrénica e triste, a Espanha?[3]

[Who, throughout the centuries, and obeying which programmes and culture planning has built our identity, or originality, or difference – as you wish – in this almost always over-simplistic opposition between Portugal and Spain that is so often schizophrenic and sad?][4]

The question is similar here. Just take the Iberian Peninsula instead of Portugal, and Spain instead of Europe. Therefore: by whom, when, and obeying which programmes or plans – and for what needs – has the difference of Iberia regarding Europe been invented?[5]

According to some, at one extreme, this difference is achieved by the will of *destiny*, or a *vocation* (an essentialist conception); on the other extreme, with a pragmatic conception, this construction is guided by a political-cultural project, a 'plan'. I propose to call these phenomena 'the anxiety of difference' (for those outside the Peninsula) and 'the anxiety of unity' (for those inside the Peninsula), the two faces of the construct.

The construction of difference regarding the Other, that is, Europe, makes us highlight those features believed to *make* the difference. The construction of unity, regarding the inside, is always a 'national unity', and of course a 'national identity', shutting out or excluding the diversities in order to be 'one', 'unique', 'specific', or 'different'. From this arises another question: who established, when, and with what elements, the boundaries of this 'inside'?

3   Maria Fernanda de Abreu, 'De que lado o espelho? Das teorias às práticas comparatistas no estudo das relações literárias entre Portugal e Espanha', in Gabriel Magalhães, ed., *Actas do Congresso RELIPES III: 18, 19 e 20 de Abril de 2007* (Covilhã: Universidade da Beira Interior, 2007), 443.

4   All quotations originally in Spanish, Portuguese or French have been translated by the editors.

5   According to Itamar Even-Zohar, 'The Role of Literature in the Making of the Nations of Europe: A Socio-semiotic Study', *Applied Semotics/Sémiotique appliquée* 1/1 (1996), 39–59 (a lecture given at the University of Santiago de Compostela, May 1993).

The anxiety of unity. What unity?
A truly regional diversity in the Iberian Peninsula

While recognizing, in the preface to a reprint of *História da Civilização Ibérica* dated 1954,[6] the absolute success of the work, as much in Portugal as in Spain, as '[u]ma das mais imponentes construções do pensamento de toda a nossa história intelectual'[7] [one of the most imposing constructions of thought of our entire intellectual history], Fidelino de Figueiredo peremptorily stresses the fact that it is not a 'History' of Iberian civilization, but an 'interpretative essay', 'cujo escopo principal foi apresentar a visão de Oliveira Martins'[8] [whose main scope was to present Oliveira Martins' vision]. In fact, it is '[um] ensaio de filosofia da história dos povos peninsulares, considerados no seu paralelismo e na sua travação dinâmica'[9] [a philosophical essay on the history of the peninsular peoples, considered in their parallelism and their dynamic slow down].

It is therefore an essay that presents itself as *História*, and that was thought of as the narration 'de uma unidade típica e circunscrita à península hispânica, na qual se fundem as várias evoluções nacionais, contidas nesse quadro geográfico'[10] [of a typical unity, confined to the Hispanic peninsula, upon which the various national developments contained in that geographical frame are based]. Fidelino de Figueiredo calls it an author's 'visão' [vision] and a 'demonstração' [demonstration] of such unity is '[a] primeira que se produziu' [the first to be produced], he says.[11]

But he still points out that both the 'sentimento geográfico' [geographical feeling] and the 'sentimento histórico' [historical feeling] of that unity

---

6   Joaquim Pedro de Oliveira Martins, *História da Civilização Ibérica*, pref. Fidelino de Figueiredo [1954] (Lisbon: Guimarães & C.ª Ed., 1984 [1879]).

7   Fidelino de Figueiredo, 'Prefácio', in J. P. de Oliveira Martins, *História da Civilização Ibérica* (Lisbon: Guimarães & C.ª Ed., 1984 [1954]), XV.

8   Figueiredo, 'Prefácio', XIII.

9   Figueiredo, 'Prefácio', XIV.

10   Figueiredo, 'Prefácio', XIII.

11   Figueiredo, 'Prefácio', XIII.

'tardou séculos a formular-se e vitalizar-se em força política' [took centuries to formulate itself and to vitalize into political strength], eventually asserting that 'nunca chegou ao pleno reconhecimento'[12] [it never achieved full acknowledgment]. The independence movements, well active in our days, do nothing but reinforce the suspension marks that Fidelino made explicit by the mid-twentieth century.

Looking at this literary field, I myself explored it some years ago and called it '[l]a-mise-en-scène d'une identité ibérique dans quelques écrivains portugais contemporains'[13] [the *mise-en-scène* of an Iberian identity in contemporary Portuguese writers], especially concerning Miguel Torga, Saramago and Natália Correia. I analysed the collective identitarian construction that Miguel Torga's book, *Poemas Ibéricos* [Iberian Poems],[14] masterfully exemplifies, with the use of elements that are territorial and ethnical, mythical, historical and symbolic.

Regarding the title of my essay, and considering that in this volume other scholars also take into account Saramago's book *A Jangada de Pedra* [The Stone Raft], I would like to stress the fact that the first title the novelist had for his book was *Pele de Touro* [Bull's Skin], which is a well-known metaphor used by the geographer Strabo when referring to the Iberian Peninsula in the first century. Only later did someone inform Saramago that this was already the title of a very important and foundational book of Catalan culture, *La pell de brau*, by Salvador Espriu (1960).[15]

It is clear that the changing of the title brought a new significance with it, since the metaphor of the *raft* contains a prospective sense that was absent in the *bull's skin*. And we may recall some words by the geographer Orlando Ribeiro:

---

12 Figueiredo, 'Prefácio', XIII–XIV.

13 Lecture delivered as part of a journey for post-graduate studies, on 'Stéréotypes culturels et constructions identitaires', organized by C.I.R.E.M.I.A. (Centre Interuniversitaire de Recherche sur l'Éducation et la Culture dans le Monde Ibérique et Ibero-Américain), at the University of Tours (France), on 22 March 2003.

14 Miguel Torga, *Poemas Ibéricos* (Coimbra: Coimbra Editora, 1965).

15 Salvador Espriu, *La pell de brau/A Pele de Touro*, trans. Manuel Seabra (bilingual edn) (Lisbon: Dom Quixote, 1960).

No fim do neolítico e no começo da época do bronze, um fermento de vida local levedou [...] no que podemos considerar a fachada atlântica da Península (Portugal, Galiza e seus confins não castelhanos). Mas as relações desta civilização são menos com o centro da Ibéria ou com o Levante mediterrâneo do que com outras finisterras atlânticas – a Bretanha, o País de Gales, a Irlanda, a Escócia – prelúdio de uma vocação de remotos caminhos do mar.[16]

[By the end of the Neolithic and beginning of the Bronze Age, there was a new stimulation of local life [...] in what we may call the Atlantic seaboard of the Peninsula (Portugal, Galicia and its non-Spanish borders). But the relations of this civilization have less to do with the centre of Iberia or the Eastern Mediterranean than other Atlantic shores – Britain, Wales, Ireland, Scotland – a prelude to a calling for remote sea paths.]

Later, he will state that somehow the unity of the Peninsula was mainly due to the fact that it is a 'península que é como a miniatura dum continente'[17] [a peninsula that is like a miniature continent]. That was what Strabo saw as a bull's skin, and which Saramago transformed into a 'jangada de pedra' [stone raft]; in fact, in his fiction, it is a stone raft that breaks away from the continent, heads south, and settles between South America and Africa.[18]

In this particular case, it is also worth noting that the term 'Iberian' which we are using for the Peninsula is not, in any way, consensual, because its connection to Iberia would exclude those regions of the peninsula that have little or no connection to the ancient *iberos*. That is why some preferred the designation 'Hispánica', instead of 'Ibérica', and Jorge de Sena, a Portuguese scholar and writer as well as a Hispanist, recalls 'la vieja Hispania-Mater' [the old Hispania Mater].[19]

16   Orlando Ribeiro, *Portugal, o Mediterrâneo e o Atlântico. Esboço de Relações Geográficas*, 5th edn (Lisbon: Sá da Costa, 1987 [1947]), 104.
17   Ribeiro, *Portugal*, 131.
18   José Saramago, *A Jangada de Pedra* (Lisbon: Caminho, 1986).
19   Jorge de Sena, 'Hispanismo: archipiélago de glorias y vanidades en el mar–océano de la ignorancia universal', in Alan M. Gordon and Evelyn Rugg, eds, *Actas del sexto congreso internacional de hispanistas celebrado en Toronto del 22 al 26 de agosto de 1977* (Toronto: Departament of Spanish and Portuguese, University of Toronto, 1980),

On the other hand, Arturo Casas, in an essay published in 2003 entitled 'Sistema interliterario y planificación historiográfica a propósito del espacio geocultural ibérico' [Interliterary System and Historiographical Planning As Regards the Iberian Geocultural Space], within the project *A Comparative History of Literatures in Iberian Peninsula*, stated that 'a falta de mejor solución, se emplea el adjetivo peninsular en un sentido amplio' [lacking a better solution, the adjective *peninsular* is used in a broad sense], and that, in that context, 'tampoco se hará cuestión aqui sobre la idoneidad o el grado de aceptabilidad de la etiqueta ibérico'[20] [neither will we question here the appropriateness or acceptability of the label *Iberian*].

Today, I think I can repeat what I wrote in 2007:

> Claro que, como todos sabemos, no último quartel do século XIX, Oliveira Martins e Antero contribuíram, de forma marcada e determinante, para o sentimento desta homogeneização 'ibérica' ou 'peninsular'. Sem esquecer Garrett que, no contexto das construções identitárias romântico-liberais, muito tinha já feito nesse sentido.[21]

> [Of course, as we all know, in the last quarter of the nineteenth century Oliveira Martins and Antero made a distinctive and decisive contribution to the feeling of this 'Iberian' or 'peninsular' homogeneity. Not to mention Garrett, who, in the context of romantic-liberal constructions of identities, had already done much.]

These writers' mythical-historical-literary narratives are built to support the idea of a 'Peninsular people' or an 'Iberian civilization' (the titles of Antero's and Oliveira Martins's works), claiming such particularities as a 'peninsular sense of liberty', 'individualism', and 'genius'. In the words of Antero de Quental: 'Logo na época romana aparecem os caracteres essenciais da raça peninsular: espírito de independência local, e originalidade de génio inventivo'[22] ['Already in the Roman period there had appeared

19–25 <http://asociacioninternacionaldehispanistas.org/actas/AIH_06_1.pdf> accessed 8 September 2012.

20 Arturo Casas, 'Sistema interliterario y planificación historiográfica a propósito del espacio geocultural ibérico', *Interlitteraria* 8 (2003), 68–97, n. 6.

21 Abreu, 'De que lado o espelho?', 440.

22 Antero de Quental, *Causas da Decadência dos Povos Peninsulares*, int. Delfim Brito (Lisbon: Guimarães Ed., 2001 [1871]), 19.

the essential features of the Peninsular race: a spirit of local independence, and an originality of inventive talent'].[23] But in the last three centuries they have lost these 'features'. Separated, excluded and underestimated by Europe, they have, nonetheless, to 'follow' Europe. This is what Eduardo Lourenço has to say about this *cultural drama*:

> Era desta Europa [*mitificada*] e desta cultura que, na sua heróica ingenuidade ibérica, Antero de Quental esperava uma resposta que conferisse *sentido* à sua interrogação do enigma da História e do nosso destino nela.[24]

> [It was from this [*mythified*] Europe and this culture that, in its heroic Iberian ingenuity, Antero de Quental expected an answer that gave *sense* to his question on the enigma of History and our destiny in it.]

Fidelino de Figueiredo also alerted us to the inexistence of a 'full acknowledgement' of the Iberian Peninsula's unity, in the 'geographical feeling' as much as in the 'historical feeling', which he had defined (in 1954) as 'um drama encenado no quadro geográfico'[25] [a drama staged within the geographical frame].

The anxiety of difference. Building the difference

There is a general sense of rejection from Europe, and this is how the Peninsula has felt during the last centuries: the object of rejection, contempt, marginalization and exclusion from Europe.

Rejection and contempt are Romantic feelings. Marginalization and exclusion are mostly social – and sociological – perceptions of today. But

23   Antero de Quental, 'Causes of the Decline of the Peninsular Peoples in the Last Three Centuries', trans. Richard Correll, *Portuguese Studies* 24/1 (2008), 68.

24   Eduardo Lourenço, *Nós e a Europa ou as Duas Razões* (Lisbon: Imprensa Nacional–Casa da Moeda, 1988), 34.

25   Figueiredo, 'Prefácio', 13.

I think that none of us could say that the latter have replaced the former. It seems that we have adopted them, without being able to erase their predecessors. And if the political and economic integration in the 'European Community' was perhaps a means of liberation from such atavistic bandages, it is also possible that the present financial crisis brings those old feelings back to life, converting them to identity traits, and incorporating them into their narratives.

We can find many expressions of this sensation of rejection – from the point of view of the rejected, and not of the rejecter – in the first phase of Portuguese Romanticism, such as in the programmatic texts by Garrett and Herculano, but also, already by the end of the nineteenth century, with the authors of Geração de 70 [Generation of 1870]. Antero, in the aforementioned lecture, plainly justifies this rejection and contempt on what he calls a 'peninsular decadence'. He also asks if the Iberian difference, in the literary field, is a result of 'caracteres essenciais da raça peninsular'[26] ['the essential features of the Peninsular race'][27] or, in essence, of geopolitical circumstances, such as late Romanticism, absolute monarchies, or the French invasions.

At the origin of Comparative Studies on peninsular literatures (referring only to the Portuguese and the Spanish ones), even if under a definite programme, and proposing to follow Paul Van Tieghem's 'new verb' and his form of comparatism, Fidelino de Figueiredo starts by telling us the legend of Pyrene, a mythic narrative of heroism and love which appears in the very title of his study.[28]

Eduardo Lourenço, in his turn, states the following about the Spanish *difference*:

---

26   Quental, *Causas*, 19.
27   Quental, 'Causes', 68.
28   Fidelino de Figueiredo, *Pyrene: ponto de vista para uma introducção á história comparada das literaturas portuguesa e espanhola* (Lisbon: Empresa Nacional de Publicidade, 1935).

É certo que a Espanha nunca deixou de exprimir essa 'diferença'. Em termos osten-
tatórios. A esse título se unem umas às outras figuras tão distintas como Rodrigo,
Calderón, Inácio de Loyola, Teresa de Jesus, El Greco, Goya, Buñuel ou Picasso,
incorporações sucessivas do seu evidente agonismo, do seu gosto e da sua paixão
pelo que é extremo. Nos seus grandes indivíduos, que o são não o sendo à maneira
europeia, o povo espanhol é um dos raros povos da terra, se não o único – que é
sujeito da sua própria História. [...] Seria uma tristeza sem nome que *essa vocação
para o 'incomparável', única na Europa*, essa nota individualista, mesmo no domínio
que menos a consente, como o religioso, soçobrasse no caos resplandecente de uma
'novidade' suscitada por atrasado mimetismo de culturas que não possuem a espes-
sura da que criou D. Quixote.[29]

[It is true that Spain never refrained from expressing that 'difference' in ostenta-
tious terms. In that regard they unite themselves to other distinguished figures such
as Rodrigo, Calderón, Inácio de Loyola, Teresa de Jesus, El Greco, Goya, Buñuel or
Picasso, successive incorporations of their evident agonism, from their taste and
passion for what is extreme. In their great individuals, which they are by not being
the European way, the Spanish people are one of the rare peoples of earth, if not the
only – that is subjected to their own History. [...] It would be profoundly sad if *that
vocation for the 'incomparable', unique in Europe*, that individualistic note, even at
the domain that less acquiesces it, such as the religious, collapsed in the resplendent
chaos of a 'novelty' raised by the delayed mimicry of cultures that do not possess the
thickness of the one created by Don Quixote.]

Therefore, setting the difference and the recognition of that difference,
with the aim of exhibiting a unique identity, inside and outside Iberia, has
been the goal of the cultural and literary historiography of the Iberian
Peninsula as a whole: '[Uma] vocação para o incomparável, única na
Europa' [A vocation for the incomparable, unique in Europe]? Which
comparatist theory, within the literary field, would sustain such a formulation today?

29   Lourenço, *Nós e a Europa*, 82–3; emphasis added.

To be in Europe without being Europe

In an essay devoted to studying the specificity of Portuguese literature, Jacinto do Prado Coelho accounts, in an incisive sentence, for something that the Peninsula inhabitants have felt for a long time: 'Portugal partilha com a Espanha o sentimento estranho de estar na Europa não sendo Europa'[30] [Portugal shares with Spain the strange feeling of being in Europe without being Europe].

It is a feeling that, in one way or another, has been surfacing since at least the first Romanticism, and since the harsh beginnings of the post-liberal victory: from Garrett to Alexandre Herculano, the renovator of Portuguese historiography, to the men of the Geração de 70 including Eça de Queirós and Antero de Quental. This feeling is possibly one of the causes for the reflections on the 'causes of decadence' undertaken by this last author. It is certainly the case given the tone of the conference delivered by Jorge de Sena at the Sixth International Congress of Hispanists (Toronto, 22–26 August 1977), entitled 'Hispanismo: archipiélago de glorias y vanidades en el mar-oceano de la ignorancia universal' in which, among other things, he stated:

> Una consecuencia [de la Cortina de Hierro que ha cercado la península y las naciones hermanas de América] que sigue siendo una obsesión ibérica y Latinoamericana, es la llamada meditación sobre el ser español, o brasileño, o mejicano, u otro cualquiera, cuando el problema concreto no es la meditación sobre el ser, sino el hacer para ser. [...] Y bien, enfrentemos el hecho que, después de todo, ninguno de nosotros ignora: como pueblos o como investigadores de un complejo peculiar de culturas, o de uno de sus aspectos lingüísticos o literarios, nos rodea un océano de malevolencia o de candida ignorancia. Muy simplemente estamos excluidos.[31]

---

30   Jacinto do Prado Coelho, *Originalidade da Literatura Portuguesa* (Lisbon: Instituto de Cultura Portuguesa, 1977), 34.
31   Sena, 'Hispanismo', 21–4.

[A consequence [of the Iron Curtain that surrounded the peninsula and its sister nations in America] that continues to be an Iberian and Latin American obsession, is the so-called meditation about being Spanish, or Brazilian, or Mexican, or any other, when the specific problem is not the meditation about being, but rather what needs to be done to be. [...] And well, let us face a fact which, after all, none of us ignores: as a people or as researchers of a peculiar complex of cultures, of its linguistic or literary aspects, we are surrounded by an ocean of malevolence or candid ignorance. We are quite simply excluded.]

So being, and following the recognition of this exclusion, he strongly urges: 'Debemos insistir y luchar por nuestro mutuo entendimiento, nosotros, las gentes que hablamos las lenguas desarrolladas en la vieja Hispania Mater'[32] [We must insist on and fight for our mutual understanding, we, the people who speak the languages that grew in the old Hispania Mater].

In fact, Europe is rarely thought of, today as in the last few centuries, as an identity from the Iberian Peninsula. And when that happens, the author of such a reflection is someone with some sort of feeling of 'belonging' to that land and geography, even if, for different reasons, such as cosmopolitanism or exile, they also 'belong' to other countries. This is the case of Claudio Guillén, in the essay 'Europa: ciencia e inconsciencia'[33] [Europe: Science and Unconsciousness], where he gives us further data and arguments to take into consideration, all of them invoked from the prudent and smart presupposition that 'Europa es un conjunto movedizo, de perfil cambiante, pero que sin embargo se reconoce a sí misma, física e históricamente'[34] [Europe is a shifting set with a changing profile, but nevertheless it recognizes itself physically and historically].

Immediately after this, he asks himself: '¿Se reconoce pero no se conoce? Digamos por ahora que su deslinde es problemático, móvil y muchas veces indefinido'[35] [Does it recognize itself without knowing itself? Let's say for now that its boundaries are problematic, movable, and often

32   Sena, 'Hispanismo', 24.
33   Claudio Guillén, 'Europa: ciencia e inconsciencia', in *Múltiples moradas* (Barcelona: Tusquets, 1998), 368–426.
34   Guillén, 'Europa', 371.
35   Guillén, 'Europa', 371.

indeterminate]. The arguments come to show, above all, the elusiveness, and mainly the mobility in definitions and characterizations of Europe, and the Iberian Peninsula's relations with it. So, for instance, there is the idea that 'Europa es una península de Asia dirigida hacia el Océano Atlántico' [Europe is an Asian peninsula directed towards the Atlantic Ocean] (Noblot, *Géographie Universelle*, 1725), which leads Guillén to apply to the Peninsula the expressive metaphor of 'Rompeolas de este movimento'[36] [a seawall to this movement]. Curiously or not, the Portuguese author José Cardoso Pires had written in 1971 that '[o] português está preso à Europa pela ponta, pelo que sobra dela, para não se deixar devolver aos oceanos que descobriu com muita honra'[37] [the Portuguese cling to Europe by its tip, by what is left of it, so they are not returned to the oceans they discovered with such great honour]. In the current economic, historical and political circumstances, it is equally interesting to attain the metaphor the writer used (the Portuguese as mussels), and developed in the following terms:

> E nisso não é como o coral que faz pé firme num ondular de cores vivas, mercados e joalharia; é antes como o mexilhão cativo, pobre e obscuro, já sem água, todo crespo, que vive a contracorrente no anonimato do rochedo. (De modo que quando a tormenta varre a Europa é ele que a suporta e se faz pedra, mais obscuro ainda).[38]

> [And in that matter it is not like the coral that firmly stands in a ripple of lively colours, markets or jewelry; instead, it is like a captive mussel, poor and obscure, without water, all wrinkled, living against the tide in the anonymity of the rugged rock. (So that when the storm sweeps Europe it is the mussel that supports it and turns into rock, becoming even more obscure).]

36   Guillén, 'Europa', 371.
37   José Cardoso Pires, 'Lá vai o português', in *E Agora, José?* (Lisbon: Círculo de Leitores, 2003 [1971]), 13.
38   Pires, 'Lá vai o português', 13.

A European perspective. What is Europe?

Last (but, by no means, least), I see yet another topic in the key objectives of this volume that deserves exploration: the matter of the 'European perspective'. Eduardo Lourenço, in the opening words of his essay 'L'Europe et nous', states: 'En dehors de sa connotation géographique, celle des manuels et celle de De Gaulle, personne ne sait très bien ce qu'est l'Europe' [Apart from its geographic connotation, the one from manuals and from De Gaulle, nobody knows for sure what Europe is], and distinguishes 'a European Europe' from 'the other Europe'.[39]

In fact, in order to be coherent both with my epistemic attitude and with the discussion of the concept of Iberia itself, its scientific accuracy, and its value as a starting point for scientific and academic work, we have to ask ourselves about the concept of a 'European perspective' and, after all, of Europe itself: its scientific accuracy; and whether it is valid as a starting point for scientific and academic work or not.

It is Claudio Guillén, once again, who in the aforementioned essay evokes *Os Lusíadas* and, praising Lourenço's 'penetration', recalls how he, in *Nós e a Europa*, had underlined that the poem is understood 'como la invención de una mirada Europeia en cuanto mirada planetária – sobre el mundo y sobre la propia Europa'[40] [as the invention of a European gaze as a planetary gaze – over the world and over Europe itself]. He is referring to the essay 'Camões et l'Europe', a lecture pronounced at UNESCO, in 1986, where he considered the poem further as a 'miroir poétique de l'expérience de deux siécles de contactes ibériques avec le monde non-européen' [a poetic mirror of the two centuries' experience of Iberian contact with the non-European world].[41] Not everyone will agree, of course. But let us face the fact that it is worth bearing in mind, as is the importance of the 'invention

39   Lourenço, *Nós e a Europa*, 39.
40   Guillén, 'Europa', 372.
41   Lourenço, *Nós e a Europa*, 87–102.

of a European gaze' in the invention of Europe. And sometimes, as we all know, it is from the margins that bridges are built. And from distant glances.

Works cited

Abreu, Maria Fernanda de, 'De que lado o espelho? Das teorias às práticas comparatistas no estudo das relações literárias entre Portugal e Espanha', in Gabriel Magalhães, ed., *Actas do Congresso RELIPES III: 18, 19 e 20 de Abril de 2007* (Covilhã: Universidade da Beira Interior, 2007), 437–52.

Cabo Aseguinolaza, Fernando, Anxo Abuín, and César Domínguez, *A Comparative History of Literatures in the Iberian Peninsula*, 2 vols (Amsterdam and Philadelphia: John Benjamins, 2010).

Casas, Arturo, 'Sistema interliterario y planificación historiográfica a propósito del espacio geocultural ibérico', *Interlitteraria* 8 (2003), 68–97.

Coelho, Jacinto do Prado, *Originalidade da Literatura Portuguesa* (Lisbon: Instituto de Cultura Portuguesa, 1977).

Espriu, Salvador, *La pell de brau/A Pele de Touro*, trans. Manuel Seabra (bilingual edn) (Lisbon: Dom Quixote, 1960).

Even-Zohar, Itamar, 'The Role of Literature in the Making of the Nations of Europe: A Socio-semiotic Study', *Applied Semiotics/Sémiotique appliquée* 1/1 (1996), 39–59.

Figueiredo, Fidelino de, 'Prefácio', in J. P. de Oliveira Martins, *História da Civilização Ibérica* (Lisbon: Guimarães & C.ª Ed., 1984 [1954]), IX–XVI.

——, *Pyrene: ponto de vista para uma introducção á história comparada das literaturas portuguesa e espanhola* (Lisbon: Empresa Nacional de Publicidade, 1935).

Guillén, Claudio, 'Europa: ciencia e inconsciencia', in *Múltiples moradas* (Barcelona: Tusquets, 1998), 368–426.

Lourenço, Eduardo, *Nós e a Europa ou as Duas Razões* (Lisbon: Imprensa Nacional–Casa da Moeda, 1988).

Martins, Joaquim Pedro de Oliveira, *História da Civilização Ibérica*, pref. Fidelino de Figueiredo [1954] (Lisbon: Guimarães & C.ª Ed., 1984 [1879]).

Quental, Antero de, *Causas da Decadência dos Povos Peninsulares*, int. Delfim Brito (Lisbon: Guimarães Ed., 2001 [1871]).

——, 'Causes of the Decline of the Peninsular Peoples in the Last Three Centuries', trans. Richard Correll, *Portuguese Studies* 24/1 (2008), 67–94.

Pires, José Cardoso, 'Lá vai o português', in *E Agora, José?* (Lisbon: Círculo de Leitores, 2003 [1971]), 13–18.

Ribeiro, Orlando, *Portugal, o Mediterrâneo e o Atlântico. Esboço de Relações Geográficas*, 5th edn (Lisbon: Sá da Costa, 1987 [1947]).

Saramago, José, *A Jangada de Pedra* (Lisbon: Caminho, 1986).

Sena, Jorge de, 'Hispanismo: archipiélago de glorias y vanidades en el mar–océano de la ignorancia universal', in Alan M. Gordon and Evelyn Rugg, eds, *Actas del sexto congreso internacional de hispanistas celebrado en Toronto del 22 al 26 de agosto de 1977* (Toronto: Departament of Spanish and Portuguese, University of Toronto, 1980), 19–25 <http://asociacioninternacionaldehispanistas.org/actas/AIH_06_1.pdf> accessed 8 September 2012.

Torga, Miguel, *Poemas Ibéricos* (Coimbra: Coimbra Editora, 1965).

FERENC PÁL

Do the Portuguese Toot Merrily? – The Image of Portugal, Portuguese History and People in Hungary during the Nineteenth Century

I would like to begin my essay with a rather superficial image of Portugal by referring to a seemingly stereotypical phrase. It was Dezső Kosztolányi, the early twentieth-century poet, who in 1923 wrote the following in his work titled *Nyelv és lélek* [Reading Portuguese]: 'Esküszöm önöknek, hogy akkor egy szót sem tudtam portugálul. A portugálokról is csak annyit tudtam, megbízható történelmi kútfőktől, hogy vígan dudálnak' [I swear that at the time I didn't know a single word of Portuguese. And of the Portuguese themselves I only gathered – from reliable, historical sources – that they tooted merrily].[1]

This idiomatic expression, also featured in the title of my essay, is cited in several occasions ranging from colloquial speech and newspaper articles to works of literature. It first appeared in the narrative *Gavallérok* [The Cavaliers] written by the nineteenth-century realist author Kálmán Mikszáth, and was used to refer to a favourable run of cards.[2] The phrase then entered common knowledge and came to be widely used in one of the songs in Charles Lecoq's popular operetta which was based on the Portuguese theme *Day & Night* (*Le Jour et la nuit*, 1881).[3]

1   Dezső Kosztolányi, *Nyelv és lélek* (Budapest: Szépirodalmi, 1990), 55. Unless otherwise stated, all translations into English are my own.
2   'Vígan dudál a portugál' [do the Portuguese toot merrily] means that 'the run of the cards is excellent'. Kálmán Mikszáth, 'Gavallérok', in *Elbeszélések és Kisregények*, vol. 2 (Budapest: Szépirodalmi, 1960), 246.
3   As stated by Alphonse Allais (1854–1905), a French humorist, in his article 'Le soi-disant bolide de Madrid': 'De même que leurs voisins les Portugais sont toujours

Based on these facts one can conclude that the phrase did not express any kind of genuine experience. Actually, it can be viewed as a literary adaptation of a popular expression. Hungarians at that time did not have a direct experience with the Portuguese and therefore could not have an opinion about them. Their image of this nation could only stem from literary works and select historical sources. The gradually increasing popularity of Camões during the Romantic period played an important role in this process. It was further aided by a vague reference to the supposed Hungarian origin of the Portuguese monarchs[4] in his *The Lusiads*. In addition to this there were somewhat biased press reports from the second half of the century that have come to light in contemporary works.

Camões and his epic poem have been known in Hungary since the eighteenth century. Camões is looked upon as the embodiment of the Romantic ideal where the poet revolts against the authority and is ready to sacrifice anything, including his own life. At the turn of the eighteenth and early nineteenth century the writer and poet János Batsányi – with early Romantic sensitivity – mentions Camões, along with Homer, Milton, Cervantes and Dante, as one who has been to the depths of hell and died in poverty.[5]

---

gais, les Espagnols sont toujours "gnols"'. Alphone Allais, 'Le soi-disant bolide de Madrid', in *Le Bec en l'air* (Paris: Paul Ollendorff, 1897), 59.

4   Cf. Ferenc Pál, 'Megjegyzések Báró Kemény Zsigmond *Élet és ábránd* című regényének szereplőválasztásához' [Remarks to the Characters of the Novel *Life and Dreams* of Baron Zsigmond Kemény], *A Modern Filológiai Társaság Értesítője* XXIV/2 (2007), 8–13.

5   'Íme Görög, és Ángol-Országnak eget, földet, poklot megjáró s előnkbe terjesztő legfőbb Poétáji az Isteneknek ama belső, meghitt fattyai – szűkölködő szegénységben töltik elhagyatott, gyámoltalan öregségeket (Homérosz és Milton, Cervantes, Camoens, Dante)...' [The most important poets of Greece and England who visited the heavens, the earth and the hell, the confidential and familiar sons of the Gods spend their lonely, helpless declining years in poverty (Homer and Milton, Cervantes, Camoens, Dante)]. János Batsányi, 'Beszéd' [Speech], in *Régi magyar irodalmi szöveggyűjtemény* <http//209.85/135.10403.15> and <http//magyar-irodalom.elte.hu/gepesk/corpus/XVIII/patsjo18.htm> accessed 15 March 2007.

A quarter of a century later Camões is presented as more than just a Romantic poet; he is a seer, capable of almost anything when it comes to the glorification and rise of his country. Not only does he confront the royal establishment, but he is also willing to relinquish love in order to consummate his poetry. This shift in the poet's image can be explained by events in Hungarian society from the 1820s onwards. For example, leading figures during this period fought against the Habsburg regime and for the revival of the Hungarian language and ideals, and the recognition of their past. Camões and *The Lusiads* were both referred to in this struggle, even if adjusted slightly to meet certain expectations.

The image of the seer who is willing to do whatever it takes for the sake of his nation was created by the poet Ferenc Kölcsey, who evokes Camões in his treatise titled *Nemzeti hagyományaink* [National Traditions]. This contrasts with the unpatriotic poets who long for foreign lands: 'Fájdalom, mi már akkor idegen befolyásnak nagy készséggel adtunk helyt; s azalatt, míg Európának végén, az éhséggel küzdő Camoens hazája örök dicsőségének szentelte hangjait, a mi pécsi püspökünk római lanton zengette a nemzet előtt idegen szép éneket'[6] [Alas, even then we readily made way for foreign influence; while at the ends of Europe the hungering Camões sang the eternal glory of his homeland, our bishop of Pécs played unfamiliar, yet fine songs on a Roman lyre].

In János Arany's treatise titled *Irodalmi hitvallásunk* [Literary Creed] the stalwart poet is presented as swimming ashore with a manuscript of *The Lusiads* after having been shipwrecked on the turbulent sea: 'Igen, a hivatás érzete ott van amaz úszó küzdelmeiben, ki pergamen-tekercscsel fogai közt, vívja élethalál-harczát a tenger bősz hullámival, hogy megmentse művét s életét, vagy együtt veszszenek. Az úszó: Camoens, a tekercs: a *Lusiada*'[7] [Aye; a sense of vocation is present in the struggle of the swimmer, who

---

6   Ferenc Kölcsey, 'Nemzeti hagyományaink', in *Válogatott művei*, vol. I (Budapest: Szépirodalmi, 1951 [1825]), 221.

7   János Arany, 'Irodalmi hitvallásunk', in *Koszorú I. Összes Művei*, vol. XI (Budapest: Szépirodalmi, 1983), 410.

– with scroll between his teeth – faces the grim waves in fierce battle to save his work and life, or perish. The swimmer: Camões; the scroll: *The Lusiads*].

However, by the end of the eighteenth century onwards, the figure of Camões is looked upon with distinguished interest by the Hungarian nobility and intelligentsia. This is mainly due to a historical hypothesis that is spelled out in his epic poem, and becomes primarily known through its Latin, French and later German translations. In stanza 25 of the Third Canto the poet hints at the Hungarian origin of the Portuguese reigning dynasty:

> Destes Henrique, dizem, que segundo
> Filho de hum Rei de Hungria exprimentado,
> Portugal houve em sorte [...].

> [And among these one Henry, as they say,
> Of Hungary's king the well-proved second son,
> By lot had Portugal [...].][8]

The statement, which is repeated in stanza 28 of the Third Canto and stanza 9 of the Eighth Canto, had a significant impact on the Hungarian national self-esteem evolving at the time. This further raised interest in Camões, however, by 1829 – the year that marked the end of the debate surrounding the origin of the Portuguese monarchs – there was proof that the reigning dynasty was not of Hungarian, but Burgundian ancestry.

In fact, the Evangelical vicar Mihály Holéczy[9] first suggested that the reigning Portuguese monarchs originated in the Árpád-dynasty in an essay titled 'Portugalliai Henrik' [Henry of Portugal] and published in the first issue of *Tudományos Gyűjtemény* [Scientific Omnibus] in 1828. This assumption was then either supported or confuted by István Horváth,[10] a

8   Luís Vaz de Camões, *The Lusiads*, trans. J. J. Aubertin (London: C. Kegan Paul i Co. Paternoster, 1878), 126–7.
9   Mihály Holéczy, 'Portugalliai Henrik', *Tudományos Gyűjtemény* 1 (1828), 66–77.
10 István Horváth, 'Henrik Portugáliai Grófról mint Magyar Király fiáról' [On Henry, Portuguese Count, son of a Hungarian King], *Tudományos Gyűjtemény* 3 (1828), 3–70.

certain Mr Y,[11] and János Lutczenbacher,[12] among others. It was not until György Fejér, the Director of the University Library that the debate finally came to an end in 1830. It should also be noted that his treatise, *Henricus portugaline comes origine burgundus non hungarus*,[13] was intended for academia as opposed to a wider audience.

Nonetheless, the belief that the Portuguese kings were in fact of Hungarian origin stayed strong, and many nationalists held on to this favourable, yet uncertain hypothesis. A prime example is the historical novel *A portugali gróf* [The Portuguese Count] written in the style of Walter Scott and Chateaubriand by the popular author József Gaál and published in the journal *Aurora* in 1836. At the end of the novel Prince Henry, being a meritorious descendent of the Árpád-dynasty, is crowned king of Portugal.[14]

In the same year a short biography on Camões was published by a certain C.C.I. in the weekly periodical the *Nemzeti Társalkodó* [National Converser].[15] In 1841 István Eördögh wrote about the poet's exile in the Far East, including the story of his shipwreck and how the manuscript of *The Lusiads* survived.[16] At the same time, Zsigmond Kemény, a highly-reputed novelist during this period, was already working on his new Portugal-related book *Élet és ábránd* [Life and Dreams].[17] In it he wrote about the romantic relationship between the poet and Catharina de Athayde, a member of the royal court. Instead of diverging on various events, the novel focuses on the psyche of the characters, Camões's gradual process of becoming a poet and the tragedy of the protagonist's love affair. It is similar in style to

11 Mr Y, 'Vélemény Henrik portugalliai Gróf eredetéről' [Opinion about the Origin of Henry, Portuguese Count], *Tudományos Gyűjtemény* 8 (1828), 46–57.

12 János Lutczenbacher, 'Henrik Portugáliai gróf eredetéről' [About the Origin of Henry, Portuguese Count], *Tudományos Gyűjtemény* 11 (1829), 19–61.

13 György Fejér, *Henricus portugaline comes origine burgundus non hungarus* (Buda: Egyetemi Nyomda, 1830). It is a small 72-page book.

14 József Gaál, 'The Portuguese Count', *Aurora* (1836), 281–347.

15 C.C.I., 'Camoens', *Nemzeti Társalkodó* 21 (24 May 1836), 331–5.

16 István Eördögh, 'Camoens', *Athenaeum* 1/2 (1841), 8–14 and 24–30.

17 Ferenc Pál, 'Megjegyzések báró Kemény Zsigmond *Élet és Ábránd* című regényének szereplőválasztásához', *A Modern Filológiai Társaság Értesítője* XXIV/2 (June 2007), 8–13.

German Romantic works of literature and borrows motifs from Ludwig Tieck's novel *Tod des Dichters* [The Death of the Poet], Friedrich Halm's one-act play *Camoens* and Almeida Garrett's epic poem *Camões*. It also depicts how the genius turns against conventions and refuses to lead a comfortable life. In order to fulfil his full potential as a poet he also rejects love and prefers to face suffering and a miserable death.

In the preface to his novel[18] Zsigmond Kemény emphasizes that his aim was not to write a picaresque novel, but rather present the self-fulfilment of a poetic genius. His descriptions of various places – Sintra and the surroundings of the Mafra National Palace in the first part, then Lisbon in the third – are all authentic. The plot summary of the epic poem also indicates that Kemény knew Portugal and Camões's work well. Nonetheless, he slightly altered certain facts for the sake of greater emotional impact. The Mafra National Palace is presented in a somewhat anachronistic way and the scene of the aforementioned shipwreck is moved from the Mekong region to the estuary of the Tagus. There is also Catharina de Athayde who remains alive. What is more, she does not even grow old during the poet's twenty-year-long voyages throughout the Far East. Furthermore, Camões's masterpiece is published by his friends only after his death.

Eventually the narrative poem *Louis de Camoens* was published in 1863 by Pál Jámbor under the pseudonym Hiador.[19] It consists of 143 stanzas, each of which are eight lines long, and recounts the poet's captivity, miraculous escape and return home. In other words, it contains all of the key elements that are significantly different from those works which rely on and enrich conventional biographies. The poet manages to free himself from the prison of a Far Eastern despot, flees onto a ship, but is shipwrecked. He is then found on a deserted island by King Sebastian, who went searching for his beloved poet. On their way back Camões reads the poem to the king after having salvaged the leather bag containing *The Lusiads* manuscript from the sea.

---

18   Ferenc Papp, 'Élet és Ábránd', in Kisfaludy-Társaság, ed., *Báró Kemény Zsigmond hátrahagyott munkái* (Budapest: Franklin, 1914), 45–72.

19   Pál Jámbor, *Hiador versei* (Oblath Leo: Szabadka, 1863).

Bearing all of this in mind it should come as no surprise that the Hungarian readership fully embraced not only the poet, but his epic poem as well, since both became known during the early nineteenth century and were closely associated to the patriotic efforts of the time. As Ferenc Toldy, the literary historian, wrote: 'A költő nagy egyénisége, e hív és honszerelmi lelkesedés valóságos synpathetikai hatást bír gyakorolni [a magyarokra]' [The poet's character and patriotism were highly appealing to the Hungarians].[20]

This explains why the translated version of *The Lusiads*, published in 1865, was altered considerably by Gyula Greguss.[21] Following in the footsteps of those Hungarian poets who strove to create a national mythology (like Sándor Aranyosrákosi Székely, Mihály Vörösmarty and János Arany) and with similar intentions to Macpherson, he turned the late Renaissance epic poem – in which the God of Christianity and ancient gods feature alike – into one with a nationalistic tone. For example, instead of Mars one encounters the Lord of Wars (Hadúr), and instead of Neptune the reader is presented with the Lord of Water-waves (Habúr), along with imaginary figures from Hungarian mythology.

After the struggle for independence, the interest in Camões decreased somewhat. From the 1870s onwards Portugal was featured regularly in the press, but newspapers only reported diplomatic or royal events because the country was regarded as being less exotic than Brazil or Africa. This obviously influenced the image of the Portuguese people, which is apparent in the works of two contemporary authors, Kálmán Mikszáth and Mór Jókai. While the former, in addition to the previously cited expression, wrote about what the Portuguese queen wore on her feet in his novelette titled *Mindenki lépik egyet* [Everyone Takes a Step], references to Portugal feature in six different novels written by the latter. In *A kalózkirály* [The Pirate King] and *Akik kétszer halnak meg* [Those Who Die Twice] the reader can find out about Portuguese colonization and bullfights, whereas the others

---

20 Introductory words to an extract of *The Lusiads* published in 1860. Cf. Rózsa Zoltán, org., *Magyar-portugál kapcsolatok* (Budapest: ELTE BTK, 1987), 40.

21 Gyula Greguss, *Camoens Luziádája* (Budapest: Athenaeum, 1874).

(*Egy hírhedett kalandor a XVII. Századból* [An Infamous Adventurer from the 17th Century]; *Eppur si muove*; *Fráter György* [Brother George]; *A magyar nemzet története regényes rajzokban* [The History of Our Nation in Fictional Images]) mention ambassadors, princes, queens and princesses, but there are no merry common folks. As a result – presumably because of these queens and ambassadors – Portugal is regarded by Hungarians as a distant, noble, somewhat cheerless country.

This can be exemplified by a few twentieth-century pieces of literature. In an extract taken from Dezső Pataki's novel *Anton Ixel*, which was published in the third issue of *Nyugat* [West] in 1937, a meticulously tidy house is likened to the boots of a Portuguese general.[22] It is likely that Tibor Déry also drew inspiration from the same tradition given that one of his short-story collections was titled *A portugál hercegnő* [Portuguese Princess]. In Zoltán Egressy's recent play *Portugál – nyolc dráma* [Portuguese] the country is referred to as a pretty, yet sad foreign place that the protagonist wants to visit:

> MASNI: És mit akarsz Portugáliában?
> [...]
> BECE: Megnézem őket. Jó nép az. Ők találták fel a teát például. Meg a vázát, meg a legyezőt.[23]

> [RIBBON: And what will you do in Portugal?
> [...]
> BECE: I'll check them out. They're nice people. They invented tea and vases. And fans.]

Another such example comes from Péter Esterházy's latest novels, where a representative of the Portuguese nobility is featured. It reads: 'Esti Kornél [...] mindig egy nő miatt van Portugáliában, mindig ugyanazon nő miatt van Portugáliában, egy már nem fiatal portugál bárónő miatt van Portugáliában,

---

22   Dezső Pataki, *Anton Ixel. Nyugat*, CD-ROM (Budapest: Arcanum Adatbázis, n.d.).
23   Egressy Zoltán, *Portugál – nyolc dráma* (Budapest: Ant-ko KKT, 2005). Project Gutenberg <http://ebooks.gutenberg.us/Wordtheque/hu/AAACAX.TXT> accessed 30 April 2012.

akibe, ahogy mondani szokás, halálosan szerelmes'[24] [Kornél Esti [...] went to Portugal because of a woman, he's always there because of a woman, always because of the same woman, he's in Portugal because of a somewhat aging baroness, with whom, as it's commonly referred to, he's desperately in love].

On the whole it can be concluded that Portugal became a part of Hungarian common knowledge in the nineteenth century. Learned readers knew about Camões and his epic poem ever since the end of the eighteenth century. The First Canto had already been translated by Sándor Aranyrákosi Székely[25] in 1818, even if from a German version. There were other literary figures who spoke the Portuguese language, such as Gyula Greguss, who translated Camões' primary work from the original. Ede Somogyi also translated *O Mistério da Estrada de Sintra* [The Mystery of Sintra Road] by Eça de Queirós from Portuguese in 1886.[26] We can also assume that there was a deeper understanding of Portugal, its history and literature based on the number of related works, relevant entries in the *Great Pallas Lexicon* (1893–7) and the close to 40 pages that discussed Portuguese literature in volume 2 of the *History of World Literature* (published by the Franklin Association in 1905). There is also Vilmos Huszár's essay which portrays the Portuguese as being distinct from the Spanish in the following way:

A fényes ég, a melegen sütő nap, az erdőben, folyóban gazdag és buján termékeny föld – a nép egyéniségére nem maradtak hatástalanul, sőt mindjobban kifejlesztették lelkének alapsig'átságát, a mely legjellemzőbben a portugál ember elégikus puhaságában, szentimentális rajongásában, melancholikus epekedésében és mindenekfölött örökösen szerelmes tenyészetében nyilvánul.[27]

---

24 Péter Esterházy, 'A Gyula-töredék', *Bárka* 5 (2007) <http://www.barkaonline.hu/szepirodalom/17-pr/322-a-gyula-t> accessed 17 November 2007.

25 A lost manuscript or publication. Cf. <wiki.miner.hu/Székely_Sándor> accessed 10 September 2011.

26 Eça de Queirós and Ramalho Ortigão, 'A cintrai ut titka' [The Mystery of Sintra Road], trans. Ede Somogyi, *Pesti Hírlap* (19 June to 29 July 1886).

27 Vilmos Huszár, 'Portugálok', in Gusztáv Heinrich, ed., *Egyetemes Irodalomtörténet*, vol. II (Budapest: Franklin–Társulat, 1905), 752–3.

[The bright sky, the warm sunshine, the endless forests and countless rivers, the fertile land all had an influence on the character of this nation. Moreover, this all developed its basic mentality, which is most apparent in the Portuguese peoples' rueful tenderness, sentimental devotion, melancholic longing and forever loving nature.]

Nonetheless, it was only Camões and his epic poem that managed to become widely known, primarily due to social, political and historical reasons.

Works cited

Allais, Alphone, 'Le soi-disant bolide de Madrid', in *Le Bec en l'air* (Paris: Paul Ollendorff, 1897), 57–61.

Arany, János, 'Irodalmi hitvallásunk', in *Koszorú I. Összes Művei*, vol. XI (Budapest: Szépirodalmi, 1983).

Batsányi, János, 'Beszéd', in *Régi magyar irodalmi szöveggyűjtemény* <http//209.85/ 135.10403.15> and <http//magyar-irodalom.elte.hu/gepesk/corpus/XVIII/ patsjo18.htm> consulted 15 March 2007.

Camões, Luís Vaz de, *The Lusiads*, trans. J. J. Aubertin (London: C. Kegan Paul i Co. Paternoster, 1878).

C.C.I., 'Camoens', *Nemzeti Társalkodó* 21 (24 May 1836), 331–5.

Eördögh, István, 'Camoens', *Athenaeum* 1/2 (1841), 8–14 and 24–30.

Esterházy, Péter, 'A Gyula-töredék', *Bárka* 5 (2007) <http://www.barkaonline.hu/ szepirodalom/17-pr/322-a-gyula-t> consulted 17 November 2007.

Fejér, György, *Henricus portugaline comes origine burgundus non hungarus* (Buda: Egyetemi Nyomda, 1830).

Gaál, József, 'The Portuguese Count', *Aurora* (1836), 281–347.

Greguss, Gyula, *Camoens Luziádája* (Budapest: Athenaeum, 1874).

Holéczy, Mihály, 'Portugalliai Henrik', *Tudományos Gyűjtemény* 1 (1828), 66–77.

Horváth, István, 'Henrik Portugáliai Grófról mint Magyar Király fiáról', *Tudományos Gyűjtemény* 3 (1828), 3–70.

Huszár, Vilmos, 'Portugálok', in Gusztáv Heinrich, ed., *Egyetemes Irodalomtörténet*, vol. II (Budapest: Franklin–Társulat, 1905).

Jámbor, Pál, *Hiador versei* (Szabadka: Oblath Leo, 1863).

Jókai Mór, *Összes művei*, CD-ROM (Budapest: Arcanum Digitéka/Arcanum Adatbázis Kft. Kiadása, n.d.).

Kölcsey, Ferenc, 'Nemzeti hagyományaink', in *Válogatott művei*, vol. I (Budapest: Szépirodalmi, 1951 [1825]).

Kosztolányi, Dezső, *Nyelv és lélek* (Budapest: Szépirodalmi, 1990).

Lutczenbacher, János, 'Henrik Portugáliai gróf eredetéről', *Tudományos Gyűjtemény* 11 (1829), 19–61.

Mikszáth, Kálmán, 'Gavallérok', in *Elbeszélések és Kisregények*, vol. 2 (Budapest: Szépirodalmi, 1960).

——, *Összes művei*, CD-ROM (Budapest: Arcanum Digitéka/Arcanum Adatbázis, n.d.).

Mr Y [??], 'Vélemény Henrik portugalliai Gróf eredetéről', *Tudományos Gyűjtemény* 8 (1828), 46–57.

Pál, Ferenc, 'Megjegyzések Báró Kemény Zsigmond *Élet és ábránd* című regényének szereplőválasztásához', *A Modern Filológiai Társaság Értesítője* XXIV/2 (June 2007), 8–13.

Papp, Ferenc, 'Élet és Ábránd', in Kisfaludy-Társaság, ed., *Báró Kemény Zsigmond hátrahagyott munkái* (Budapest: Franklin, 1914), 45–72.

Pataki, Dezső, *Anton Ixel. Nyugat*, CD-ROM (Budapest: Arcanum Adatbázis, n.d.).

Queirós, Eça de, and Ramalho Ortigão, 'A cintrai ut titka', trans. Ede Somogyi, *Pesti Hírlap* (19 June to 29 July 1886).

Zoltán, Egressy, *Portugál – nyolc dráma* (Budapest: Ant-ko KKT, 2005). Project Gutenberg <http://ebooks.gutenberg.us/Wordtheque/hu/AAACAX.TXT> accessed 30 April 2012.

Zoltán, Rózsa, org., *Magyar-portugál kapcsolatok* (Budapest: ELTE BTK, 1987).

DEREK FLITTER

North and South: Iberian Identity Formation in Romanticism and Post-Romanticism

Schlegelian Romantic theory provided, in its postulation of an all-embracing intimate relationship between individual and national community, for an essential dualism in imaginative consciousness and literary figuration, between, on the one hand, a 'Northern' temperament and outlook characterized by introverted metaphysical speculation and, on the other, a fundamentally expressive and impassioned 'Southern' counterpoint. Madame de Staël's *De l'Allemagne* succinctly encapsulated this, identifying the first as the personal correlation of northern Europe's emblematic physical geography in its remoteness and disposition to withdraw within itself, and the second as similarly conditioned by the continental south, impelled outward by the warmth of its vital passion.

As Romantic theory cohered in Spain in the decade of the 1820s, we find any number of writers resolutely restating this essential dualism: in the pages of the Barcelona journal *El Europeo*, for example, in the words of the Italian émigré Luigi Monteggia.[1] After the fall of the Roman Empire, the invasion of southern Europe by the northern tribes brought with it, as he stated it, the lugubrious ideas and imaginative bent produced by the experience of life in a sterner climate. Later in the decade, Donoso Cortés would reveal himself to be profoundly influenced by this basic contention in the contribution to the debate characteristically known as the 'Cáceres speech'. In referring to Byron, he describes the essential tenor of the English poet's lyric in the following terms:

---

1   Luigi Monteggia, 'Romanticismo' [1823], in Ricardo Navas-Ruiz, ed., *El romanticismo español. Documentos* (Salamanca: Anaya, 1971), 33–42.

Byron hace resonar a la musa de Inglaterra con los grandes acentos de su sublime
melancolía y la hace gemir con los profundos gemidos del infortunio y del dolor. Todo
es vago en sus producciones: el velo misterioso que las cubre hace que, replegándonos
sobre nosotros, contemplemos el misterio de nuestro *yo moral*; el fatalismo de las
pasiones que arrastran a sus personajes con una mano de hierro por los escollos de
la vida, nos prepara a que contemplemos silenciosos cómo se huyen los límites del
tiempo y cómo se abre el abismo de la eternidad. Todo en él nos recuerda nuestra
nada; todo es terrible y misterioso como el hombre; todo está velado con el velo
de la naturaleza y sellado con el sello de la contemplación. Ha pintado las pasiones
que nos desgarran con su lucha y ha enseñado a los poetas modernos cuál debe ser
el objeto de sus cantos.

[Byron makes the English muse resound with the high accents of his sublime melancholy and makes her moan with the deep moans of misfortune and pain. Everything
is vague in his productions: the mysterious veil that covers them causes us to retire
within ourselves and contemplate the mystery of our *moral selves*; the fatalism of the
passions which drag his characters with an iron grip through the shoals of existence
prepares us to contemplate in silence how the limits of time flee away and how the
abyss of eternity opens. Everything in him reminds us of our nothingness; everything is terrible and mysterious like man himself; everything is veiled with the veil
of Nature and sealed with the seal of contemplation. He has painted the passions
which tear us with their struggle and he has taught modern poets what should be
the object of their songs.][2]

I have suggested elsewhere that Donoso, like Monteggia's editorial col-
league on *El Europeo* Ramón López Soler, effectively mitigates and contains
Byron's air of metaphysical uncertainty by ascribing the despairing tones
of his lyric to the confines of Edmund Burke's aesthetic Sublime. When
López Soler wrote the prologue to his 1830 historical novel *Los bandos de
Castilla*, ostensibly a reworking of Walter Scott, he would supply a Spanish
readership with what amounted to an imaginative template for the configuration of Spain's Romantic literary muse. This extensive passage is so
central to my purpose that I cite it in full in the original:

2   Quoted and translated into English in Derek Flitter, 'The Immortal Byron in Spain:
     Radical and Poet of the Sublime', in Richard Cardwell, ed., *The Reception of Byron
     in Europe, Vol. I: Southern Europe, France and Romania* (London and New York:
     Thoemmes Continuum, 2005), 133; emphasis in the original.

Libre, *impetuosa, salvaje* por decirlo así, tan admirable en el osado vuelo de sus ins-piraciones como sorprendente en sus sublimes *descarríos*, puédese afirmar que la literatura romántica es el intérprete de aquellas pasiones *vagas* e *indefinibles* que, dando al hombre un *sombrío* carácter, lo impelen hacia la *soledad*, donde busca en el *bramido* del mar y en el silbido de los vientos las imágenes de sus *recónditos* pesares. Así, pulsando una lira de ébano, orlada la frente de *fúnebre* ciprés, se ha presentado al mundo esta musa *solitaria*, que tanto se complace en pintar las *tempestades* del uni-verso y las del corazón humano; así, cautivando con mágico prestigio la *fantasía* de sus oyentes, inspírales, *fervorosa*, el deseo de la *venganza*, o enternécelos, *melancólica*, con el *emponzoñado* recuerdo de las pasadas delicias. En medio de *horrorosos hura-canes*, de noches en las que apenas se trasluce una luna amarillenta, reclinada al pie de los *sepulcros*, o errando bajo los arcos de antiguos alcázares y monasterios, suele elevar su peregrino canto semejante a aquellas aves *desconocidas*, que sólo atraviesan los aires cuando parece anunciar el *desorden* de los elementos la *cólera* del Altísimo o la *destrucción* del Universo.[3]

[Free, *impetuous* and *wild*, so to speak, and as admirable in the daring flight of its inspirations as surprising in its sublime *wanderings*. One can say that Romantic lit-erature is the interpreter of such *vague* and *indefinable* passions that, giving man a *gloomy* character, drive him towards *solitude*, where he seeks, in the *roaring* of the sea and the whistling winds, the images of his *hidden* sorrows. And so, playing an ebony lyre, with her forehead fringed by *funeral* cypress, was this *lonely* muse introduced to the world; she, who's equally pleased in portraying the *tumults* of the universe and those of the human heart. And so, captivating her listeners' *fantasy* with a magi-cal prestige, she inspires in them, *earnestly*, the wish for *revenge*, or else she softens them, with *melancholy*, with the *poisoned* memory of past delights. Amid *horrific hurricanes*, and nights that show but the glance of a yellowish moon, reclining over the graves or wandering under the arches of ancient palaces and monasteries, she wants to raise her chant, rare as that of birds *unknown* that seem to only cross the skies announcing the *disorder* of the elements, the *wrath* of the Almighty or the destruction of the Universe.][4]

3   Ramón López Soler, 'Los bandos de Castilla, o el Caballero del Cisne. Prólogo' [1830], in Ricardo Navas-Ruiz, ed., *El romanticismo español. Documentos* (Salamanca: Anaya, 1971), 101–7; emphasis added.
4   Unless otherwise stated, all quotations were translated into English by Amândio Reis.

This passage stands out for the insistent, formulaic even, quality of its enunciation and rhetoric. It dovetails very closely, as will be immediately apparent, with Donoso's slightly earlier evocation of Byron, but, more importantly, reminds us of one really crucial factor. In the development of Romanticism, especially Romantic theory, in Spain, there were a small number of judgements that acquired a sense of incontestable doctrinal truth: that European literary history could be separated into discrete periods of Classicism and Romanticism; that the natural *habitus* of the latter was the Christian Middle Ages, privileged by its elevated spirituality; that the mediaeval *romancero* and the theatre of the Spanish Golden Age were intimately representative of Spain's distinctive literary genius, products of an authentic collective imagination and mindset. To these, however, needs to be added one further component: the asseveration that while Classicism represented Beauty, Romanticism was the literary province of the Sublime. In the gestation period of Spain's Romanticism, it is perhaps the prevalence of the literary Sublime as an aesthetic procedure that is ultimately the most far-reaching ingredient, something which arguably has greater resonance even than the predilection for things mediaeval.

If we return to López Soler's prologue, we can see on even a cursory first acquaintance that the majority of the words that make up its effusive declaration appear to have been chosen precisely for their location within the sphere of the Sublime, that they have been chosen categorically to distinguish that sphere from the attributed tranquillity and equanimity of its Classical, 'beautiful' counterpart. We can swiftly enumerate many of them. Virtually every detail of these words reflects the thorough-going bipartite divisions made by Burke in his distillation and formulation of the Sublime and in his polarized distinctions of it from the Beautiful: light is beautiful, darkness is sublime; harmony is beautiful while disorder is sublime; joy is beautiful but pain and terror are sublime; and a long etcetera. What could be more sublime, if we take one extended and slightly mischievous example deriving from the López Soler prologue, than finding oneself alone, at night, in the midst of a terrifying storm, among the tombstones surrounding a ruined, reputedly haunted, castle, burdened by the painful consciousness of lost love?

Related to all of this, it goes without saying, is the calculated strategic effect upon the desiring reader, the reader who demands emotional thrills and spills and who wishes to experience, vicariously, the turmoil that closely defines the text in front of them: the phrase 'cautivando con mágico prestigio la fantasía de sus oyentes' [captivating her listeners' fantasy with a magical prestige] undoubtedly possesses further implications. In English literature Jane Austen had already forcefully satirized it in *Northanger Abbey*, but the predilection was alive, well and thriving in a Spain which had yet to have the eye of the Romantic storm break over it.

I want to consider another dimension here, one which is readily apparent once we add this almost obsessive fondness for the Sublime to the characteristic distinction between North and South that I alluded to at the start. Nothing should surprise us about the fact that Spain, coming to Romanticism late, embraces a form of Romanticism conditioned by motif, often dualistic motif. What is perhaps more striking is the degree in which López Soler's prologue acts as a paradigm for illustrations of Romantic inspiration. A few key examples, taken from well-known poems of the Spanish 1830s, especially initial lines that forcefully establish a meaningful locus for the Romantic lyric, will render the point beyond doubt.

Firstly, the verses that initiate Patricio de la Escosura's luridly atmospheric narrative poem 'El bulto vestido de negro capuz' [The Shadow Wearing a Black Cap]: 'El sol a occidente su luz ocultaba,/de nubes el cielo cubierto se vía;/furioso en los pinos el viento bramaba,/rugiendo agitado Pisuerga corría'[5] [The western sun hid its light,/one saw the sky covered with clouds;/the wind howled furious at the pines,/roaring and shaken it ran Pisuerga]. Light and sound effects are conjugated in order to consciously establish the dominant correlation between the storms of nature and those of the human heart: tempestuous nature as the essential background to tumultuous passion. José Bermúdez de Castro's emblematically named 'El

---

5   Patricio de la Escosura, 'El bulto vestido de negro capuz', in Eugenio de Ochoa, ed., *Apuntes para una biblioteca de escritores españoles contemporáneos*, vol. 1 (Paris: Baudry, Librería Europea, 1840), 500.

día de difuntos' [The Day of the Dead] is similarly pregnant with pathetic fallacy couched in the most blatant terms:

> Noviembre empezaba, la tarde era fría,
> Las nubes se alzaban cual negro vapor,
> Por entre los pinos el viento gemía
> Al lejos silbando con grito de horror.
>
> Las hojas marchitas que arranca la brisa
> Ruedan entre polvo con triste gemir,
> Y mágicas danzas, fantástica risa
> Imitan sus vueltas, su duro crujir.[6]
>
> [November began, the evening was cold,
> Like black smoke the clouds rose,
> The wind moaned through the pines
> Whistling at far in a cry of horror.
>
> The withered leaves that the breeze tears
> Roll in the dust with a sad moan,
> And magical dances, fantastical laughs,
> They imitate in their turns, in their hard crunch.]

Possibly the most familiar example would come from a poet whose verse, in its semantic concentration, regularly accumulated densely suggestive uses of the aesthetic Sublime. The opening lines of Espronceda's experimental narrative poem 'El estudiante de Salamanca' [The Student of Salamanca] create the perfect backdrop for the supernaturally entailed drama that is to follow:

> Era más de medianoche,
> antiguas historias cuentan,
> cuando en sueño y en silencio
> lóbrego, envuelta la tierra,

---

6   José Bermúdez de Castro, 'El día de difuntos', in Eugenio de Ochoa, ed., *Apuntes para una biblioteca de escritores españoles contemporáneos*, vol. 1 (Paris: Baudry, Librería Europea, 1840), 99–102.

los vivos muertos parecen
los muertos la tumba dejan.
Era la hora en que acaso
temerosas voces suenan
informes, en que se escuchan
tácitas pisadas huecas,
y pavorosas fantasmas
entre las densas tinieblas
vagan, y aúllan los perros
amedrentados al verlas;
en que tal vez la campana
de alguna arruinada iglesia
da misteriosos sonidos
de maldición y anatema,
que los sábados convoca
a las brujas a su fiesta.
El cielo estaba sombrío,
no vislumbraba una estrella,
silbaba lúgubre el viento,
y allá en el aire, cual negras
fantasmas, se dibujaban
las torres de las iglesias.[7]

[It was past midnight,
As ancient stories tell,
when in sleep and dark
silence covered the earth,
the living dead appear,
the dead their tombs leave.
It was the time when perhaps
fearful voices might sound
deformed, when tacit
hollow footsteps are heard,
and frightening ghosts
between the thick darkness
roam, and dogs howl
frightened at their sight;

7   José de Espronceda, 'El estudiante de Salamanca', in *Obras poéticas completas* (Madrid: Aguilar, 1972), 373–4.

at the time when the bell
of some ruined church
might mysteriously sound
like a curse and anathema
that on Saturdays summons
the witches to their party.
The sky was gloomy,
with no glimpse of a star,
mournful whistled the wind,
and there in the air, like black
ghosts, were drawn
the church towers.]

Espronceda enunciates a veritable roll call of the distinctive features of the Sublime. It could not be otherwise given the nature of his subject matter, which serves merely to illustrate the reciprocal relationship between setting and content that effectively dominated the literature of the whole of the period. The setting is such that the narrative which follows is not just appropriate and desired but indispensable, while the subject matter itself, that of the socially and morally ostracized anti-hero led to his death by a spectral figure who personifies his past villainy, could only truly be enacted in just such an ambiental scenario.

It might be said that practically the totality of the texts comprising the canonical works of Spain's Romantic drama can be ascribed to the same pattern: *Don Álvaro* (1835), *El trovador* (1836) and *Don Juan Tenorio* (1844) being principal among them, and the climactic scene of Rivas's play being the most extravagant example. The troubadour Manrique even dreams of himself inhabiting almost precisely the locale evoked by López Soler a few years earlier; the reminiscence is especially strong in Act IV, Scene VI, ll. 186–94: 'Trémulo como el viento en la laguna/triste brillaba el resplandor siniestro/de amarillenta luna./Sentado allí en su orilla y a tu lado/pulsaba yo el laúd, y en dulce trova/tu belleza y mi amor tierno cantaba,/y en triste melodía/el viento que en las aguas murmuraba/mi canto y tus suspiros repetía'[8] [Trembling like wind in the lagoon/sad shone the sinister glow/of yellowish moon./There, sitting on the bank and by your side/strummed I the lute, and in sweet lay/your beauty and my tender love I sung,/and in a sad melody/the wind that whispered in the waters/ repeated my song and your sighs].

The aesthetic Sublime becomes then something of an indispensable requirement, a *sine qua non* of the creative processes inherent in Spanish Romanticism. It is, furthermore, a crucial contributory ingredient of many examples of more personal lyric, poems cast in the first person that describe and evoke the nature of poetic inspiration. If we take one final example, we see it as a defining recurrent metaphor in the Galician poet Nicomedes-Pastor Díaz's piece entitled, significantly, 'Mi inspiración' [My Inspiration]:

> Cuando hice resonar mi voz primera
> Fue en una noche tormentosa y fría;
> Un peñón de la cántabra ribera
> De asiento me servía;
> El aquilón silbaba;
> La playa y la campiña estaban solas;
> Y el Océano rugidor sus olas
> A mis pies estrellaba.
>
> No brillaban los astros en el cielo,
> Ni en la tierra se oía humano acento;
> Estaba escuro, silencioso el suelo,
> Y negro el firmamento.
> Sólo en el horizonte
> Alguna vez relámpagos lucían;
> Y al mugir de los mares respondían
> Los pinares del monte.[9]

8 Antonio García Gutiérrez, *El trovador*, ed. Carlos Ruiz Silva (Madrid: Cátedra, 1997), 168–9.

9 Nicomedes-Pastor Díaz, 'Mi inspiración', in José María Castro y Calvo, ed., *Obras completas de D. Nicomedes-Pastor Díaz*, 3 vols (Madrid: Atlas, 1969–70), ii.

[When I firstly made my voice resound
It was a cold and stormy night;
A rock of the Cantabrian shore
        Served me as a seat;
        The north wind whistled;
The beach and the country were alone;
And the roaring Ocean crashed
        His waves at my feet.

No stars shone in the sky,
Neither on earth was heard a human sound;
It was dark, the earth quiet,
        And the skies black.
        Only in the horizon
Lightning stroke from time to time;
And the roaring of the seas was answered
        By the mountain forests.]

Díaz's poem introduces some new and further implications. While what I
have been describing as López Soler's affective template for the *habitus* of
the Romantic muse has, in the earlier examples, been employed as a schema
for narrative poetry or as ambiental formula for Romantic theatricality
and staged performance, it has been part and parcel of a larger design in
which the recreation of an historically distant, usually remote past, has
been factored in as a further means of literary idealization and escapism,
as part of a stratagem to dispel the limitations of everyday modern experience in favour of a time, place and phantasmagorical reality conceived
as more elevated, as truly Sublime. In many ways, the chosen settings of
Spanish Romanticism replicate, in Iberian terms, the preferred locus and
effects of the English writing that is perhaps most authentically the voice
of Burke's Sublime: Macpherson's Ossian poems. Recalling an earlier and
more heroic age and employing idealized yet elusively recognizable landscapes, their dream-like quality is given comparable life and depth. Díaz's
poem is different in that it configures the Sublime as belonging to the
Spanish nineteenth century and lived at first hand.

    What I think I have been indirectly suggesting throughout is that
among the preferred polarities and dualisms of Romantic theory as

conceived and expressed in Spain – the very terms 'Classical' and 'Romantic', the nationalistic preference for the native Golden Age against prescriptive neo-Classicism, the fondness for the Middle Ages – there is one further fundamental *binomio* in which Romanticism has unquestionable associations with North, not South. In short, it is the North which encapsulates and projects the Sublime. With the personal lyric of poets like Díaz, the poetics of Spain's own 'septentrión' is consolidated. Nicomedes-Pastor's evocation of Galicia's Cantabrian coast has potent affinities of geography and outlook with Ossian's Hebrides which Spain's southern periphery could never authentically supply. The historic heartland of Castile, mediated by historical distance and the refractive powers of the imagination, might act as a surrogate but without achieving the lyrical immediacy of Spain's own North.

To flesh out this basic contention, some contingent factors might be adduced here. When García Villalta staged his Spanish translation of *Macbeth* in Madrid in 1836, for example, it was commended especially for its 'authentic' recreation of mediaeval Scotland in its all-pervading mists and storms but also in its depiction of Shakespeare's witches and other supernatural paraphernalia: see particularly the review by Enrique Gil y Carrasco.[10] This seemed to be deemed as convincing as contemporary forms of *costumbrismo*. Another consideration is that those works by English Romantic authors to enjoy significant influence and repute in Spain were, principally, Macpherson's Ossian poems and Scott's *Ivanhoe*; of Byron's works it would be 'Manfred' which enjoyed the greatest acclaim, while it is not coincidental that Keats (surprisingly) and Wordsworth (less so) were never really understood in the Spanish nineteenth century. One last point is that when Bécquer, Spain's quintessential writer of metaphysical abstraction, enters the frame in the 1860s, it is the landscapes of Soria within his prose and verse which seemed most roundly to characterize his entire literary enterprise: the Soria of 'El rayo de luna' [The Moonbeam], the landscapes of 'El monte de las ánimas' [The Hill of Souls], his relationship with Toledo.

---

10   Enrique Gil y Carrasco, *Obras completas de don Enrique Gil y Carrasco*, ed. Jorge Campos (Madrid: Rivadeneyra, 1954), 421.

The poetic configuration of a Spanish 'septentrión' would have more far-reaching ramifications in the final decades of the century, and a new channel for North and South would be created. The Galician *Rexurdimento* was, after all, to be predicated upon resolute differentiation: in Rosalía de Castro between Galicia and Castile, predicated in almost apocalyptic terms, and, of more relevance in the present context, in Eduardo Pondal's declamation of a separate Celtic heritage. Galicia's Celtic remains become a vehicle for the distillation of Pondal's poetic and political vision, the wild landscapes of Bergantiños a means of transposing Ossian's bardic commemoration of Caledonian resistance to imperial Rome to a modern Spanish context. Ossian's Sublime becomes a Galician Sublime inhabited by reminiscences of the region's past and an ostensible way of proclaiming its differentiated Atlantic entailments against a dominant Mediterranean culture. The rub, as it were, in the Iberian nineteenth century, is that Spain's *Volksgeist*-informed historical Romanticism is restored, in microcosm and reductively, in Pondal's vision for Galicia. Rather than a falsely universal-izing and prescriptive neo-Classicism seeking to hold in thrall an autoch-thonous tradition, it is Spain's Mediterranean culture which is viewed as having enslaved, and continuing to enslave, the Celtic heritage of its north-western seaboard. Pondal plays insistently on the note of Ossian's Sublime in configuring Galicia's identity, especially in his evocation of the Terra de Xallas: 'Cautivo do barro,/con fonda tristura/dixérase o bardo/ que soña antre as uces/co tempo pasado'[11] [Prisoner of the clay,/in deep sadness,/ one would say of the bard/who dreams amongst the heather/of times past]. In Pondal's verse the essential paradigm of López Soler's pro-logue is recalled to life; the imagined landscape of that text breathes freely in Pondal's recapturing of his solitary walks in the wilds of Bergantiños, but the 'recónditos pesares' [hidden sorrows] of López Soler's Romantic muse are reconfigured as a lament for Galicia's lost Celtic heritage, and it is not the anguish of the individual's lost love which defines his song but of a lament for an entire tradition. In the 'Salvaxe val de Brantoa' [Wild Valley of Brantoa], Pondal's bard, in profound communion with the natural

11   Eduardo Pondal, *Queixumes dos pinos*, ed. Xavier Senín (Vigo: Galaxia, 1985), 13.

landscape, is rendered acutely conscious of that lost past; as the landscape itself explains to him in Pondal's poem:

> Esa indecisa inquietude,
> cando me ves, bardo amigo,
> suidades son dunha patria
> que un día a alma perdío;
> son misteriosas lembranzas
> do desterrado afrixido,
> que se acorda da súa terra,
> en terra allea cautivo,
> e quer volver outra vez
> ós patrios eidos amigos.[12]

> [This undecided disquietness
> you see in me, bard friend,
> is the lacking of a country
> once lost by the soul;
> these are mysterious memories
> of the aflicted outcast
> who recalls his homeland
> whilst captive in others',
> and wants to come back again
> to the friendly birth place.]

The aesthetic Sublime, the poetic figuration of the North, in the generations after Romanticism proper, acquires different life and unsuspected new depths, called to reinforce the imaginative projection of a differentiated Celtic Galicia. Romanticism lives on, but in regional guise, in another flight from centre to periphery, into the intimacies of a transcendent poetic consciousness that is at the service, like the Romantic Sublime had previously been, of cultural resistance.

---

12 Pondal, *Queixumes dos pinos*, 24.

Works cited

Bermúdez de Castro, José, 'El día de difuntos', in Eugenio de Ochoa, ed., *Apuntes para una biblioteca de escritores españoles contemporáneos*, vol. 1 (Paris: Baudry, Librería Europea, 1840), 99–102.

Díaz, Nicomedes-Pastor, 'Mi inspiración', in José María Castro y Calvo, ed., *Obras completas de D. Nicomedes-Pastor Díaz*, 3 vols (Madrid: Atlas, 1969–70), 11.

Escosura, Patricio de la, 'El bulto vestido de negro capuz', in Eugenio de Ochoa, ed., *Apuntes para una biblioteca de escritores españoles contemporáneos*, vol. 1 (Paris: Baudry, Librería Europea, 1840), 500.

Espronceda, José de, 'El estudiante de Salamanca', in *Obras poéticas completas* (Madrid: Aguilar, 1972), 373–4.

Flitter, Derek, 'The Immortal Byron in Spain: Radical and Poet of the Sublime', in Richard Cardwell, ed., *The Reception of Byron in Europe, Vol. I: Southern Europe, France and Romania* (London and New York: Thoemmes Continuum, 2005), 129–43.

García Gutiérrez, Antonio, *El trovador*, ed. Carlos Ruiz Silva (Madrid: Cátedra, 1997).

Gil y Carrasco, Enrique, *Obras completas de don Enrique Gil y Carrasco*, ed. Jorge Campos (Madrid: Rivadeneyra, 1954).

López Soler, Ramón, '*Los bandos de Castilla, o el Caballero del Cisne*. Prólogo' [1830], in Ricardo Navas-Ruiz, ed., *El romanticismo español. Documentos* (Salamanca: Anaya, 1971), 101–7.

Monteggia, Luigi, 'Romanticismo' [1823], in Ricardo Navas-Ruiz, ed., *El romanticismo español. Documentos* (Salamanca: Anaya, 1971), 33–42.

Pondal, Eduardo, *Queixumes dos Pinos*, ed. Xavier Senín (Vigo: Galaxia, 1985).

JUAN M. RIBERA LLOPIS

Centre–Peninsular Considerations on Catalan Literary Regeneration: An Everlasting Code?*

I. Premises and predictions

In the following pages we will deal with a series of documents that offer a certain centre–Peninsular – Castilian-Spanish, that is – discourse on Catalan contemporary literary Regeneration, which, as we will show, also receives response from Catalan writers. This discourse seems to diachronically perpetuate a code imposed by the *central system*. This code, composed by a group of *topoi* which will be summarized in the conclusions of these texts, has the following effects:

- *it obstructs* Iberian or Spanish literary polyphony;
- *it neutralizes* the centripetal minorization of Catalan literature from within the Peninsular *interliterary community* itself;
- *it conditions* the *projection* of this same literary tradition on its historical *interliterary community*.

This code therefore constructs itself as a way for the *Castilian-Spanish cultural system* to establish, perpetually and for its own benefit, the concept of *centre* as a synonym of *power* that is opposed to the notion of *periphery* which then, so it seems, should be linked to *dependence* or *submission*.

---

* This essay was translated from Spanish by Santiago Pérez Isasi.

II. Spanish voices and Catalan counterparts

In an inverse chronological order, we start our review of the verbaliza-
tion of this discourse, code and *topoi*, with a Spanish intellectual from the
second half of the twentieth century: Pedro Laín Entralgo (1908–2001).
His bio-ideological profile progresses from his early post-war Francoism
to a 'political Humanism', highly praised by his commentators, which, if
applied to the Spanish post-war reality, included an early interest in Spanish
cultural plurality. This evolution would finally lead him to the category
of *liberal humanist* and *democratic intellectual*, a category to which he was
catapulted during the transition to democracy, and in which he was gladly
accepted by the political left (PSOE).

This last co-ordinate explains the presence of Pedro Laín Entralgo
at the encounter for Castilian and Catalan writers, which was held in
Sitges in 1981. By looking at his interventions during this encounter, we
see him defend Spanish diversity,[1] and the Catalan tradition within it.
We even *understand* the exclusive use of the Catalan language by some of
the Catalan writers:

---

1   'Revisar, en lo que tenga de tradicional y recibida, nuestra idea de España, para
     sustituirla por otra más adecuada a su rica diversidad. Con sus bienandanzas y sus
     malandanzas debe pesar sobre nosotros, por supuesto, todo lo que ha sido nuestra
     historia común. Pero la crítica de ella y el proyecto que sobre esta crítica deba fundarse
     no se limitarán, como desde el regeneracionismo y la generación del 98 viene siendo
     tópico, a lo que en nuestro común destino ha sido unificante' [Review our idea of
     Spain, to the extent that it is a received tradition, to substitute it for a new one which
     is more adequate to its rich diversity. With its good and bad fortune, our common
     history must of course weigh on us. But its criticism and the project founded on this
     cricism will not restrict itself, as it has been the case since the *Regeneracionismo* and
     the Generation of 1898, to the unifying aspects of our common destiny]. Pedro Laín
     Entralgo, 'Ponencia. El diálogo de 1951', in *Relaciones de las culturas castellana y cata-
     lana. Encuentro de intelectuales. Sitges, 20–22 diciembre 1981* (Barcelona: Generalitat
     de Catalunya/Departament de la Presidència, 1983), 117. Unless otherwise stated, all
     translations were made by the editors of this volume.

[M]uchos escritores catalanes, pudiendo usar con notoria maestría la lengua castellana, se resistiesen a emplearla aquí. No hablo, claro está, de los que resueltamente
eligieron la expresión castellana, como Pi i Margall, Balmes o el segundo D'Ors, y
tampoco de los que, como, Maragall o Rusiñol, al menos en cuanto prosistas, indis-
tintamente recurrieron a uno y otro modo de expresarse. [...] Hablo tan sólo, baste
la mención del alto nombre de Espriu, de los que, como respuesta al mal trato que
entonces recibía su lengua materna y literaria, voluntariamente optaron, en cuanto
literatos, por una 'mudez castellana'. Con toda decisión comprendí y comprendo esa
actitud. Pero sólo a medias diría mi sentir si ocultase mi satisfacción advirtiendo que,
pese a todo, era en ellos general la capacidad para escribir un excelente castellano.[2]

[Many Catalan writers, who can skilfully use the Spanish language, resist to using
it here. I am not, of course, talking about those who resolutely chose a Spanish
expression, such as Pi i Margall, Balmes or the second D'Ors, neither of those who,
like Maragall or Rusiñol, at least as prose writers, indistinctly used one or another
language as a means of expression. [...] I am just talking about those – let the mention of Espriu suffice – who, as writers, opted for a 'Spanish mutism' as a response to
the mistreatment that their native and literary language was suffering at the time. I
understood and continue to understand this attitude with all my heart. But I would
only speak half my mind if I hid my satisfaction about the fact that, despite everything, they were generally able to write in excellent Spanish.][3]

But we can also hear him point out that there have been other Catalan writers who were correctly bilingual in Catalan and Spanish, or who made good
use of the Spanish language, if not for their literary works. This makes him
desire a Catalan-Spanish bilingualism,[4] which should always be understood as being 'from Catalan to Spanish'. This literary bilingualism, in these
specific terms, had already been mentioned by Laín Entralgo in 1960, in

2   Laín Entralgo, 'Ponencia', 114.

3   Unless otherwise stated, all quotatios were translated into English by Santiago Pérez
    Isasi.

4   '[V]ivir en una España en la cual los catalanohablantes, definitivamente liberados
    de la tan comprensible actitud de defensa a que aquí mismo se ha referido el padre
    Batllori, no tengan el menor inconveniente en usar el castellano todo lo bien que sepan
    hacerlo' [To live in a Spain in which the Catalan-speaking people, definitively liber-
    ated from the very comprehensibly defensive attitude referred to by father Batllori,
    don't have the slightest inconvenience in using the Spanish language to the best of
    their abilities]. Laín Entralgo, 'Ponencia', 115.

his prologue to Joan Maragall's prose works in Spanish. In that text, he considered this literary bilingualism to be founded on a well-established social bilingualism, and he even proposed it as a historical solution:

> En pocas regiones de Europa constituye el bilingüismo un hecho social tan real y patente como en Cataluña. Descartada una muy exigua fracción de la población rural, todos los catalanes son capaces de usar fluida y correctamente, con su propio idioma, el que Castilla inventó y hoy es de todos los hispano-hablantes. [...] ¿qué papel puede representar el castellano en el actual bilingüismo de Cataluña? ¿Habrá de ser tan sólo un instrumento útil para la expresión social de cuanto en la vida del hombre parece más tópico y negocioso? Los catalanes verdaderamente fieles a su idioma propio, ¿son acaso incapaces de pronunciar y de escribir en castellano 'palabras vivas'? ¿Deberán renunciar, en consecuencia, al empleo literario del habla de Castilla?[5]

> [In very few regions of Europe is bilingualism such a real and clear social fact as in Catalonia. With the exception of a very small fraction of the rural population, all Catalans are able to use, as fluently and correctly as their own language, the one that Castile invented, and which is nowadays used by all Spanish speakers. [...] What role may Castilian play in the current bilingualism of Catalonia? Will it just be a useful tool for the social expression of the most topical and industrial aspects of life? Those Catalans who are faithful to their own language, are they, by any chance, incapable of uttering and writing 'living words'? Should they, therefore, renounce to the literary use of the Castilian language?]

We may ask ourselves about the root or pattern of this discourse, which tends to perpetuate itself. To that end, we will attend to what we consider to be the constitutional period of the Catalan literary system (1875/7–1939), after the diglossic minorization of Catalan culture in the sixteenth and seventeenth centuries and the first steps of the *Renaixença*. Furthermore, this period corresponds to the growing normalization of the Peninsular interliterary dialogue, as it is full of personal exchanges, mutual translations, literary criticism published in newspapers or theatre productions, both in Spanish and in Catalan, within the Castilian-Spanish sphere. This overlapping double reality would contribute to the existence of Castilian writers

---

5   Pedro Laín Entralgo, 'Pròleg', in Joan Maragall, *Obres completes. Obra castellana* (Barcelona: Editorial Selecta, 1981), 17.

who wrote in Spanish in favour of Catalan literature and its development; but even in those cases, we still perceive certain reluctance between the lines. In this spectrum, Marcelino Menéndez y Pelayo (1856–1912) is an example of an intellectual who was favourable to the interest and approximation towards Catalan culture: he was, indeed, a Romance Philologist educated in Manuel Milà i Fontanals's school and indebted, as was the parallel trend of 'Iberismo', to Alexandre Herculano's comprehension of the Iberian Peninsula as a 'system'. In the texts that we will study here, we find his judgement to be reasoned on the base of the distinction between 'political' and 'literary' nationality; in 1878, speaking specifically on the limits of the concept of Spanish language and literature, he wrote:

> [C]onviene distinguir entre *nacionalidad* política y nacionalidad literaria [...]. Si de algo conviene huir en crítica es de ese afán de considerar encerradas todas las fuerzas vivas de un pueblo en una unidad panteística, llámese *estado, genio nacional, índole de raza*. [...] [A] nadie se ocultará que el espíritu y el *genio nacional* en literatura deben de ser algo distinto del Estado político [...]. Es preciso tomar las nacionalidades como las han hecho los siglos, con unidad en algunas cosas y *variedad* en muchas más, y sobre todo en la lengua y la literatura.
>
> Sentado pues que existe una nacionalidad literaria, cuyos lindes, rayas y términos no siempre son los impuestos por tratados y combinaciones diplomáticas [...] resta apurar cuándo comienza esta literatura y en qué señas hemos de conocerla y distinguirla de las demás antiguas y modernas. Aquí entra para algunos el poner la unidad literaria en la *lengua*, carácter, a la verdad mucho menos vago y contradictorio que el de *Estado*, pero todavía insuficiente. En primer lugar y concretándonos a nuestro estudio ¿existe, por ventura, una lengua *española*?, ¿es castizo, ni propio, ni adecuado este nombre? ¿le usaron alguna vez nuestros clásicos?[6]

> [It is convenient to distinguish between political and literary *nationality*. [...] If criticism should avoid something, it is the efforts to consider all the living strengths of a people in one single pantheistic unity, be it *state, national character, race nature*. [...] No one can deny that the spirit and the *national character* in literature must be something different from the political State. [...] It is necessary to take nationalities as the centuries have, considering them as unities in some aspects and as variety in many others, and especially in language and literature.

6   Marcelino Menéndez y Pelayo, *Obras completas. Estudios y discursos de crítica histórica y literaria*, vol. I (Madrid: CSIC, 1941), 4–5; emphasis in the original.

Accepting, then, that there are literary nationalities, whose limits, frontiers and boundaries are not always those established by treaties and diplomatic combinations, [...] we must still consider when this specific literature starts and how we are to know it and distinguish it from all the other ancient and modern ones. Some would then base literary unity on *language*, which is really an element that is less vague and contradictory than the *State*, but insufficient nonetheless. Firstly and focusing on our own study, does a *Spanish* language exist? Is it genuine, proper or adequate to use this name? Did our classic authors ever use it?]

From this conviction stems an intellectual project, in Catalan, that even dealt with the Catalan linguistic and literary Restoration in 1888, from the very centre of the contemporary Catalan cultural system, in the celebration of the *Jocs Florals*.[7] This attitude also makes itself evident in his successive studies on the works of some prominent figures of Catalan culture at that time.

This defense of Catalan culture, however, was counterbalanced by some precautions, even in writers that were in its favour. Francisco M.ª Tubino (1833–88) was a federalist, and in 1880 published in Spanish one of the first histories of the literary *Renaixença* in Catalonia, Valencia and the Balearic Islands, as to stimulate national honour and mutual knowledge

7   'Rompuda la tradició [...] sols un miracle patent podia salvar la parla catalana de sa ruina i afanyosa descomposició i del aviliment en que per forsa ha de caure la llengua que, abdicant la corona imperial de la ciencia y de la poesia, 's resigna als usos de trivial é dialecte.//Y aquest miracle Deu volgué que's cumplís. Deu que va fer curables als individuos y als pobles, y que'ls torna la memoria quant los hi fa mes falta, consentí que *la morta* s'aixequés de son sepulcro y comensés a parlar com si fos viva.//Y aquí la teniu, Senyora, llansant de sos llavis lo doll de la paraula armoniosa y eterna' [Once the tradition was broken [...] only a miracle could save the Catalan language from its ruin and its steady decomposition, and from the unavoidable humiliation in which a language necessarily falls when, abdicating from the Imperial crown of science and poetry, it resigns itself to trivial and dialectal uses.//And God wanted this miracle to happen. God, who heals individuals and peoples, and gives them their memory back when they are in greatest need of it, allowed the *dead* to exit its tomb and speak as if she was alive.//And here we have her, throwing from its lips the stream of harmonious and eternal words]. Marcelino Menéndez y Pelayo, *Obras completas. Estudios y discursos de crítica histórica y literaria*, vol. V (Madrid: CSIC, 1942), 112; emphasis in the original.

within Spain.[8] Intertwined in his texts, however, we perceive his fear that at least in Catalonia this literary regeneration may go hand in hand with political Catalanism and 'anti-españolismo':

> [R]enacimiento catalanista y antipatía a Castilla se han convertido en sinónimos para muchos de los que cultivan la poesía o la prosa, no para todos, porque separándose de los que así discurren, hay quienes hallan compatible aquella esflorescencia con el patriotismo a que todos como hijos de España estamos obligados.[9]

> [Catalanist revival and antipathy for Castile have become synonyms for many of those who write poetry or prose; not for all of them, because, separating themselves from those who think such, there are others who find that flowering compatible with the patriotism that is mandatory for us all as the sons of Spain.]

> Tiene hoy, pues, su ideal el grupo literario que en Cataluña asocia las letras a la política y menosprecia la práctica del arte por el arte. En sus manos, la poesía como la prosa, son trascendentales; esto es, constituyen un medio, no un fin, siquiera ese medio encubra un problema de tanta gravedad, que su sola contemplación infunde legítimos temores y muy hondas dudas en los ánimos menos asustadizos y pusilánimes.[10]

> [Today in Catalonia literary groups that associate arts to politics and belittle the practice of art for art's sake have their way. In their hands, both poetry and prose are transcendental; in other words, they constitute a means and not an end, even if this

---

8   'La intención que nos guía es honrada, el sentimiento que nos impulsa noble y generoso, la preparación con que nos hemos fortificado la más conveniente. Queremos destruir prevenciones irritantes, allanar dificultades enojosas, promover simpatías fecundas, hacer resaltar méritos y triunfos que honran a la nación entera, honrando a las localidades donde inmediatamente se manifiestan' [Our true intention is honourable; the feeling that moves us is noble and generous; the preparation with which we have fortified ourselves, the most convenient. We want to destroy irritating prejudices, to smooth annoying difficulties, to promote fruitful sympathies, to highlight merits and triumphs that honour the whole nation, honouring the regions in which they most immediately manifest themselves]. Francisco M.ª Tubino, *Historia del renacimiento literario contemporáneo en Cataluña, Baleares y Valencia*, ed. Pere Anguera (Pamplona: Urgoiti Editores, 2003), 6.

9   Tubino, *Historia*, 377.

10 Tubino, *Historia*, 438.

means covers such a serious problem, that its mere contemplation inspires legitimate fears and deep doubts even in the least fearful and timid souls.]

[S]e sobrepongan al idioma nacional, que es eje de todos los españoles, como no se intenta oponer una patria localizada a la gran patria que a todos comprende, y cuyos intereses debemos todos sustentar.[11]

[That they might superimpose [them] to the national language, which is the axis of all Spaniards, just like a localized homeland is not opposed to the greater homeland that includes us all, and whose interests we must all support.]

Against this risk, Tubino advocates in favour of this movement only as far as it works in benefit of the Spanish civilization, of which everything Catalan can only be a variant:

[L]a verdadera situación de las cosas: el renacimiento literario catalanista no ha menguado en nada, el benéfico influjo de la civilización española en aquellas hermosas comarcas del territorio nacional; ni los catalanistas, excepción hecha de las individualidades que perciben todo a través de un velo pesimista, creen que el bienestar de su tierra es incompatible con la aproximación cada día mayor, de los elementos provinciales y nacionales, sin detrimento de los unos ni de los otros.[12]

[The true state of things: the Catalan literary revival has not diminished in anything the beneficial influence of the Spanish civilization in those beautiful regions of the national territory; not even the catalanist, with the exception of those who see everything through a veil of pessimism, believe that the well-being of their land is incompatible with the progressive approximation of the provincial and national elements, without the detriment of one another.]

Españoles bajo todos conceptos los autores que trabajan en semejante renovación, no es de extrañar que los partos de su ingenio o de sus talentos, ofrezcan el sello de la cultura propia, y que si se distinguen como una variedad, con caracteres propios, débase esto al uso de un modo de lenguaje que, siendo congénere del idioma nacional, separa de él lo bastante, para figurar por sí en el círculo de los novo-latinos.[13]

---

11   Tubino, *Historia*, 417.
12   Tubino, *Historia*, 417.
13   Tubino, *Historia*, 435.

[Being Spanish from all points of view the authors that work on such renovation, it shouldn't surprise us that the product of their wits and talents bear the sign of their own culture, and that, if they are distinguished as a variety with specific characteristics, this is due to a type of language which, being a relative of the national one, is still different enough from it to stand on its own in the circle of neo-Latin languages.]

In this last text, Francisco M.ª Tubino refers to the Catalan 'linguistic variety', which should not collide with the 'national language'. We should therefore consider if, at least partially, the historical prevention against Catalan literature is enrooted in linguistic differentiation, which is presented by the Spanish system both as a differential element of Catalonia, and as a difficulty and an excluding limitation for Castilian-Spanish.

Emilia Pardo Bazán (1851–1921), another literary figure who was in favour of Catalan restoration, unmasks, in a letter from 1884 written to Narcís Oller (1846–1930), the alleged difficulty for an educated person to read Catalan, while at the same time she is aware that only very few Castilian literary personalities will make the effort to read in that language:

Efectivamente no se necesitan grandes estudios para entender y poder gozar con la lectura de las obras catalanas, portuguesas y gallegas, y sin embargo, amigo mío, ¿Cuántas personas encuentra V. que Menéndez, Pereda y yo, se deleitan con los versos y libros catalanes, no habiendo nacido ahí o con un libro portugués o gallego? Yo lo juzgo torpeza o ineptitud, pues nada es más fácil o fue más fácil para mí que empecé a leerlo. Me acuerdo de haber devorado un cuaderno de la *Renaixensa* donde venía una novelita catalana ¿qué falta hace para eso cátedra ni diccionario?[14]

[It is not, indeed, necessary to study much to understand and enjoy the reading of Catalan, Portuguese or Galician works, and yet, my friend, how many people do you find, apart from Menéndez, Pereda and myself, who take pleasure on reading Catalan verses or books, not being born there, or with a Portuguese or Galician book? I find it to be laziness or ineptitude, since nothing is easier or was easier for me, since I started reading it. I remember devouring a booklet from the *Renaixensa* which contained a Catalan novel; there's no need of studies or dictionaries for that.]

---

14   Nelly Clemessy, 'Une Correspondance littéraire: Emilia Pardo Bazán à Narciso Oller', in *Aspects des civilisations ibériques: Amerique Latine, Espagne* (Saint-Etienne: Université de Saint-Etienne/CIEREC, 1979), 183.

This is the reason why, in other occasions, she regrets that the lack of translations into Spanish may restrict the desirable dissemination of Catalan works.[15] This framework also explains why another author sympathetic towards the Catalan regeneration, Juan Valera (1824–1905),[16] requested a translation into Spanish of a work by a Catalan author that had been highly praised to him and which he was eager to read: in 1904 Blanca de los Ríos (1862–1956) wrote to Caterina Albert i Paradís – Víctor Català (1869–1966) that Valera had asked her to act as a 'bad translator', possibly because she had Catalan origins and because she did not suffer from the aforementioned linguistic prejudices.[17]

With very similar arguments, even a liberal and realist writer such as Benito Pérez Galdós (1843–1920) recriminates the Catalan author Narcís Oller, in a letter from 1884, for not writing in Spanish, or at least getting his works translated, considering the high literary merits of these works which he was able to perceive after a struggling reading in the Catalan original. He considers this persistence in writing in his own language as a mere homage or debt to 'local exclusivism': 'Es un verdadero crimen que V. no haya escrito este libro (*La Papallona*) en castellano, ó traducídolo,

---

15   'Sólo me pesa que la obra esté en catalán: y bien sabe Dios que no es egoísta este pesar, por que con excepción de algunos términos yo puedo gozarla; pero la inmensa mayoría de los españoles no está en este caso' [I can only regret that this work is in Catalan; and God knows this regret is not selfish, since I can enjoy it with the only exception of a few expressions; but this is not the case for the majority of Spaniards]. Clemessy, 'Une Correspondance littéraire', 175.

16   '[I]nclinadísimos a hacer coro a los encomiadores de todo lo catalán' [Very inclined to giving echo to the praisers of everything that is Catalan], written in 1890 by Juan Valera, 'El renacimiento clásico de la literatura catalana', in *Obras completas. Crítica literaria, estudios críticos. Historia y política. Miscelánea*, vol. II, preliminary study by Luis Araujo (Madrid: M. Aguilar, 1942), 798.

17   'Hablé también – aquí en Madrid – de la obra de V. a D. Juan Valera y me mostró tanto deseo de conocerle y tanta pena de no entender el catalán, que será posible que me preste yo a hacer de *mala* traductora de *Dramas rurals* para complacer al maestro' [I also spoke, here in Madrid, about your work to D. Juan Valera, and he was so eager to know you and so sorry for not speaking Catalan that I may offer myself as a *bad* translator of *Dramas rurals* to please the master]. Juan M. Ribera Llopis, *Projecció i recepció hispanes de Caterina Albert i Paradís* (Girona: CCG Edicions, 2007), 32.

después de haber rendido al exclusivismo local el tributo de la prioridad'[18] [It is truly a crime that you haven't written this book (*La Papallona*) in Spanish, or translated it, after having given the tribute of priority to the local exclusivism].

From this premise, Galdós arrives at the identification of – political? – Catalanism and – only literary? – *Renaixença*, denying all value to this enterprise, and inviting Oller to access the Castilian-Spanish language, presenting it as a favourable threshold towards a greater intellectual universalism and a better dissemination of his literary works.

> Lo que sí le diré es que es tontísimo que V. escriba en Catalán. Ya se irán Vds. curando de la manía del catalanismo y de la *renaixensa*. Si es preciso, por motivos que no alcanzo, que el catalán viva como lengua literaria, deje V. a los poetas que se encarguen de esto. La novela debe escribirse en el lenguaje que pueda ser entendido por mayor número de gente. Los poetas que escriban para si mismos, déjelos V. con su manía, y véngase con nosotros. Le recibiremos á V., en el recinto de nuestro Diccionario, con los brazos abiertos.[19]

> [I will only say that it is very silly of you to write in Catalan. You will one day get cured of this infatuation of catalanism and *renaixensa*. If it is necessary, for reasons that I do not understand, that Catalan survives as a literary language, let the poets deal with that. Novels must be written in a language that is understood by more people. Let the poets write for themselves, leave them with their fixation and come with us. We will welcome you into our Dictionary with open arms.]

In her letter exchanges with Víctor Català, Concha Espina (1869–1955) defended a similar passage to Spanish, in favour of a wider recognition in Spain and America. For instance, in a letter from 1919:

> [E]l honor de ver su prosa castellana y exquisita en las páginas madrileñas [...] En cuanto V. se proponga escribir en castellano, traducirse sí a misma, se asombrará V. de lo que logra y se verá V. en la cumbre del éxito en España y América. [...] Yo quisiera que no unos cuantos elegidos sino todo el gran público de España y América la

---

18 W. H. Shoemaker, 'Una amistad literaria: la correspondencia entre Galdós y Narciso Oller', *Boletín de la Real Academia de Buenas Letras* III (1963–4), 266.

19 Shoemaker, 'Una amistad literaria', 267.

conociese y admirase a V. en cuanto vale: haré lo poco que yo pueda por conseguirlo
y a medida que las circunstancias me lo permitan. Espero y confío en que V. me
ayude y me lo conceda.[20]

[The honour of seeing your exquisite Castilian prose in the papers from Madrid. [...]
As soon as you start writing in Spanish, translating yourself, you will be amazed by
what you can achieve and you will find yourself at the top of success in Spain and
America. [...] I would like that not only a chosen few, but a wider audience, knew you
and admired you as you deserve: I will do my best to obtain that, to the extent allowed
by the circumstances. I hope and expect that you will help me and grant me this.]

In another letter from 1921 she insisted that her shift into Spanish – knowing
how well she was able to write in it thanks to their long letter exchanges –
would not be difficult, and that it would always be better than somebody
else's translations.[21] And again, in a letter from 1923, she argued that this
linguistic transit into Spanish would not only be good for the distribu-
tion of her works in and from Madrid, but also help her understand how
harmful it was, for her own works, to comply with – literary and political? – Catalanism:

Insisto, amiga mía, en que *debe* V. escribir en castellano y editar sus libros en Madrid
para que vayan a todas las partes del mundo. No le agradecerá a V. nunca ni le pre-
miará jamás el catalanismo ese acatamiento perjudicial de sus obras, son fuertes, son

---

20 Ribera Llopis, *Projecció*, 32–3.
21 '[N]o tiene derecho a encerrar su inspiración en una sola lengua, poco extendida, como
    la catalana. El idioma familiar de V. es de noble abolengo, respetable y hermoso, pero
    de escasa circulación, al traducirla a V. la perjudican, de seguro, y además V. habla y
    escribe un castellano rotundo y fuerte, aunque la modestia de V. tema lo contrario.
    Todo será que su esfuerzo se discipline un poco a la consulta de los diccionarios: el
    ingenio de V. saldrá triunfante y *Gil Blas* tendrá a mucho honor publicar su novela'
    [You don't have the right to confine your inspiration to just one language, and one
    that is not very widespread, such as Catalan. Your language has a very noble ancestry,
    respectable and splendid, but very little circulation; you are with no doubt harmed
    when translated and, in addition, you speak and write a sound and strong Spanish,
    even if your modesty might make you fear the contrary. You would only need to make
    an effort of discipline with the dictionary: your talent would be victorious and *Gil
    Blas* would be honoured to publish your novel]. Ribera Llopis, *Projecció*, 32–4.

bellas ... y son poco conocidas fuera de Cataluña. Se lo digo a V. con rudeza curativa y porque le profeso la más leal y pura de las admiraciones.[22]

[I insist, my friend, that you *must* write in Spanish and publish your books in Madrid for them to travel to all parts of the world. Catalanism will never thank or reward this submission which is harmful for your works; they are strong and beautiful ... and very little known outside Catalonia. I speak to you with healing roughness because I profess the most loyal and pure admiration for you.]

III. Catalan responses

Let us consider now how the Catalan writers respond or position themselves in relation to this discourse of attraction and reluctance. We will respect and leave out of these considerations the cases of Catalan writers who did, in fact, opt for bilingualism, a topic that would require special attention and a case-by-case approach, from Eugeni D'Ors to Terenci Moix, among many others.

Catalan authors had of course the option of reaffirming their own tradition, always with a reassured respect for Castilian literature and were only allowed to project themselves on that literature through translation or through sporadic linguistic excursions. This is the case of the previously mentioned Víctor Català, who, in a letter from 1946 written to Maximiano García Venero (1907–75) justified his only volume of short stories in Spanish as an 'incursión fuera de mi coto vedado': a limited trip outside her own literary territory into a strange land from which, it seems, she does not conceive writing, since literature should always grow inside its own cultural system.

> Creyéndolo así y creyendo al mismo tiempo que era sino su deber, un derecho natural de los que amamos a la España una y múltiple exponer públicamente nuestros puntos de vista para que se examinaran y contrastaran posibilidades, yo me había permitido

22   Ribera Llopis, *Projecció*, 32–4; emphasis in the original.

destinar a 'Retablo' un largo prólogo (casi había sido esto uno de los motivos deter-
minantes de mi incursión fuera de mi coto vedado)...[23]

[Thus thinking and believing at the same time that it was if not a duty, a natural right
of those who love a united but multiple Spain to publicly expose our points of view
to be examined and contrasted, I had allowed myself to devote a long prologue to
'Retablo' (this was almost one of the decisive reasons for this incursion out of my
own territory).]

This intervention allows us to perceive the complex situation of Catalan
intellectuals and creators moving in Castilian-Spanish circles, even when
their approach was devoted to a Spanish and Peninsular interliterary reen-
counter. This was also documented in 1911 by Joan Maragall (1860–1911),
who, when debating with Miguel de Unamuno (1864–1936) on how to put
forward the project for a *Revista Ibérica* [Iberian Journal], noticed some
preventions against an alleged implied Catalanism of the project among
less informed individuals in Madrid, especially since the journal was to be
published in Barcelona:

Y usted hará esa *Revista Ibérica* y todos le ayudaremos; aquí a cuantos he hablado de
ello se han entusiasmado con la idea y estoy seguro de que por esta parte no faltará
cooperación. También he sondeado algún editor. Se me ha hecho observar – y encuentro razón en ello – que si la revista salía de aquí en seguida parecería a muchos de ahí
cosa de catalanismo, algo así como un rodeo para ir disimuladamente a lo nuestro.
Y esto aislaría en seguida la empresa, podía asfixiarla. Eso debe salir de Madrid – me
han dicho. Pero al salir de Madrid, ¿no será bastante para apartar a los portugueses,
que – en lo que he podido observar – hablarles de algo con España es hablales de cosa
del diablo? ¿Qué le parece a usted de esto? ¿Y si saliera de Portugal?[24]

[And you will make that *Revista Ibérica* and we will all help you; everyone to whom
I have spoken about it here is enthusiastic about the idea, and I am sure that you
will not be short of co-operation on that end. I have also approached some editors.
I have been pointed out, and I find it reasonable, that if the magazine came out
here it would immediately seem to many as something related with catalanism, like

23   Ribera Llopis, *Projecció*, 55.
24   Joan Maragall, *Obres completes. Obra castellana* (Barcelona: Editorial Selecta, 1981),
      943.

a detour to surreptitiously go on with our thing. And this would quickly isolate this endeavour, it could asphyxiate it. This must be published in Madrid – so they tell me. But if it is published in Madrid, won't that suffice to disengage the Portuguese, for whom, I have noticed, talking about doing something with Spain is like a deal with the devil? What do you think of this? And what if it came out in Portugal?]

IV. 'Topoi' of Castilian-Spanish centre–Peninsular discourse

From *centre* and *power* – always opposed to *periphery* in its corresponding double meaning – the *political nationality* imposes itself over the *national* or *literary nationality* with the former being conceived as totalitarially *Spanish* from the *Castilian axis*. From this perspective and with these co-ordinates, we perceive a *Spanish cultural system* or *Spanish civilization* to which *all other peripheral cultures* within its common historical framework must submit. This system may *condescend* with them but only if the given linguistic alienation, *literary bilingualism* or *translations* (always from language and culture B towards language and culture A) are accepted as a necessary means. In any case, this threshold does not eliminate the offer to definitively abandon language and culture B in favour of language and culture A. Such an offer is considered to lead to a higher linguistic richness (since language A is considered a *prestigious language*) and to a wider and *universal* projection of their works. On the other hand, language and culture B – Catalan, in our case – is defined as a vehicle for restricted *local interests*.

This type of proposal may generate from the Catalan side, as we showed in the previous section, a creative and exclusive reaffirmation of their own cultural system. Even when understanding is sought with a cultural system that is respectfully treated as a neighbour or even as a brother, it is not possible to ignore that they are moving in a common historical space full of reluctance towards one or several of its components. They may try, it is true, to agree with the *whole* from their respective *peripheries* (peripheral not only in the geographical sense), but not necessarily from a perspective of *dependence*.

Works cited

Clemessy, Nelly, 'Une Correspondance littéraire: Emilia Pardo Bazán à Narciso Oller',
in *Aspects des civilisations ibériques: Amerique Latine, Espagne* (Saint-Etienne:
Université de Saint-Etienne/CIEREC, 1979), 169–89.

Laín Entralgo, Pedro, 'Ponencia. El diálogo de 1951', in *Relaciones de las culturas castellana y catalana. Encuentro de intelectuales. Sitges, 20–22 diciembre 1981* (Barcelona:
Generalitat de Catalunya/Departament de la Presidència, 1983), 108–19.

——, 'Pròleg', in Joan Maragall, *Obres completes. Obra castellana* (Barcelona: Editorial
Selecta, 1981), 13–31.

Maragall, Joan, *Obres completes. Obra castellana* (Barcelona: Editorial Selecta, 1981).

Menéndez y Pelayo, Marcelino, *Obras completas. Estudios y discursos de crítica histórica
y literaria*, vol. I (Madrid: CSIC, 1941).

——, *Obras completas. Estudios y discursos de crítica histórica y literaria*, vol. V (Madrid:
CSIC, 1942).

Ribera Llopis, Juan M., *Projecció i recepció hispanes de Caterina Albert i Paradís* (Girona:
CCG Edicions, 2007).

Shoemaker, W. H., 'Una amistad literaria: la correspondencia entre Galdós y Narciso
Oller', *Boletín de la Real Academia de Buenas Letras* III (1963–4), 247–306.

Tubino, Francisco M.ª, *Historia del renacimiento literario contemporáneo en Cataluña,
Baleares y Valencia*, ed. Pere Anguera (Pamplona: Urgoiti Editores, 2003).

Valera, Juan, 'El renacimiento clásico de la literatura catalana', in *Obras completas. Crítica
literaria, estudios críticos. Historia y política. Miscelánea*, vol. II, preliminary study
by Luis Araujo (Madrid: M. Aguilar, 1942), 798–800.

LEONARDO ROMERO TOBAR

Juan Valera's Iberism

Juan Valera (Cabra, 18 October 1824 – Madrid, 19 April 1905) is one of the Spanish writers who have most clearly and completely expressed the wealth and complexity implicit in the idea of Iberism, a word which, incidentally, whilst in use prior to the publication of his first public writings (leaving aside his poetry) was repeated with noteworthy frequency in some of his work.[1] As there is no natural explanation for Valera's bilingualism, his perspective must be the result of his experiences in Portugal and Brazil and are, above all, a result of his untiring intellectual curiosity which focused on the international presence of Hispanic civilization. This tendency has been commented on by a number of critics (Figueiredo,[2] Ares Montes,[3] Cuenca Toribio,[4] Corredoira Rodríguez,[5] Dias and Morillo[6]). The following pages add to this body of thought, and seek to follow a systematic and diachronic explanation of how Juan Valera constructed his vision of Iberism.

1   The Real Academia Española's CORDE lexicographic programme cites the first recorded use of 'iberismo' as fourteen examples of the word used in a series of articles by Juan Valera published in 1861–2.

2   Fidelino de Figueiredo, 'A lusophilia de Don Juan Valera', *Revista de Historia* XV (1926), 282–94/XVI–XVII (1927–8), 75.

3   José Ares Montes, 'Juan Valera y *Os Lusiadas*', *Revista de Filología Española* LVI (1973), 53–65.

4   José Manuel Cuenca Toribio, 'Don Juan Valera, iberista', in Matilde Galera, ed., *Actas del Primer Congreso Internacional sobre don Juan Valera* (Cabra: Ayuntamiento, 1997), 95–106.

5   María Teresa Corredoira Rodríguez, *Visión de Portugal en Juan Valera (análisis de un desencanto)*, PhD thesis (Salamanca: Universidad de Salamanca, 1999).

6   Eduardo Mayone Dias and Antonio Morillo, *Juan Valera ante Portugal (dos formas de pensar en un mismo hombre)* (Newark, DE: Juan de la Cuesta, 2005).

Valera's time in Portugal and Brazil

The young diplomat arrived in Portugal for the first time to work at the Spanish Embassy in Lisbon, a post he took up on 26 August 1850. Two days later he sent a letter to his mother in which he described his sea voyage from Cadiz and his first impressions of the Portuguese capital 'que se extiende sobre la orilla izquierda del Tajo, y está en declive en la falda de varias montañas coronadas de palacios y jardines. Hermosa posición, pero no tanto como la de Nápoles'[7] [which expands on the left bank of the river Tagus and lies on the slopes of several mountains crowned by palaces and gardens. A beautiful location, but not as much as that of Naples]. His first look at the country and its people was contradictory. Despite the fact that his letters mention a real interest in the book markets and intellectual elite, he ironically noted (a constant element in his epistolary confidences about all countries) the less pleasant aspects he witnessed in the Portuguese people and their customs.[8]

7   Juan Valera, *Correspondencia*, ed. Leonardo Romero, dir. M.ª A. Ezama and E. Serrano, vol. 1 (Madrid: Castalia, 2002), 112. Unless otherwise stated, all quotations were translated into English by the editors.

8   The sarcastic nature of the first impressions upon his arrival are clear in the letters from his first months in Lisbon. We have, for example, the one he wrote to Serafín Estébanez Calderón on 24 January 1851: 'La instrucción aquí es muy superficial y enteramente francesa. Vista nuestra España desde Portugal parece más grande en todo que la Inglaterra vista desde España. La política es aquí tan mezquina y personal que da asco; no saben sino llamarse ladrones; el conde de Thomar paréceme hombre vulgarísimo y sus enemigos aún más vulgares' [Education here is very superficial and entirely French. Our Spain, seen from Portugal, seems bigger in all aspects than England seen from Spain. Politics here are so mean and personal that it is disgusting; they know nothing but to call one another 'thief'; the Count of Thomar seems to me a very vulgar man, and his enemies even more vulgar]. Valera, *Correspondencia*, vol. 1, 139. These venting observations, which were typical of the curious impertinence of the traveller of 'impresiones', were strictly censored by Valera himself when they came from rushed travellers who were visiting Spain (the Marques of Custine, for example). The value of these opinions should not be taken as the sole vision of Portugal, as certain readers of his correspondence have done.

Valera's literary vocation drove him to read such classics as Camões, but he also established personal relationships with contemporary writers including José María Latino Coelho, Alexandre Herculano, Joaquim Pedro Oliveira Martins and João Baptista Almeida Garret, translating one of his poems into Castilian (*El ángel y la princesa*), and sending it in a letter to his sister Sofía on 14 October. It was also included in the publication of a poetry collection entitled *Poesías* in 1858.

During this first Lisbon period, the information he passed on to his correspondents regarding his diplomatic work gives the impression that he had to occupy himself with practical questions such as Hispano-Portuguese commercial relations and projects focusing on channels of communication which facilitated the transit of goods and people between the two countries. Nonetheless, he continued to make his observations concerning the attitude of the Portuguese towards Spain and the possibilities that existed for a closer relationship between the two. By way of example he outlined governmental difficulties in regulating free passage along the River Duero in a letter to Estébanez Calderón:

> [D]ominados como están sus ánimos por rancias preocupaciones y por antigua enemistad y recelo contra los españoles, quienes suponen ellos, sólo desean enseñorearse de los estados de Portugal con el pretexto del comercio; y esto no contradice lo que en otra le escribí de lo mucho que nos quieren y desean la unión los portugueses, pues unos son los que piensan así, jóvenes en general, y otros los que ponen mano en las cosas del Gobierno.[9]

9 Valera, *Correspondencia*, vol. 1, 148. The above mentioned letter is dated 19 February 1850. On the seventh Valera had also written to Estébanez, giving his impression regarding future relations between Spain and Portugal: 'Soy con Vd. en pronosticar que se acerca la época en que los Estados de Portugal y España se fundirán en uno. En Madrid apenas hay quien se ocupe de esta idea; aquí hay muchos, casi todos los hombres de saber y de corazón que siempre están pensando en ella; y a pesar de las rancias preocupaciones y enemiga del vulgo a los castellanos esperan que se realice [...]. El periódico luso-hispano que se publica en Lisboa con el intento de preparar los caminos porque los tiempos se acercan, es por desgracia *impar congressus Achilli* [...]. Yo también, aunque por mí solo nada valgo, con el apoyo de Vd. me tendré en más y contribuiré en cuanto esté de mi parte a la prosperidad y buen nombre de la *Revista de Mediodía*' [I agree with you in the prediction that the time is close when

[Dominated as their spirits are by ancient worries and old enmity and mistrust towards Spaniards, who, they suppose, only want to take over the Portuguese territory with the excuse of commerce; and this does not contradict what I once wrote about how much the Portuguese love us, and how much they desire the [Iberian] union, since there are some, young in general, that feel such, and others that control the duties of the Government.]

Valera lived in Lisbon until September 1851, when he was transferred to the Spanish Embassy in Rio de Janeiro. It was here that he had his first contact with the Americas and the former Portuguese colony, an experience that placed him before a multi-racial slave-owning society. He stayed in Brazil until September 1853, when he returned to Europe, stopping over in Lisbon. Although his second stay in the Portuguese capital was brief and implied breaking a prior marriage commitment, it did allow him to resume his contact with his writer friends. These circumstances led him to the idea for a magazine which would defend the cause of Iberism, for which Valera sought help from the seemingly ever-present Estébanez Calderón:

> Se trata nada menos que de fundar una revista, la *Revista Ibérica*, que se publicará cada quince días, desde 1.° de enero de 1854, y contendrá 64 páginas de impresión por cada número. Latino Coelho, el joven más entendido y literato de Portugal se encarga de dirigir la revista, y yo le he prometido enviarle de España la mitad de los artículos en castellano. La otra mitad será portuguesa, y la escribirán el mismo Latino, Serpa, Corvo, Lopes de Mendoza, Herculano y otros de los que por sus escritos alcanzan aquí más fama. La revista sostendrá sólo indirecta y prudentemente la idea de la unión, y de política militante hablará con gran cautela y reposo en la revista de la quincena.[10]

---

the states of Portugal and Spain will become one. In Madrid almost nobody talks about this idea; here there are many, most of them men of wisdom and heart, who are always thinking about it; and despite the old worries and enmity of the masses against the Spaniards they wish that it becomes real [...]. The luso-hispanic journal published in Lisbon with the intention of preparing the way because these times are near is unfortunately *impar congressus Achilli* [...]. I too, even if am nothing by myself, with your help will grow stronger and contribute in what I can to the prosperity and good name of this *Revista de Mediodía*]. Valera, *Correspondencia*, vol. 1, 145.

10   Valera, *Correspondencia*, vol. 1, 266–7.

[It is no less than the creation of a new journal, the *Revista Ibérica*, which will be published every fifteen days, from 1 January 1854, and will continue 64 pages in each number. Latino Coelho, the wisest young writer in Portugal, is in charge of the direction of the journal, and I have promised to send him half of the articles in Spanish. The other half will be Portuguese, and will be written by Latino himself, Serpa, Corvo, Lopes de Mendoza, Herculano and others who have gained fame here with their works. The journal will only indirectly and prudently support the idea of union, and active politics will be dealt with with great caution in the fortnight issue of the journal.]

Valera's return to Spain saw him maintain an eloquent correspondence over a period of months with Latino Coelho, who suggested the inclusion of Caldeira do Casal Ribeiro and Sinibaldo de Mas in the project, even if he attenuated 'la desacertada idea de hacer a las claras la propaganda ibérica y de ponerle este apellido a la revista' [the unfortunate idea of doing clear Iberian propaganda and giving that surname to the journal] as for various reasons 'la idea de la unión ha llegado a hacerse sospechosa en España al Gobierno y a la Reina'[11] [the idea of union has become suspicious in Spain for the Government and the Queen]. The planned *Revista Ibérica*, also known at other moments as *La Aurora Ibérica* and *Revista de Lisboa* – all of which were titles used by Valera and his friends – did not materialize, although a few years later the idea took shape in the form of another cultural magazine, the *Revista Peninsular*, published in Lisbon between 1855 and 1856 and with which Valera was also involved.

The *Revista Peninsular*[12] focused on Hispano-Portuguese cultural relations, an area that had been the objective – albeit in a more cosmopolitan manner – of the *Revista Española de Ambos Mundos* (Paris and

---

11   Valera, *Correspondencia*, vol. 1, 285. In another paragraph of this letter Valera writes: 'La gente del gobierno sospecha y va propagando por ahí que todo el iberismo de don Sinibaldo nace de que no le envían a ninguna parte de ministro plenipotenciario; ibérico y antidinástico es para muchos una misma cosa' [The people in the Government suspects and propagates all around that Mr. Sinibaldo's Iberism stems from the fact that he is not sent anywhere as a plenipotenciary minister; 'Iberist' and 'antidynastic' are synonyms for many people].

12   This magazine should not be confused with another of the same title edited by Andrés Borrego and published in Madrid in 1838.

Madrid, 1853–5) and which was intended to echo the *Revue des deux mondes*. Literature was one of the richest areas for the *Revista Peninsular*, whose implicit pan-Iberist objectives were never in doubt. The magazine was published in Lisbon although the combined efforts of writers from the two countries was the driving force behind its existence, unlike the other journalistic projects mentioned earlier which never saw the light of day. Juan Valera was responsible for publicizing the new publication, asking family and friends to take out subscriptions. This is the case of José Areas, who would later become his father-in-law, and his half-brother José Freuller. He also had, of course, an extensive number of his own collaborations on hand, ranging from serious literary criticism to the laying bare of pranks and frauds[13] as well as ideological and moral discussions on the idea of 'progreso' [progress] or the humanitarian debate 'sobre la trata de negros' [on the trade of black men].

In the publicity letter he sent to Mr. Areas he precisely set out those who would make up the team of journalists and what the aim of the magazine would be:

> Nada prometemos, porque no nos gusta la tal palabrería de los prospectos, pero yo puedo asegurar a Vuestra merced que escribirán en nuestra revista, de los escritores portugueses, Herculano, Castillo, Lopes de Mendoça, Mendes-Leal, Latino-Coelho y Rebello de Silva, y entre los españoles Gayangos, Adolfo de Castro y otros muchos de nota. El fin de la revista será establecer una especie de comunicación y hermandad literaria entre Portugal y España, haciendo, al mismo tiempo por que se conozcan y aprecien nuestros libros en el extranjero, para lo cual se publicarán de ellos detenidas y juiciosas críticas.[14]

> [We do not promise anything, because we don't like the babbling of pamphlets, but I can assure you that our journal will include, among the Portuguese writers, Herculano, Castillo, Lopes de Mendoça, Mendes-Leal, Latino-Coelho and Rebello de Silva, and among the Spaniards Gayangos, Adolfo de Castro and many others of such high level. The aim of the journal will be to establish a way of communication

---

13   Leonardo Romero Tobar, 'Supercherías de textos antiguos en el siglo XIX', in
      J. Álvarez Barrientos, ed., *Imposturas literarias españolas* (Salamanca: Universidad
      de Salamanca, 2011), 109–26.

14   Valera, *Correspondencia*, vol. I, 275.

and literary brotherhood between Portugal and Spain, contributing, on the other hand, for our books to be known abroad, to which end detailed and sensible reviews will be published.]

As far as the spreading of Iberism was concerned, a number of other periodicals began to appear which, from both an ideological and literary cultural perspective and that of the pragmatism required in public works and business interests, continued to proclaim the mutual collaboration between Spain and Portugal, and even a utopian political union of the two countries which was a subtext in many Iberist proposals. We should remember publications such as the decidedly intellectual *Revista Ibérica de Ciencias, Política, Artes e Instrucción Pública* (Madrid, 1861–3), as it is no coincidence that its editor was Professor Francisco de Paula Canalejas, or the longer-lasting *Revista Peninsular–Ultramarina de Caminos de Hierro, Telégrafo, Navegación e Industria* (Madrid, 1857–66).

Valera returned to Lisbon for a third time as Minister Plenipotentiary from March 1881 to July 1883, after a rewarding diplomatic career that had taken him to a number of countries, marrying the daughter of the diplomat Jose Areas and publishing some of his most internationally successful novels. The excellent professional reputation that preceded him and his family connections through his marriage further complemented the solid maturity of his international political outlook. The ironic tone he used when referring to the Portuguese in his private letters and when talking about his expectations with regard to the Iberist movement continued. Nonetheless, in his role as a diplomat he had to prepare the official reports that the Spanish Embassy sent to the Minister of State, and his points of view had to be expressed in the most objective terms possible.[15]

15   Having recently taken charge of his diplomatic posting he reiterated his disrespectful views of the Portuguese in letters he wrote in 1881 to Tamayo y Baus and Menéndez Pelayo, both of whom were colleagues from the Real Academia Española and men of his confidence.

Ana Navarro[16] was able to locate the reports that Valera sent to his political superior, who incidentally was the Marquis of la Vega de Armijo. These contained qualified opinions that appeared in his early and juvenile writings on Iberism and coincided with the European political analysis of the time. By way of example, here are two paragraphs from a report dated 4 October 1881:

> Desde luego se advierte en esto del iberismo que, si el recelar tiene fundamento, le ponen mil veces más los portugueses que los españoles; esto es, que la mayoría de los ibéricos ha estado y sigue estando siempre aquí y no en España. En Portugal es desmedido el amor de la patria, y no hay un hombre solo que no desee su independencia, integridad y grandeza; pero muchos de los que son más patriotas son también ibéricos en virtud de ese amor y ese deseo [...]. El iberismo portugués en cualquiera de sus grados no nace de indignidad sino de amor a la patria, de aborrecimiento a Inglaterra y de la convicción de que Inglaterra ha hecho y seguirá siempre haciendo pagar muy caro su apoyo a Portugal. Toda la razón del iberismo portugués se cifra, a mi ver, en estas palabras de Teófilo Braga: 'Nuestra servidumbre a Inglaterra no puede ser perpetua; las naciones pequeñas tienen el derecho de ser libres y autónomas; nos aturden con el miedo tradicional de España para entregarnos a Inglaterra con las manos atadas'.[17]

16   Ana Navarro, 'La correspondencia diplomática de Valera desde Francfort, Lisboa, Washington y Bruselas. IV: Portugal [1881–III–24 to 1883–VII–31]', *Cuadernos para Investigación de la Literatura Hispánica* 20 (1995), 255–349.

17   Navarro, 'La correspondencia diplomática', 280–1. The quote attributed to Braga has somewhat mitigated the historical-mythological emphasis that the young Valera, writing in 1851, found in other testimonies by Herculano and Garrett: 'Garrett ha dicho en una de sus obras que los portugueses son españoles, tan españoles como los aragoneses y los castellanos, y Herculano en su Historia desengaña a sus compatriotas del antiguo error en que vivían de que los lusitanos son los antiguos portugueses, y prueba hasta la evidencia que no hay tal cosa, y que Portugal no tiene nombre, ni gente propia, ni historia hasta el año 1140 en que principia la suya' [Garrett has said in one of his works that the Portuguese are Spaniards, as Spaniards as the Aragonese or the Castilians, and Herculano in his History opens his compatriots' eyes about the old mistake in which they lived, that the Lusitanians were the ancient Portuguese, and he proves with evidence that there is no such thing, and that Portugal does not have a name, nor a people, nor a history until the year 1140 in which it starts]. Valera, *Correspondencia*, vol. 1, 145.

[In this issue of Iberism we observe that, if distrust has any foundation, it is found a thousand times stronger in the Portuguese side than in the Spanish side; in other words, that the majority of Iberists has been and still is here and not in Spain. Love of the homeland is disproportionate here, and there is not one person who doesn't want its independence, integrity and greatness; but many of those who are more patriotic are also Iberists as a result of this love and desire [...]. Portuguese Iberism in any of its degrees is not born from indignity but from love of the homeland, from hatred towards England and from the conviction that England has made and will continue to make Portugal pay a high price for its support. All the reason of Portuguese Iberism is summed up, in my opinion, in these words by Teófilo Braga: 'Our servitude towards England cannot be perpetual; small nations have the right to be free and autonomous; we are stunned with the traditional fear of Spain, only to be handed over to England with tied hands'.]

Valera's last family letter from Portugal, dated 7 September 1883, concluded the comprehensive information that he had provided to his correspondents regarding formal relations between the two States. This information served to contrast the scarce references made to other Portuguese writers, with the exception of mention to his close friendship with Latino Coelho. On 25 February 1883 he wrote the following to Menéndez Pelayo: 'Tal vez me lance, sin dar mi nombre, a publicar en *El Día* (de Madrid) una serie de artículos sobre la literatura portuguesa de ahora'[18] [I may take the leap of publishing, without giving my name, in *El Día* (de Madrid) a series of articles about contemporary Portuguese literature]. As far as I have been able to ascertain, nothing ever came of this thought.

Juan Valera and the Iberist movement

The history of the Iberist movement in the nineteenth century is sufficiently well-known, both in terms of the implications of its political commitments and its profile as a utopian imaginary to which men of action would seek

18   Valera, *Correspondencia*, vol. III, 488.

refuge in those situations they deemed convenient,[19] making it somewhat impertinent to sketch out a summary here. Both the organizations that co-operated in the project's expansion – the 'Club Democrático Ibérico' from Paris in 1848, the 'Liga Hispano-Lusitana' from 1855 and a number of other associations – as well as the periodicals that supported them were not few in number and effectively contributed to the mutual knowledge of the two countries. I will limit myself here to mentioning just a few names of the Spaniards with which Valera discussed Iberism in his most forceful writings in which he set out his views and personal attitude.

The first of these was a multifaceted Catalonian intellectual, the unconventional traveller and diplomat Sinibaldo de Mas (1809–68), whose pro-Iberist pamphlet appeared in 1852 in Lisbon anonymously translated, although the translator must have been Latino Coelho; the Castilian text from 1854 was titled *La Iberia. Memoria sobre la unión pacífica y legal de Portugal y España.*

Although José Simões Dias did not include him within his repertory of Spanish pan-Iberists (*As Peninsulares* [The Peninsular Songs], 1876),[20] Arturo de Marcoartú should be borne in mind since a pamphlet published in 1859 included a series of his articles that had appeared in the *Revista Peninsular–Ultramarina.* Those articles argued that the pan-Iberist movement was part of a more general unionist tendency that was becoming more popular in mid-nineteenth century Europe. His first assertion – 'la fusión de las nacionalidades es la aspiración de los pueblos' [the fusion of nationalities is the aspiration of peoples] – took his discourse toward commercial and pragmatic proposals that were not at variance with an idealistic exaltation of the phenomenon of fraternity between nations that, for him, was the 'idea cristiana que en este país que circundan los

19   For a non definitive summary of this complex process, see Gabriel Magalhães, 'Visita guiada à Casa Ibérica (1801–1900)', in Gabriel Magalhães, ed., *RELIPES. Relações Linguisticas e Literárias entre Portugal e Espanha desde o Início do Século XIX até à Actualidade* (Covilhã and Salamanca: Universidade da Beira Interior/Celya, 2007), 47–124.

20   José Simões Dias, *As Peninsulares: collecção das obras poéticas* (Viseu: Liv. Academica, 1876).

mares y los Pirineos abraza con fervor la joven España, saluda alborozada la joven Portugal, y se llama la joven Iberia; santa unión prometida por la geografía y por la historia, por la identidad de razas y de idiomas, por la religión y las costumbres'[21] [the Christian idea that this country which is surrounded by the seas and the Pyrenees fervently embraces the young Spain, joyfully greets the young Portugal, and its name is young Iberia; a sacred union promised by geography and history, by the identity of races and languages, by religion and habits].

Other authors of writings inflamed with an Iberism based on Castilian hegemony – such as Pío Gullón in his pamphlet *La fusión ibérica* [The Iberian Fusion] (1861) – or travellers who produced very accurate profiles of the places they visited – as in Pedro Calvo Asensio's book *Lisboa em 1870* [Lisbon in 1870] – aroused less interest in Valera the diplomat, of whose Iberism it is necessary to highlight his position as observer of collective tendencies and behaviour based on tired stereotypes of disagreements and the artist's vision of the world. This encountered a profound and stimulating sense of fraternity toward future collaboration thanks to the writers in the two official languages in Spain and Portugal who have been able to imbue their work with literary and human amplitude. On a number of occasions reference was made to the bilingualism of Galician and medieval Castilian writers – King Alfonso X or the Troubadour Macías for example – and the Portuguese Renaissance, as mentioned in a letter to Estébanez Calderón dated 12 November 1853:

> ¿(Usted) no podría escribir unos artículos sobre los escritores portugueses que han publicado obras en lengua castellana, y hablar de las obras de Gil Vicente, Camoes, Faria e Souza, Jorge de Montemayor, Melo, etc.; no como autores de historia el uno y de comedias el otro, sino como portugueses todos que han manejado con primor la lengua castellana?[22]

---

21 Arturo de Marcoartú, *El iberismo ó la fusión de las nacionalidades por la paz: la confederación postal de la Península*, ed. 'Revista Peninsular–Ultramarina' (Madrid: Imp. de Tomás Núñez Amor, 1859), 5.

22 Valera, *Correspondencia*, vol. I, 273.

[Would if be possible for you to write some articles on Portuguese writers who have published works in Spanish, and talk about the works of Gil Vicente, Camões, Faria e Souza, Jorge de Montemayor, Melo, etc.; not as authors of history, in one case, or comedies, in the other, but as Portuguese all of them who have skillfully used the Spanish language?]

By the end of the century, Valera discussed his pamphlet entitled *Portugal contemporáneo* [Contemporary Portugal] (1889) with publicist Rafael María de Labra, disagreeing once again on the impatience to establish an immediate union between the two States.[23]

The never-born magazines that I have referred to earlier, and specifically the publications with which Valera had a close relation – the *Revista Ibérica* (1861–3) for example – attest to the seriousness with which he outlined his personal position regarding the complex Iberist movement of the time. In the *Revista Ibérica* he published 'España y Portugal', one of its most outstanding pieces on the subject, as a series of nine articles which was concluded in *El Contemporáneo*, the newspaper of Madrid owned by the Marquis of Salamanca and Albareda in which Valera played a key role; the *Revista Ibérica* only published seven of the articles from the series. Nevertheless, regardless of this double version of a piece of work in which the value lies in its ideological basis, the most important factor in this piece of journalism is that it puts forward one of the clearest ideas in its concept of a single political space in the Iberian Peninsula, the distinction between 'nación' [nation] and 'Estado' [State]. To a large extent, the articles are a replica of the pamphlet by Pío Gullón entitled *La fusión ibérica*.[24]

---

23   Juan Valera, '*Portugal contemporáneo*. Consideraciones acerca del libro de este título publicado por Rafael María de Labra', in *Obras completas*, vol. II (Madrid: Aguilar, 1947; originally published in *La España moderna* [February 1890]), 807–12.

24   Pío Gullón's seriously distorted unionist strategy was emphatically highlighted in the conclusion to a piece of writing in which he argued that at the forthcoming festival of Saint James 'el eco de las salvas a Santiago resuene coetáneamente en Madrid y en las bocas del Tajo, la bandera española tremole a la vez en Baleares y en las Azores' [may the echos of the salutes to Santiago resound simultaneously in Madrid and at the mouths of Tagus river, may the Spanish flag wave at the same time in the Balearic

The series of nine articles takes as its point of departure an undeniable truth as far as the author is concerned, that the political unification of Italy or Germany arose from very different situations:

> En la Península que habitamos hay dos naciones distintas, portuguesa y española. Si hubiera dos Estados y una sola nación, los Estados fácilmente se fundirían. Lo difícil, o punto menos que imposible, es fundir las nacionalidades. Así es que nosotros, aunque siempre hemos tenido un amor entrañable a la idea de la unión ibérica, más hemos creído que esta idea es una aspiración sublime, casi irrealizable, o realizable solo en un remoto futuro, que un plan político, para cuya realización y cumplimiento están ya preparados los ánimos y las cosas.[25]

> [In the Peninsula we inhabit there are two different nations, the Portuguese and the Spanish one. If there were two states and just one nation, these states would easily come together. What is difficult, or almost impossible, is to join nationalities. This is why we, who have always had a deep love for the idea of Iberian union, believe that this idea is more a sublime aspiration, almost unrealizable, or realizable only in a distant future, than a political plan for whose realization and fulfilment are souls and things prepared.]

However, as far as the longed-for Iberian union was concerned he recognized that on the Iberian Peninsula 'hay dos naciones y hay dos dinastías nacionales'[26] [there are two nations and two dinastic nationalities] whose reality cannot be ignored, as Pío Gullón suggested, in the same way that economic conditions in the two countries are not equivalent either. Nevertheless, despite these difficulties, Valera was convinced that Spanish and Portuguese Iberism had to undergo a rebirth and progress 'con pausa y sosiego a la unidad. Por sus pasos y grados naturales, como único medio de recobrar en las circunstancias presentes del mundo la fuerza y preponderancia perdidas'[27]

Islands and the Azores]. Pío Gullón, *La fusión ibérica* (Madrid: Imp. de Gabriel Alhambra, 1861), 56.

25 Juan Valera, 'España y Portugal' [articles published in *El Contemporáneo* and *Revista Ibérica*, 15–VIII–1861 to 30–I–1862], in *Obras completas*, vol. III (Madrid: Aguilar, 1947), 675.

26 Valera, 'España y Portugal', 679b.

27 Valera, 'España y Portugal', 690a.

[with pause and calm towards unity. By its natural steps and degrees, as the only way to recover in the present world circumstances the lost strength and preponderance], a path in which writers would have to play a key role. Valera wrote a number of articles on ancient and modern Portuguese literature, published in various newspapers and magazines from 1869 until just a few years before his death (see the relation between the texts referred to in the 'Works Cited' section at the end of this essay). In all his Iberist articles, Valera made it very clear that commercial and economic interests needed to follow a path of delicate political and diplomatic negotiations and that the historic reality of unity was a long way off.

In a number of writings Juan Valera insisted on the view that the definitive historical rupture between the two countries was sealed with the secessionist events of 1640, a reaction against the politics of the Count-Duke of Olivares who deposed the Castilian king in Portugal, Felipe III, replacing him with Juan IV of Braganza. For example, his manuscript titled 'Plan de una historia de España y Portugal'[28] outlined an integrated index for what was to be a joint history of Spain and Portugal, arriving at the date on which

> la separación de Portugal y Castilla, en 1640, la larga guerra que hubo entonces, auxiliados los portugueses por naciones extranjeras y otras varias causas, concurren a que Portugal se separe de España, no sólo política sino como carácter y condición de pueblo. La historia de Portugal no es en realidad otra que nuestra historia sino de 1640 en adelante.[29]

> [the separation of Portugal and Castile, in 1640, and the long war that happened then, the Portuguese aided by foreign nations, and other causes, contribute to Portugal drifting away from Spain, not only politically but in its character and its conditions as a people. The history of Portugal is not different from our own until 1640.]

28   His editor Cyrus de Coster proposed that this Unified History be written between 1868 and 1878.

29   Juan Valera, 'Plan de una historia de España y Portugal [manuscript]', in Cyrus de Coster, ed., *Obras desconocidas de Juan Valera* (Madrid: Castalia, 1965), 361.

It is in his critical summary of the third edition of Oliveira Martins' *História da Civilização Ibérica* [History of the Iberian Civilization] (1879) where he succinctly sets out his wide-ranging concept of what terms such as *patria, nación, nacionalidad* and *civilización* should mean, viewpoints he had also detailed in earlier works.[30]

Thanks to this differentiation we can understand the theoretical and political difficulties that Valera foresaw in contemplating the immediate union of Spain and Portugal and its greater integration within the wider notion of *civilización*. When Valera received the third edition of the Portuguese intellectual's work, with its dedication from the author with whom he had a very close relationship,[31] he dedicated an extensive commentary to him in the *Revista de España* (1887–VIII–25 to 1887–X–25), volumes CXVII and CXVIII.[32] In this exegetical piece, the most pertinent section is the one reproduced below, in which he establishes the idea that the most solid base for Iberian union has to be based on the Hegelian notion of 'civilization':

> Es evidente, pues, que en la formación de todo pueblo entran dos elementos distintos, que nos atrevemos a llamar la naturaleza y la idea. Hasta la fusión de esos dos elementos no surge por completo el *pueblo* distinto y bien determinado; pero antes hay algo como base de ese pueblo; antes hay la *patria*, el suelo en que hemos nacido, cuyo clima y demás condiciones naturales influyen poderosamente en la formación de la nación futura. Sobre ese suelo y bajo el influjo de su clima y demás naturales circunstancias viene, como el andar de los siglos, a constituirse la *nacionalidad*, merced a la fuerza plasmante de la Historia, la cual trae el otro elemento que hemos llamado la idea, obra del espíritu [...].
>
> La Historia, tomando las palabras en su más recto sentido, es sobrenatural, lo que el espíritu va creando y añadiendo a la naturaleza [...]. La verdadera Historia nace con la conciencia del ser humano, es hija de su espíritu, es el desarrollo de su

30   Leonardo Romero Tobar, 'Romanticismo e idea de España en Juan Valera', in *Nación y nacionalismo* (Madrid: Fundación Ortega y Gasset), forthcoming.

31   Ana María García Martín and Pedro Serra, 'Oliveira Martins visto por intelectuais espanhóis nas correspondências de Juan Valera e Marcelino Menéndez y Pelayo', *Revista da Universidade de Coimbra* 30 (1999), 159–73.

32   Juan Valera, 'Reseña de *Historia de la civilización ibérica* de J. P. Oliveira Martins', in *Obras completas*, vol. III (Madrid: Aguilar, 1947), 812–42.

idea. La cual se apropia y humaniza la naturaleza de dos modos: comprendiéndola en la mente y transformándola o añadiendo a ella lo que el espíritu humano va poco a poco creando [...].

Todo el conjunto de cosas que crea el espíritu humano se llama civilización, y dentro de esta civilización general están las *nacionalidades* con sus diversos caracteres, miras, fines y propósitos. Una *nación* es, pues, obra de arte, creación de nuestra voluntad o de nuestro ingenio.[33]

[It is obvious, then, that in the formation of any people there are two elements, which we will dare to call nature and idea. Until the fusion of these two elements, the *people* as a distinctive and determined entity does not exist; before that there is *homeland*, the land in which we are born, whose climate and other natural conditions influence powerfully in the formation of the future nation. On this land and under the influence of this climate and all the other natural circumstances, with the passing of centuries, the *nationality* is formed, thanks to the purifying force of History, which brings the other element which we called the idea, a product of the spirit [...].

History, if we understand it in its straightest sense, is supernatural: what the spirit creates and adds to nature. [...] True History is born with the human consciences, it is born from the spirit, it is the development of its idea. And it appropriates and humanizes nature in two ways: understanding it in the mind and transforming it, or adding to it what the human spirit creates little by little. [...]

All the things that the human spirit creates is called civilization, and inside this civilization are the *nationalities* with their diverse characters, motives, objectives and purposes. A *nation* is, therefore, a work of art, a creation of our will or our talent.]

The prudent, even distanced enthusiasm that Valera always showed with regard to the *fusión ibérica* grew in the 1880s and the 'fin de siglo', a historic moment in which the various strains of nationalism gaining ground in Spain also failed to arouse his interest.

It should therefore be remembered that throughout his writing career he had stressed the close relation between the two schools of Iberian literature, the Portuguese and the Castilian. Here he insisted on the literary aspect, an area in which he also showed he was fully aware of the current situation, both in terms of the publishing of ancient poetic texts and his knowledge of recent literary output. The synthesis of his concept of Iberism as having the idea of *civilización* at its centre is outlined in his last novel,

33   Valera, 'Reseña de *Historia*', 832b–833a; emphasis added.

Morsamor (1899).[34] For Valera, this synthesis of renaissance culture within a Spanish and Portuguese context cured the former of their pessimism after the 'Desastre' [Disaster] of 1898 and imbued both nations with the enthusiasm of classical authors[35] like Camões, quoted at various points throughout the book, who prophezied in his epic poem: 'Cesse tudo o que a Musa antiga canta,/que outro valor mais alto se alevante'[36] ['Abandon all the ancient Muse revered/A loftier code of honour has appeard'].[37]

In his last piece of writing – the official speech to be given to mark the three hundredth anniversary of the first publication of the *Quijote*, solemnly celebrated in Madrid in 1905 – Juan Valera stated that Camões 'presintió y adivinó todo el valer, toda la maravillosa trascendencia de las hazañas que portugueses y castellanos habían realizado para magnificar y completar en nuestra mente el concepto de la creación o de las incomprensibles obras divinas'[38] [foresaw and guessed all the value, all the marvellous transcendence of the great deeds achieved by the Portuguese and Spaniards to magnify and complete in our mind the concept of the Creation or of the incomprehensible divine work].

---

34   Juan Valera, *Morsamor*, ed. Leonardo Romero Tobar (Sevilla: Fundación José Manuel Lara, 2003; originally published Madrid: Fernando Fé, 1899).

35   Alongside the Spanish heroes who appear in this adventure novel concerning the circumnavigation of the earth, a number of Portuguese characters appear or are evoked, such as Damião de Góis, Gil Vicente and Bernardim Ribeiro.

36   Valera, *Morsamor*, 3.

37   Luís Vaz de Camões, *The Lusíads*, trans. Landeg White (Oxford: Oxford University Press, 1997), 3.

38   Juan Valera, 'Consideraciones sobre el "Quijote". Discurso escrito por encargo de la Real Academia Española y leído por D. Alejandro Pidal el día 8 de mayo de 1905', in *Obras completas*, vol. III (Madrid: Aguilar, 1947), 1252b.

Works cited

Ares Montes, José, 'Juan Valera y *Os Lusiadas*', *Revista de Filología Española* LVI (1973), 53–65.

Camões, Luís Vaz de, *The Lusíads*, trans. Landeg White (Oxford: Oxford University Press, 1997).

Corredoira Rodríguez, María Teresa, *Visión de Portugal en Juan Valera (análisis de un desencanto)*, PhD thesis (Salamanca: Universidad de Salamanca, 1999).

Cuenca Toribio, José Manuel, 'Don Juan Valera, iberista', in Matilde Galera, ed., *Actas del Primer Congreso Internacional sobre don Juan Valera* (Cabra: Ayuntamiento, 1997), 95–106.

Dias, Eduardo Mayone, and Antonio Morillo, *Juan Valera ante Portugal (dos formas de pensar en un mismo hombre)* (Newark: Juan de la Cuesta, 2005).

Dias, José Simões, *As Peninsulares: collecção das obras poéticas* (Viseu: Liv. Academica, 1876).

Figueiredo, Fidelino de, 'A lusophilia de Don Juan Valera', *Revista de Historia* XV (1926), 282–94/XVI–XVII (1927–8), 75.

García Martín, Ana María, and Pedro Serra, 'Oliveira Martins visto por intelectuais espanhóis e nas correspondências de Juan Valera e Marcelino Menéndez y Pelayo', *Revista da Universidade de Coimbra* 30 (1999), 159–73.

Gullón, Pío, *La fusión ibérica* (Madrid: Imp. de Gabriel Alhambra, 1861).

Magalhães, Gabriel, 'Visita guiada à Casa Ibérica (1801–1900)', in Gabriel Magalhães, ed., *RELIPES. Relações Linguisticas e Literárias entre Portugal e Espanha desde o Início do Século XIX até à Actualidade* (Covilhã and Salamanca: Universidade da Beira Interior/Celya, 2007), 47–124.

Marcoartú, Arturo de, *El iberismo ó la fusión de las nacionalidades por la paz: la confederación postal de la Península*, ed. 'Revista Peninsular–Ultramarina' (Madrid: Imp. de Tomás Núñez Amor, 1859).

Navarro, Ana, 'La correspondencia diplomática de Valera desde Francfort, Lisboa, Washington y Bruselas. IV: Portugal', *Cuadernos para Investigación de la Literatura Hispánica* 20 (1995), 255–349.

Romero Tobar, Leonardo, 'Supercherías de textos antiguos en el siglo XIX', in J. Álvarez Barrientos, ed., *Imposturas literarias españolas* (Salamanca: Universidad de Salamanca, 2011), 109–26.

——, 'Romanticismo e idea de España en Juan Valera', in *Nación y nacionalismo* (Madrid: Fundación Ortega y Gasset), forthcoming.

Valera, Juan, 'Consideraciones sobre el "Quijote". Discurso escrito por encargo de la Real Academia Española y leído por D. Alejandro Pidal el día 8 de mayo de 1905', in *Obras completas*, vol. III (Madrid: Aguilar, 1947), 1245–58.

——, *Correspondencia*, ed. Leonardo Romero, dir. M.ª A. Ezama and E. Serrano, 8 vols (Madrid: Castalia, 2002–9).

——, 'De los más notables poetas portugueses que han escrito en castellano', in Cyrus de Coster, ed., *Obras desconocidas de Juan Valera* (Madrid: Castalia, 1965; originally published in *Revista de España* I [28 April 1868]), 185–209.

——, 'El regionalismo filológico en Galicia', in *Obras completas*, vol. II (Madrid: Aguilar, 1947; originally published in *El liberal* [22 August 1896]), 907–10.

——, 'España y Portugal', in *Obras completas*, vol. III (Madrid: Aguilar, 1947), 675–95.

——, 'Il canzoniere portoghese della Biblioteca Vaticana, meso a stampa da Ernesto Monaci, La Academia', in *Obras completas*, vol. II (Madrid: Aguilar, 1947; originally published on 1 April 1877), 475–9.

——, 'Las Cantigas del Rey Sabio. Disertación leída 12 febrero 1872, ante la R. A. E. en una junta que honró con su presencia el Emperador del Brasil, en Memorias de la Real Academia Española, 1873', in *Obras completas*, vol. III (Madrid: Aguilar, 1947 [1872]), 1115–30.

——, *Morsamor*, ed. Leonardo Romero Tobar (Sevilla: Fundación José Manuel Lara, 2003; originally published Madrid: Fernando Fé, 1899).

——, 'Plan de una historia de España y Portugal', in Cyrus de Coster, ed., *Obras desconocidas de Juan Valera* (Madrid: Castalia, 1965), 347–62.

——, '*Portugal contemporáneo*. Consideraciones acerca del libro de este título publicado por Rafael María de Labra', in *Obras completas*, vol. II (Madrid: Aguilar, 1947; originally published in *La España moderna* [February 1890]), 807–12.

——, 'Reseña de *Don Cristóbal de Moura, primer marqués de Castel-Rodrigo*, por Alfonso Danvila', in *Obras completas*, vol. II (Madrid: Aguilar, 1947; originally published in *El imparcial* [2 and 9 July 1900]), 1012–19.

——, 'Reseña de *Doña Felipa Moniz de Melo, mujer de Colón* de Nicolás Florentino', in Cyrus de Coster, ed., *Obras desconocidas de Juan Valera* (Madrid: Castalia, 1965; originally published in *El centenario* II [1892]), 369–76.

——, 'Reseña de *Historia de la civilización ibérica* de J. P. Oliveira Martins', in *Obras completas*, vol. III (Madrid: Aguilar, 1947), 812–42.

——, 'Viagens na Galiza por I. F. Silveira da Mota', in *Obras completas*, vol. II (Madrid: Aguilar, 1947; originally published in *La España moderna* [March 1890]), 812–14.

MARIA GRACIETE BESSE

Iberism Reconfigured: Between Passion and Utopia*

> La Relation n'est pas confusion ou dilution. Je peux changer en échangeant
> avec l'autre sans me perdre pourtant ni me dénaturer.
> — ÉDOUARD GLISSANT, 'Il n'est de frontière qu'on n'outrepasse',
> *Le Monde diplomatique*, October 2006

In Édouard Glissant's perspective, the Relation constitutes the foundation
for a poetical and philosophical reflection that allows us to rethink the
question of identity in an operational form. The Antillean writer considers
Western hegemonic thought to be based on the certainty of a 'root-identity'
with a 'totalitarian' nature that kills everything around it.[1] In order to

---

* This essay was translated from Portuguese by Rui Vitorino Azevedo.

1 Just as Édouard Glissant affirms: 'Gilles Deleuze et Félix Guattari ont critiqué les
notions de racine et peut-être d'enracinement. La racine est unique, c'est une souche
qui prend tout sur elle et tue alentour; ils lui opposent le rhizome qui est une racine
démultipliée, étendue en réseaux dans la terre ou dans l'air, sans qu'aucune souche y
intervienne en prédateur irrémédiable. La notion de rhizome maintiendrait donc le
fait de l'enracinement, mais récuse l'idée d'une racine totalitaire. La pensée du rhizome serait au principe de ce que j'appelle une poétique de la Relation, selon laquelle
toute identité s'étend dans un rapport à l'Autre' ['Gilles Deleuze and Felix Guattari
criticized notions of the root and, even perhaps, notions of being rooted. The root
is unique, a stock taking all upon itself and killing all around it. In opposition to this
they propose the rhizome, an enmeshed root system, a network spreading either in
the ground or in the air, with no predatory rootstock taking over permanently. The
notion of the rhizome maintains, therefore, the idea of rootedness but challenges
that of a totalitarian root. Rhizomatic thought is the principle behind what I call the
Poetics of Relation, in which each and every identity is extended through a relationship with the Other']. Édouard Glissant, *Poétique de la relation* (Paris: Gallimard,

substitute it, Glissant finds inspiration in Deleuze and Guattari and first proposes the idea of a 'rhizome-identity' which accepts differences and the possibility of a harmonious relationship with the Other. This involves an understanding that is devoid of any mythical or ideological prejudices and is capable of creating 'escape lines' that allow us to overcome the limits of essentialness. It also lets us conceive the Relation from a non-system that is open to the complexity of diversity. The Relation 'relie (relaie), relate'[2] ['relinks (relays), relates'][3] by articulating the 'opacities' without denaturing a single identity. It does not have an ideological fixity, making us therefore pass from the simplicity of a 'One-World' to the complexity of a 'Whole-World' (*Tout-Monde*)[4] that is open to sharing without uniformity or amalgams.

Glissant widely developed this idea at the opening session of a conference that took place in Paris in 2009. It was dedicated to the relationship between Iberian and Ibero-American cultures and included the participation of Maria Fernanda de Abreu and Eduardo Lourenço. The Portuguese essayist affirmed at that time that the European construction had allowed at least one 'pequeno milagre'[5] [small miracle] which was well visible in the closer rapprochement between Portugal and Spain. In fact, in his opinion, Spain 'é o outro lado da lua que faz parte de nós próprios e onde vamos descobrir possibilidades de confronto, de contraste'[6] [is the other side of

---

1990), 23; Édouard Glissant, *Poetics of Relation*, trans. Betsy Wing (Ann Arbor: University of Michigan Press, 1997), 11.

2   Glissant, *Poétique*, 187.

3   Glissant, *Poetics*, 173.

4   This concept is defined by Édouard Glissant in the following terms: 'J'appelle Tout-Monde notre univers tel qu'il change et perdure en échangeant, et, en même temps, la "vision" que nous en avons' [I call Whole-world our universe as it changes and maintains itself through its changes, and, at the same time, the vision that we have of it]. Édouard Glissant, *Traité du tout-monde* (Paris: Gallimard, 1997), 176.

5   Maria Graciete Besse, org., *Cultures lusophones et hispanophones: penser la relation* (Paris: Indigo & Côté-Femmes, 2010), 23. Unless otherwise stated, all quotations were translated into English by Rui Vitorino Azevedo.

6   See the interview conducted by Maria Manuel Baptista on 20 February 2004 in: Maria Manuel Baptista, ed., *O Outro Lado da Lua. A Ibéria Segundo Eduardo Lourenço* (Porto: Campo das Letras, 2005), 25.

the moon that is a part of ourselves and where we go to discover the possibilities of confrontation or contrast].

The complex relations between the two peninsular countries as well
as their European integration continue to be discussed today after they
have fuelled numerous controversies that were crystallized in the second
half of the nineteenth century. They were all about the Iberian question
and infatuated such writers as Antero de Quental and Oliveira Martins,
among many others. It almost always oscillated between 'utopia e distopia'[7] [utopia and dystopia] with great repercussions in each respective
socio-cultural imaginary.

In order to address the question of Iberian and European identity,
within the scope of its historical and literary rhizomatic reconfiguration,
we will swiftly tread the path that goes from Antero de Quental's utopian
passion of the nineteenth century to José Saramago's invented allegory
of the peninsular raft[8] without forgetting the Iberian suspension and
strangeness denoted by João de Melo.[9]

The dialogue of knowledge: the ideal and the risk

The Iberist theses are grounded on the utopianism from the Enlightenment
era and the rising nationalisms that mainly emerge during times of crisis.
They pervade the works of several thinkers from the nineteenth century
who come to elaborate a project for a peninsular union based on common
geographical and cultural references. For instance, there is the book by
José Félix Henriques Nogueira titled *Estudos sobre a Reforma Agrária em*

---

7   This aspect was widely developed by Maria da Conceição Meireles Pereira, 'Iberismo
     e Nacionalismo em Portugal da Regeneração à República. Entre utopia e distopia',
     Revista de História das Ideias 31 (2010), 257–84.

8   José Saramago, *A Jangada de Pedra* (Lisbon: Caminho, 1986).

9   João de Melo, *O Homem Suspenso* (Lisbon: Dom Quixote, 1996); *O Mar de Madrid*
     (Lisbon: Dom Quixote, 2006).

Portugal [Studies about Land Reform in Portugal], which suggested, as early as 1851, that Portugal should look for 'na Federação com os outros povos peninsulares a força, a importância e a verdadeira independência' [the force, importance and true independence in the Federation along with the other Iberian peoples].[10] However, as several historians have already shown, it is mainly after 1852 that the discussion encompassing Iberism starts to develop with the publication of *La Ibéria*, by the Catalan diplomat Sinibaldo de Mas in which he calls for a pacific union of a monarchic nature.[11]

The Geração de 70 [Generation of 1870] resumed this theme passionately without, however, bringing anything new to it.[12] Antero de

10   As Maria da Conceição Meireles Pereira observes about Henriques Nogueira, and despite the fact that he is one of the main Portuguese republicanism theorists, he 'manifestou-se a favor da via monárquica, justificando que a aceitava se esta fosse a forma de viabilizar a união peninsular a mais curto prazo, isto é, os fins elevados da união justificavam os meios por que se realizasse. Segundo este autor, a futura Federação Peninsular deveria obedecer à divisão provincial já consagrada pelo tempo e pela tradição, sendo constituída por 15 estados: Portugal e as 14 províncias espanholas' [expressed himself in favour of the monarchy, justifying that he accepted it if it enabled the peninsular union in the shortest possible time. That is, the high goals of the union justified the necessary means to carry it through. According to this author, the future Peninsular Federation should obey the provincial division which had already been consecrated by time and tradition. This would be constituted by 15 states: Portugal and the 14 Spanish provinces]. Maria da Conceição Meireles Pereira. 'Concepções e avatares do Iberismo no Portugal finissecular – do federalismo republicano ao ecletismo dos republicanos', in Victor Martínez-Gil, ed., *'Uns apartats germans': Portugal i Catalunya/'Irmãos Afastados': Portugal e a Catalunha* (Palma: Instituto Camões/Lleonard Muntaner Editor, 2010), 85–110.

11   This opuscule was translated into Portuguese by Latino Coelho. It has three editions from 1852 to 1856, in addition to five Spanish editions until 1860. For more on this see Fernando Catroga, 'Nacionalistas e Iberistas', in José Mattoso, ed., *História de Portugal*, vol. 5 (Lisbon: Estampa, 1993), 563.

12   According to Gabriel Magalhães, 'o iberismo dos principais protagonistas da Geração de 70, corresponde muito mais ao desenvolvimento de uma tradição do que a uma qualquer inovação ou radical ruptura' [the Iberism from the main protagonists of the Generation of 70 corresponds much more to the development of a tradition than to any kind of innovation or radical rupture]. Cf. 'A atitude ibérica da Geração de 70. Variações na unidade', *Península. Revista de Estudos Ibéricos* 4 (2007), 161. For

Quental published an opuscule in 1868 that was marked by the influence of Proudhon.[13] It was titled *Portugal perante a Revolução de Espanha* [Portugal and the Spanish Revolution] and enthusiastically proposed the creation of a peninsular federal republic. A few years later, during the renowned Casino's conference of 1871, the philosopher-poet resumed the same ideal and considered it necessary to end with inquisitorial Catholicism, absolutism and colonialism once and for all. In other words, these three factors were responsible for the economic and political failure of the Iberian Peninsula and he exaltedly proclaimed the creation of a 'federação republicana de todos os grupos autonómicos, de todas as vontades soberanas'[14] [republican federation with all of the autonomic groups, from all of the sovereign wills].

In Oliveira Martins's *História da Civilização Ibérica* (1879), he defends the existence of a single peninsular soul formed by two distinct political entities, but with a geographic, social and cultural unity and common

---

this scholar, the Generation of 70 reveals, in fact, three distinct attitudes towards the Iberian problem. Thus, Antero's 'iberismo teórico' [theoretical Iberism] opposes Oliveira Martins's 'iberismo concreto' [concrete Iberism] and Queirós's 'anti-iberismo' [anti-Iberism]. In fact, Eça de Queirós, who in his youth shared the ideologies of Quental and Oliveira Martins, quickly revealed to be the less Iberist of the three. He often transmitted in his novels a stereotypical vision of Spanish culture, namely in relation to the female characters. He even proposed a difference between the two peoples when considering, with some arrogance, that 'metade do sangue espanhol é africano; [enquanto] todo o sangue português é de raça latina' [half of the Spanish blood is African; [while] all of the Portuguese blood is of the Latin race]. Eça de Queirós in *O Distrito de Évora* 10 (10 February 1867), 1, cited in Maria da Conceição Meireles Pereira, 'Relações entre Portugal e Espanha no 3.º quartel do século XIX – os aspectos cultural e económico', *População e Sociedade* 6 (2000), 105.

13   In Óscar Lopes's view, the Proudhonian ideology was 'a última das utopias oitocentistas [...] com os olhos postos na I Internacional dos Trabalhadores, na Comuna de Paris, nas probabilidades de uma república em Espanha' [the last of the nineteenth-century utopias [...] with all eyes on the I International Workers Convention, at the Paris Commune, in the probabilities of a republic in Spain]. Cf. Antero de Quental, *Vida e Legado de uma Utopia* (Lisbon: Caminho, 1983), 12.

14   Antero de Quental, *Prosas Sócio-Políticas*, ed. Joel Serrão (Lisbon: Imprensa Nacional–Casa da Moeda, 1982), 296.

Berber roots combined with Latin influence. If in 1879 the historian still believed in the creation of an 'organismo social ibérico' [Iberian social organism], the truth is that the exacerbation of the 'questão colonial' [colonial issue] at the end of the nineteenth century will undo his enthusiasm. In 1907, Ribera i Rovira, who defended a unified Iberia with three autonomous nationalities: Portugal, Castile and Catalonia, considered that the failure of this ideal was essentially due to the evident utopian nature.[15]

Iberism never found a true political or economic application despite its passionate intensity.[16] Instead, it motivated the creation of associations that defended a 'nacionalismo exacerbado' [exacerbated nationalism][17] that multiplied pejorative visions about the Spanish who were presented as 'sanguinários' [bloodthirsty] and threatening. This contrasted with the soft Portuguese customs which generated stereotypes where the neighbour inevitably assumed the frightening figure of the Other. At the same time, caricature representations of the Portuguese[18] emerged on the Spanish side

15   Ignasi Ribera i Rovira, *Iberisme* (Barcelona: Biblioteca Popular de 'L'Avenç', 1907).
16   First of all, according to Jorge Cagiao y Conde the failure of Iberism is due to the failure of federalism. Cf. Jorge Cagiao y Conde, 'Penser l'identité nationale dans la Péninsule Ibérique à la lumière de la relation glissantienne. Glissant fédéraliste?', in Maria Graciete Besse, org., *Cultures lusophones et hispanophones: penser la relation* (Paris: Indigo & Coté-Femmes, 2010), 231–42.
17   António dos Santos Pereira, 'O Iberismo em conceito e questão', in Gabriel Magalhães, ed., *RELIPES. Relações Linguísticas e Literárias entre Portugal e Espanha desde o Início do Século XIX até à Actualidade* (Covilhã and Salamanca: Universidade da Beira Interior/Celya, 2007), 33.
18   Gabriel Magalhães points out to an interesting symmetry on the double Iberian gaze: 'Não deixa de ser curioso constatar que, quando os Portugueses contam anedotas sobre os Espanhóis, o papel que estes desempenham é o de fanfarrão. Do mesmo modo, quando são os Espanhóis que contam graças sobre os Portugueses, é a vez de serem os lusitanos a encarnarem uma certa fanfarronice. Na realidade, estes filões humorísticos permitem-nos ver dois países – duas culturas – a olharem-se de esguelha, com um trejeito sardónico no canto dos lábios' [It is interesting to note that when the Portuguese tell anecdotes about the Spanish, the role portrayed by them is that of a boaster, in the same manner that when the Spanish tell jokes about the Portuguese, it is the Lusitanians' turn to embody a certain boastfulness. In reality, these humoristic veins allow us to see two countries – two cultures – looking at each other cross-eyed,

which converged with the lack of mutual understanding that Unamuno had previously complained about. As Sérgio Campos Matos observes, in the end the utopian and dystopic representations of Iberism configured a 'debate público sobre a nação, o seu presente, passado e futuro'[19] [public debate about the nation, its present, past and future], at a time particularly marked by the tension between the desire for regeneration and the feeling of decadence.

Closer to us and in an interview given to the *Diário de Notícias* on 15 July 2007, José Saramago affirmed: 'Não sou profeta, mas Portugal acabará por integrar-se na Espanha' [I am not a prophet, but Portugal will end up integrating Spain]. This immediately provoked a great controversy. This idea was also emphasized by the novelist in 1988 in an article titled 'O (meu) Iberismo'[20] [(My) Iberism]. In it, he moves away from the providencialist ideals as well as his nationalist roots and evokes the need for an Iberian 'harmonização dos interesses' [harmonization of interests], inscribed in a trans-Iberian global discourse, thus revealing some contact points with the Glissantian perspective of 'Whole-World'.

As Boaventura de Sousa Santos has rightly emphasized, in this 'jogo de espelhos, ora se salientam os contrastes, ora se salientam as cumplicidades'[21] [game of mirrors, either the contrasts are highlighted or the complicities are]. In effect, it is clear that there is a 'fantasma que habita a casa da Ibéria – o fantasma das suas muitas contradições, das suas infinitas desfocagens e ininteligibilidades' [ghost that inhabits the house of Iberia – the ghost of its several contradictions, of its infinite blurriness and intelligibleness],

---

with a sardonic grimace on the corner of their lips]. Gabriel Magalhães, 'Visita guiada à Casa Ibérica (1801–1900)', in Gabriel Magalhães, ed., *RELIPES. Relações Linguísticas e Literárias entre Portugal e Espanha desde o Início do Século XIX até à Actualidade* (Covilhã and Salamanca: Universidade da Beira Interior/Celya, 2007), 62.

19   Sérgio Campos Matos, 'Conceitos do Iberismo em Portugal', *Revista de História das Ideias* 28 (2007), 169.

20   José Saramago, 'O (meu) Iberismo', *Jornal de Letras, Artes e Ideias* 330 (31 October 1988), 32.

21   Boaventura de Sousa Santos, *Pela Mão de Alice. O Social e o Político na Pós-Modernidade* (Porto: Ed. Afrontamento, 1994), 55.

as affirmed by Gabriel Magalhães.[22] The 'dupla parede' [double wall] that
separates the two Iberian countries extends beyond the nineteenth century
and can be identified throughout the twentieth century and continues until
our current time. This frontier, which is very perceptible in the complex
relations between the two neighbouring cultures – besides the obvious historical reasons – could be founded on what Édouard Glissant and Patrick
Chamoiseau designated as the 'tentation du mur' [wall temptation],[23]
which is made of mutual ignorance, closing and authoritarian arrogance.

Beyond the wall: the allegory of the raft

Numerous critics have already shown how the interest for Spain can be
found in the works of a large number of Portuguese writers from the twenty-
first century.[24] Among the many paths taken, let us just remind you of some

22   Gabriel Magalhaes, 'Visita Guiada', 113.
23   In the opinion of Édouard Glissant and Patrick Chamoiseau: 'La tentation du mur
     n'est pas nouvelle. Chaque fois qu'une culture ou qu'une civilisation n'a pas réussi à
     penser l'autre, à se penser avec l'autre, à penser l'autre en soi, ces raides préservations
     de pierres, de fer, de barbelés, de grillages électrifiés, ou d'idéologies closes, se sont
     élevées, effondrées, et nous reviennent encore avec de nouvelles stridences' [The
     temptation of building walls is not new. Every time that a culture or a civilization
     has not succeeded in thinking the other, in thinking itself with the other, to think
     of the other within itself, these rigid barriers of stone, iron, barbed wire, electrified
     fences, or closed ideologies are erected, demolished, and return to us again with new
     stridency]. Édouard Glissant and Patrick Chamoiseau, *Quand les murs tombent:
     l'identité nationale hors-la-loi?* (Paris: Ed. Galaade, 2007), 7.
24   For a complete summary, see in particular in *RELIPES. Relações Linguísticas e
     Literárias entre Portugal e Espanha desde o Início do Século XIX até à Actualidade*
     (Covilhã and Salamanca: Universidade da Beira Interior/Celya): Antonio Sáez
     Delgado, 'La edad de oro, la época de Plata y el esplendor del bronce. El contin-
     uum de la modernidad y la vanguardia (1901–1935)', 125–70; Eduardo Javier Alonso
     Romo, 'Letras en tiempos de dictaduras (1936–1974)', 171–202; Cristina Maria da
     Costa Vieira, 'Fronteira Permeável (1975–2005)', 203–59. Each of these articles is

of the ways to evoke the Iberian Peninsula as a space of multiple convergences and divergences: thus, in the laudatory and mystical poem *Marânus* (1911), Pascoaes reveals the aspiration for a peninsular quest that is capable of giving a new direction to humanity; in mid-century, Miguel Torga defines Iberia as 'Terra nua e tamanha/Que nela coube o Velho Mundo e o Novo'[25] [such a large and naked Land/In which the Old World and the New fit]; in the late 1980s, Natália Correia proposes a supranationality that is Iberian and mixed.[26] But it is without a doubt José Saramago who better condenses the Iberian Utopianism in *A Jangada de Pedra*, a novel with a fabulous and telluric fracture that was meaningfully published in the year when Portugal and Spain joined the European Union.

The Iberian Peninsula – as the referential centre of an itinerary where all frontiers are annulled – is allegorically transformed into a stone raft. It is characterized by both the mobility offered to the Relation and the rhizomatic dimension of the mythemes that it focuses on in its initial trajectory (Atlantis, hell, the Flying Dutchman, the mythical barge, the labyrinth, ascension/downfall). In fact, the raft gives itself again to its Atlantic vocation and stops between Africa and Latin America, its historically natural area of conquest and integration. By doing so, it creates 'uma bacia cultural atlântica'[27] [an Atlantic cultural basin] that forces us to look south, and

accompanied by a complete bibliography on the presence of the Spanish culture in the works of Portuguese writers from the twentieth century.

25 Miguel Torga, 'Ibéria', in *Poemas Ibéricos* (Coimbra: Coimbra Editora, 1965), 7.

26 Natália Correia, *Somos Todos Hispanos*, 2nd edn (Lisbon: Ed. Notícias, 2003 [1988]), 94.

27 In an interview published in the *Jornal de Letras*, shortly after the novel's publication, José Saramago spoke about his aims in the following terms: 'Neste livro, tentei mostrar duas coisas; primeiro: a Península Ibérica tem pouco a ver com a Europa no plano cultural [...]. Segundo: há na América um número muito grande de povos cujas línguas são a espanhola e a portuguesa. Por outro lado, nascem em África novos países que são as nossas antigas colónias. Então, imagino, ou antes, vejo, uma enorme área ibero-americana, que terá certamente um grande papel a desempenhar no futuro. Esta não é uma afirmação rácica, que a própria diversidade das raças desmente. Não se trata de nenhum quinto nem sexto nem sétimo império. Trata-se apenas de sonhar [...] com uma aproximação entre os dois blocos, e com o modo de demonstrar.

questions the feeling of a sedimented European culture which was almost always very arrogant towards the peninsular peoples. However, the narrator also invents a Europe that is capable of change given that at a certain stage of the adventure some 'desassossegados' [restless] Europeans,[28] wanting to share the Iberian dream, begin to ask themselves about their own identity and write 'nós também somos ibéricos' [we too are Iberian] on the walls in every language. At the end of the plot, it is the same intervening and complicit narrator who highlights another decisive transformation: the pregnancy of 'todas ou quase todas as mulheres férteis'[29] [all or almost all fertile women]. This 'engravidamento colectivo'[30] [collective pregnancy] as a realized eschatology, brings us into the category of what is to come and into the ethical responsibility of being with the other at the same time that it emphasizes the importance of female power, which is very common in Saramago's writing.

From a formal point of view, José Saramago's novel – despite its insular theme – does not correspond exactly to the 'traditional utopia' in the Thomas More fashion where an ideal community is invented and it is dictatorially circumscribed to a closed space. On the contrary, this is a

---

Ponho a Península a vagar para o seu próprio lugar, que seria no Atlântico, entre a América do Sul e a África Central. Imagine, portanto, que eu sonharia com uma bacia cultural atlântica' [I tried to show two things in this book; first: the Iberian Peninsula has little to do with Europe at a cultural level [...]. Secondly: there is a large number of people in America whose languages are Spanish and Portuguese. On the other hand, there is the birth of new countries in Africa who are our former colonies. So, I imagine, or rather, see, an enormous Ibero-American area that will certainly have a big role to play in the future. This is not a racial affirmation which is denied by the actual diversity of races. It's not about a fifth, sixth or seventh empire. It's only about dreaming [...] about the approximation between the two blocks and about the way of demonstrating it. I have the Peninsula wandering towards its own place, which would be in the Atlantic, between South America and Central Africa. Imagine, therefore, that I had dreamt of an Atlantic cultural basin]. Inês Pedrosa, 'José Saramago: a Península Ibérica nunca esteve ligada à Europa', *Jornal de Letras, Artes e Ideias* VI/227 (10–16 November 1986), 24.

28   Saramago, *A Jangada de Pedra*, 162.
29   Saramago, *A Jangada de Pedra*, 318–19.
30   Saramago, *A Jangada de Pedra*, 319.

'concrete utopia' with an open recreation towards the future inscribed in that which the German philosopher Ernst Block designates as the 'principle of hope'.[31] It is thought in terms of a dynamics that is militant and solidarity-based and is constituted as the preview of a radically new social form. Thus, José Saramago rejects the old Sebastianist utopia and invents another order and for the first time confers a 'estatuto literário canónico' [canonic literary status] to Iberism.[32]

The questioning of identity has another form of representation in two novels by João de Melo. They were published in a ten-year interval which also illustrates an inaugural and decisive gap. But this time, the fracture is not telluric. Instead it belongs to a sentimental order, as we will see.

Identity displacement and dilution

In *O Homem Suspenso* [The Suspended Man] (1996), the writer chooses the tormented course of a Professor of Literature at the Faculty of Letters (Lisbon) as the narrative thread of the entire story. He is at the height of a profound emotional crisis and painfully rethinks his place in the world and his destiny within a Europe that has been demonized by the fear of assimilation. This is a Europe, to use the famous words of Eduardo Lourenço, for which the peninsular people have always felt 'fascínio e ressentimento'[33] [fascination and resentment].

31   Ernst Bloch (1885–1977) proposes a distinction between abstract and concrete utopias: whereas the former are unachievable, the latter are possible. For more on this subject, see *Le Principe espérance, I* (Paris: Gallimard, 1976).

32   On this point, see Helder Garmes, 'Para sempre Ibéria', *Ipotesi. Juiz de Fora* 15/1 (January–June 2011), 119–25 <http://www.ufjf.br/revistaipotesi/files//2011/06/15-Para-sempre-Iberia.pdf> accessed 4 August 2011.

33   Eduardo Lorenço defended this duplicity in the relation between Us and Europe and highlighted it again in a conference entitled 'A Península como problema europeu' [The [Iberian] Peninsula as a European Problem], given in November 2001 at the

The tormented professor defines himself as belonging to 'às pere-grinações que já só levam ao desterro'[34] [the pilgrimages that only lead to exile] as he begins a process of identity dissolution that goes through several forms of physical and mental displacement. This is quite similar to a shipwreck and also functions as a double for Fernão Mendes Pinto. In fact, the 'homem suspenso' [suspended man] seems to be condemned to nomadism, aware of being 'um religioso sem Deus, um patriota sem pátria, um exilado das suas culpas absolutas e infinitas'[35] [a religious person without a God, a patriot without a homeland, an exile from his own infi-nite and absolute guilt].

As the professor crosses Spain, he is confronted with the impossi-ble relationship with the Iberian neighbour. This is seen when he mani-fests his wish to know 'o que pensam os espanhóis de Madrid'[36] [what the Spanish of Madrid think], and only finds contempt, humiliation and misunderstanding.

In the professor's itinerary between Lisbon and Poitiers, where he is going to give a talk about identity, there is an existentialist but also political and social reflection about the meaning of Europe. It is a deter-ritorialized Europe nurtured by the constant tension between despair and the feeling of ridicule. The fluid scene that João de Melo's anti-hero moves in could very well correspond to that which the Polish sociologist Zygmunt Bauman designates as 'liquid modernity'.[37] Thus, implying the articulation of several configurations from a global world made of disjunc-tions[38] and dissonances.

Centro de Estudos Ibéricos [Centre for Iberian Studies] in Guarda, and reproduced by Maria Manuel Baptista, *O Outro Lado da Lua*, 77–83.

34   Melo, *O Homem*, 66.
35   Melo, *O Homem*, 66.
36   Melo, *O Homem*, 215.
37   Zygmunt Bauman, *Liquid Modernity* (Cambridge: Polity Press, 2006).
38   Arjun Appadurai, *Modernity at Large: Cultural Dimensions of Globalization* (Minneapolis: University of Minnesota Press, 2003).

Convergences and divergences:
the irremediable Iberian strangeness

In *O Mar de Madrid* [The Sea of Madrid] (2006), the writer moves again within the overarching topics of voyage and gazing to narrate the misadventures of a poet from Lisbon named Francisco Bravo Mamede. Somewhere in Castile, he falls in love with a Catalan novelist, Dolors Claret, whom he meets in Madrid for a university conference during a cold month of February. Despite several attempts, which include a troublesome escape to Toledo, the two lovers can never understand each other, hence illustrating the fundamental divergence that is born from that irremediable Iberian strangeness.

The accumulation of paths and experiences that develop at the rhythm of the displacement and the quality of the characters' gaze, mobilizes, as in the previous novels, a certain number of intertextual references which are predominantly of Spanish origin (Cervantes, Antonio Machado, Gómez de la Serna). At the same time, it defines a dynamics that also allows for the establishment of a painful contrast between centre and periphery, past and present. When the two peripheral writers meet at the conference in Madrid, a city that represents the Iberian centre par excellence, what brings them together is an identical fascination that evolves from the discovery of an insurmountable strangeness.

This conference, which could have allowed the participants to establish bonds, is actually presented as a ritualized space of alterity with the convergence of double images, distances, biases, tensions and especially much hypocrisy. Thus, by exploring the symbols that are constructed in two strange cultures, despite their proximity, the narrator ironically accumulates the reasons – inscribed in politics and in the history of mentalities – that explain the staunch Iberian distance and the impossibility for a Relationship. The obliqueness of his discourse manifests itself in both the bitter sarcasm as well as the ferocity of the caricature and the laughter of the humorous. It ruptures the linearity of the intrigue, making it alternate between action and reflection, or knowledge and ignorance, through a fairly rhythmic movement. With João de Melo we decisively abandon the utopian universe and situate ourselves in the hurt vision of an identity of a post-modern man, who is suspended between drama and laughter, and questions his Portuguese, Iberian, trans-Iberian and European identity that liquefies itself into a problematic rooting.

Boaventura de Sousa Santos has already observed that the Portuguese society was 'o centro de um grande império colonial e a periferia da Europa'[39] [the centre of a great imperial power and the periphery of Europe] during several centuries. He also stated that the end of the empire did not put an end to its 'carácter intermédio' [intermediate character]. Instead, it created a 'suspensão social' [social suspension] that allowed the country to enter a period of renegotiation of its position within the world system. The characters created in both of Saramago's and Melo's novels force us to rethink the necessary articulation not only between Portugal, Spain and Europe, but also with the Whole-World, in search of a Relation inscribed as a plot that is announced in the future horizon. As Glissant affirms: 'Vient le temps où la Relation ne se dit plus par une théorie de trajectoires, d'itinéraires qui se succèdent ou se contrarient, mais, d'elle-même et en elle-même, s'explose, à la manière d'une trame, inscrite dans la totalité suffisante du monde'[40] ['There is a point at which Relation is no longer expressed through a procession of trajectories, itineraries succeeding or thwarting one another, but explodes by itself and within itself, like a network inscribed in the self-sufficient totality of the world'].[41]

---

39   Santos, *Pela Mão de Alice*, 59.
40   Glissant, *Poétique*, 211.
41   Glissant, *Poetics*, 195.

Works cited

Appadurai, Arjun, *Modernity at Large: Cultural Dimensions of Globalization* (Minneapolis: University of Minnesota Press, 2003).

Baptista, Maria Manuel, ed., *O Outro Lado da Lua. A Ibéria Segundo Eduardo Lourenço* (Porto: Campo das Letras, 2005).

Bauman, Zygmunt, *Liquid Modernity* (Cambridge: Polity Press, 2006).

Besse, Maria Graciete, org., *Cultures lusophones et hispanophones: penser la relation* (Paris: Indigo & Côté-Femmes, 2010).

Bloch, Ernst, *Le Principe espérance, I* (Paris: Gallimard, 1976).

Cagiao y Conde, Jorge, 'Penser l'identité nationale dans la Péninsule Ibérique à la lumière de la relation glissantienne. Glissant fédéraliste?', in Maria Graciete Besse, org., *Cultures lusophones et hispanophones: penser la relation* (Paris: Indigo & Côté-Femmes, 2010), 231–42.

Catroga, Fernando, 'Nacionalistas e Iberistas', in José Mattoso, ed., *História de Portugal*, vol. 5 (Lisbon: Estampa, 1993), 563–7.

Correia, Natália, *Somos Todos Hispanos*, 2nd edn (Lisbon: Ed. Noticias, 2003).

Garmes, Helder, 'Para sempre Ibéria', *Ipotesi. Juiz de Fora* 15/1 (January–June 2011), 119–25 <http://www.ufjf.br/revistaipotesi/files//2011/06/15-Para-sempre-Iberia.pdf> accessed 4 August 2011.

Glissant, Édouard, *Poetics of Relation*, trans. Betsy Wing (Ann Arbor: University of Michigan Press, 1997).

——, *Poétique de la relation* (Paris: Gallimard, 1990).

——, *Traité du tout-monde* (Paris: Gallimard, 1997).

——, and Patrick Chamoiseau, *Quand les murs tombent: l'identité nationale hors-la-loi?* (Paris: Ed. Galaade, 2007).

Magalhães, Gabriel, 'A atitude ibérica da Geração de 70. Variações na unidade', *Península. Revista de Estudos Ibéricos* 4 (2007), 157–75.

——, 'Visita guiada à Casa Ibérica (1801–1900)', in Gabriel Magalhães, ed., *RELIPES. Relações Linguísticas e Literárias entre Portugal e Espanha desde o Início do Século XIX até à Actualidade* (Covilhã and Salamanca: Universidade da Beira Interior/Celya, 2007), 47–124.

Matos, Sérgio Campos, 'Conceitos do Iberismo em Portugal', *Revista da História das Ideias* 28 (2007), 169–93.

Melo, João de, *O Homem Suspenso* (Lisbon: Dom Quixote, 1996).

——, *O Mar de Madrid* (Lisbon: Dom Quixote, 2006).

Pedrosa, Inês, 'José Saramago: a Península Ibérica nunca esteve ligada à Europa', *Jornal de Letras, Artes e Ideias* VI/227 (10–16 November 1986), 24.

Pereira, António dos Santos, 'O Iberismo em conceito e questão', in Gabriel Magalhães, ed., *RELIPES. Relações Linguísticas e Literárias entre Portugal e Espanha desde o Início do Século XIX até à Actualidade* (Covilhã and Salamanca: Universidade da Beira Interior/Celya, 2007), 17–44.

Pereira, Maria da Conceição Meireles, 'Concepções e avatares do Iberismo no Portugal finissecular – do federalismo republicano ao ecletismo dos republicanos', in Victor Martínez-Gil, ed., *'Uns apartats germans': Portugal i Catalunya/'Irmãos Afastados': Portugal e a Catalunha* (Palma: Instituto Camões/Lleonard Muntaner Editor, 2010), 85–110.

——, 'Iberismo e nacionalismo em Portugal da Regeneração à República. Entre utopia e distopia', *Revista de História das Ideias* 31 (2010), 257–84.

——, 'Relações entre Portugal e Espanha no 3.º quartel do século XIX – os aspectos cultural e económico', *População e Sociedade* 6 (2000), 101–11.

Quental, Antero de, *Vida e Legado de uma Utopia* (Lisbon: Caminho, 1983).

——, *Prosas Sócio-Políticas*, ed. Joel Serrão (Lisbon: Imprensa Nacional–Casa da Moeda, 1982).

Ribera i Rovira, Ignasi, *Iberisme* (Barcelona: Biblioteca Popular de 'L'Avenç', 1907).

Romo, Eduardo Javier Alonso, 'Letras en tiempos de dictaduras (1936–1974)', in Gabriel Magalhães, ed., *RELIPES. Relações Linguísticas e Literárias entre Portugal e Espanha desde o Início do Século XIX até à Actualidade* (Covilhã and Salamanca: Universidade da Beira Interior/Celya, 2007), 171–202.

Sáez Delgado, Antonio, 'La edad de oro, la época de Plata y el esplendor del bronce. El continuum de la modernidad y la vanguardia (1901–1935)', in Gabriel Magalhães, ed., *RELIPES. Relações Linguísticas e Literárias entre Portugal e Espanha desde o Início do Século XIX até à Actualidade* (Covilhã and Salamanca: Universidade da Beira Interior/Celya, 2007), 125–70.

Santos, Boaventura de Sousa, *Pela Mão de Alice. O Social e o Político na Pós-Modernidade* (Porto: Ed. Afrontamento, 1994).

Saramago, José, *A Jangada de Pedra* (Lisbon: Caminho, 1986).

——, 'O (meu) Iberismo', *Jornal de Letras, Artes e Ideias* 330 (31 October 1988), 32.

——, *Jornal de Letras, Artes e Ideias* VI/227 (10–16 November, 1986), 24.

Torga, Miguel, 'Ibéria', in *Poemas Ibéricos* (Coimbra: Coimbra Editora, 1965), 7.

Vieira, Cristina Maria da Costa, 'Fronteira Permeável (1975–2005)', in *RELIPES. Relações Linguísticas e Literárias entre Portugal e Espanha desde o Início do Século XIX até à Actualidade* (Covilhã and Salamanca: Universidade da Beira Interior/Celya, 2007), 203–59.

PART III

Contemporary Iberia:
Plural Identities and Artistic Representation

ÂNGELA FERNANDES

Iberian and Romance Identities: Literary Representations of the Centre and the Margins

The place of an Iberian cultural identity within the Romance world seems to be a rather neglected issue, probably due to its scarcely controversial potential nowadays. The discussion of a Romance identity, with its roots in Roman classical culture and the Latin language, lost most of its allure during the twentieth century, as new topics of geocultural tension became more relevant. The Romance background is nevertheless an essential clue to understand Iberian cultures. Therefore, my aim is to reflect upon Iberian and Romance cultural identities, considering not only the Latin matrix of the Western world but also the literary dimension of such powerful ideas and images. The novel *Um Deus Passeando pela Brisa da Tarde* [A God Strolling in the Cool of the Evening], published in 1994 by the Portuguese author Mário de Carvalho (b. 1944), will be the main point of departure for this reflection, as it portrays some key issues connected with the concepts of Roman identity and Iberian difference. Moreover, we may find in this novel the debate over the relationship between the centre and the margins – in geographical, cultural and symbolic terms – as well as the discussion of the status of borderline locations, which is rather significant when considering the Iberian Peninsula. In order to delve further into this question, two other Portuguese narratives will also be considered: the opening story of the 1935 essay *Pyrene*, by the literary historian Fidelino de Figueiredo (1889–1967) and the short-story 'Joan', published in 1953 by the philosopher Agostinho da Silva (1906–1994). Both narratives depict the Peninsula as a frontier region, open to different influences that combine in multiple ways, thus building a specific identity.

The definition of an identity becomes clearer when faced with some sort of difference. In what concerns the Romance or Latin world, there are several literary examples of this confrontation with the 'non-romans', or the 'barbarians'. As we may recall, the word 'barbarian' (quite similar to other words in many European languages) has its root in the Latin *barbarus*, which comes from the Ancient Greek βάρβαρος, meaning 'foreign', or 'strange', and mimicking the sound of foreign languages. So, for the Greeks and the Romans, the barbarians were those who did not belong to their political, cultural or linguistic community, and historically, in Western cultures, the word 'barbarian' came to be used in a derogatory way to denote people with different customs and different speech, often perceived as unsophisticated, or uncivilized.[1] The representation of both the opposition and the complementary existence of the civilized and the barbarians can be traced in Western literature to the most ancient artistic evidence, namely Aeschylus's tragedy *The Persians*. Among modern examples of such ambiguous representation of 'barbarian' images, we may evoke the poem 'Waiting for the Barbarians' (1904), by the Greek poet Constantin Cavafy.[2] In this poem, we find Rome and the Romans waiting for a barbarian conquest which eventually does not happen. The explicit reference to the Roman Empire, with the forum, the senators, the emperor and so on, builds an image of the imperial power in its several distinctive elements and rules, most of which, as it is suggested, the unsophisticated barbarians will not respect nor understand: '[T]he barbarians are coming today/and they're bored by rhetoric and public speaking'.[3] The difference between the Romans and the barbarians seems to be precisely there, in 'Romanitas', 'Romanness' or the Roman way of life, whose value is hence somehow reconsidered when in the presence of new rules and a new emerging power. Actually, in the end of the poem, the barbarians do not really come, and 'some who have just returned from the border say/there are no barbarians any longer'.[4] Anyway, the menace of their coming was enough to trigger the reflection about the

---

1   Cf. Ralph W. Mathise and Danuta R. Shanzer, eds, *Romans, Barbarians, and the Transformation of the Roman World* (Farnham: Ashgate, 2011).

2   C. P. Cavafy, *Collected Poems*, ed. George Savidis, trans. Edmund Keeley and Philip Sherrard (Princeton: Princeton University Press, 1992), 18–19.

3   Cavafy, *Collected Poems*, 19.

4   Cavafy, *Collected Poems*, 19.

identity of those who were waiting. And, throughout the poem, the main aspects of Roman identity were hence put forward and emphasized, as if the danger (or the solution) coming from the border pointed more sharply towards the central and distinctive elements of 'Romanitas', of Roman (or we may say Romance) identity.

This same historical setting and this same kind of opposition between the centre and the margins of Roman identity is what we find in the Portuguese novel *Um Deus Passeando pela Brisa da Tarde* [A God Strolling in the Cool of the Evening], by Mário de Carvalho.[5] The novel's epigraph – 'Este não é um romance histórico. Tarcisis, ou, mais propriamente, o município de fortunata Ara Iulia Tarcisis, nunca existiu' [This is not a historical novel. Tarcisis, or, more properly, the municipality of Fortunata Ara Iulia Tarcisis, never existed] – seems to focus on the fictional dimension of the story, but despite this remark the narrative presents a coherent and accurate description of Roman imperial times in Hispania. The plot is clearly embedded in this setting and both historical and geographical issues are taken into account: *A God Strolling in the Cool of the Evening* may hence be read as a discussion of the Iberian place within Romance identities.

The story takes place in Tarcisis, an invented Roman city in southern Lusitania, during the times of Emperors Marcus Aurelius and Comodus, in the second half of the second century AD. We have a first person narrator, Lucius Valerius Quintius, who is an old magistrate of Tarcisis and decides to write his memoirs while in exile (in a villa not far from his hometown). The narrative tells us how, during his time as governor, Lucius had to face important challenges to his convictions and to his authority, namely the threat of the barbarians: some hordes of Moors from northern Africa entered the Iberian Peninsula, devastated the region, and besieged the town of Tarcisis.

Some historical data may now be relevant. The Romans started conquering the Peninsula in the second century BC, within a very neat

---

5   The first Portuguese edition was published in 1994 and won the Portuguese Writers' Association Grand Prize for Fiction. The novel also won the Pegasus Prize for Literature and was translated into English in 1998.

administrative system.[6] The western region generally known as Iberia, by the Greeks, became then Hispania, a specific province in the Roman world, with its distinctive features. The initial division between Hispania Citerior (nearer Hispania) and Hispania Ulterior (further Hispania), based on the distance between those regions and Rome, grew in complexity as the conquest of the territory progressed; the geographical remoteness from the centre of the Empire remained, nonetheless, a crucial topic when describing the region. Under Emperor Augustus, the Peninsula was completely conquered and Roman law and customs were then systematically widespread in Hispania, though it continued somehow as a frontier region, clearly distant from Rome, and thus rather open to any sort of barbarian influence or attack.

Unlike Cavafy's poem, in Mário de Carvalho's novel some barbarian invaders do arrive, bringing violence and destruction. But, according to the narrator, they do not represent the only, nor the most serious menace to the Roman town or to the Roman customs in Lusitania. Several other changes in social and religious domains are just as disturbing as the arrival of the Moors. We come to understand that the new Christian values, propagated by assured and bewitching people like the convert Iunia, and the new social and political organization, mostly incarnated by uncultivated people like Rufus, constitute the most obvious challenges to traditional Romanness, or 'Romanitas'.

There is a vivid description of this 'Romanitas' in Lucius's initial self portrait:

> Deixem-me cultivar esta despreocupação, a ilusão de que o mundo seguirá para sempre imperturbado e imperturbável, após um desassossego passageiro na sua ordem. Sou um senhor da terra, sou um romano, leio, cultivo-me, marco os tempos com o meu

6   Cf. the essays by Helena Paula Abreu de Carvalho, 'A construção do espaço ibérico em época romana. Conceitos, escalas e modelos de desenvolvimento', *Revista de História das Ideias* 31 (2010), 7–23, and by António Apolinário Lourenço and Alexia Dotras Bravo, 'Da Ibéria à Hispânia, da Espanha à Ibéria', *Revista de História das Ideias* 31 (2010), 285–301.

porte, os meus gestos, os meus ditos, as minhas maneiras, a minha fleuma, o meu trajo togado. Dignidade. Gravidade. Romanidade. Humanidade.[7]

[Let me cultivate this lack of concern, the illusion that the world will go on forever unperturbed and imperturbable after a temporary disturbance of its order. I am a landowner, I am a Roman, I read, I learn, I follow the rhythm of the times in my bearing, my gestures, my words, my manners, my phlegm, my toga. Dignity. Gravity. Romanity. Humanity.][8]

Despite the remote Iberian (or Hispanic) setting, and despite the fact that he sometimes feels he is just a plain countryman, '[um] provinciano hispânico'[9] ['a provincial from Hispania'],[10] Lucius clearly identifies himself with Roman values, thus suggesting that living in Rome or in Lusitania should mean exactly the same for a Roman citizen. Indeed, this was what Lucius had heard from Marcus Aurelius, when he joined the delegation from Tarcisis in an audience with the emperor, in Rome. In his memoirs, Lucius recalls the emperor's words:

[O Imperador] mencionou os vínculos de romanidade que uniam a cidade mais remota da Lusitânia a qualquer posto milotar das montanhas da Bitínia, numa uniformidade e coesão que nós estávamos ali a comprovar. E assim como a alma de cada homem era uma parcela do espírito universal e geral – acrescentou – assim cada urbe do Império, por mais pequena e distante, era comparte do génio de Roma.[11]

[He [the Emperor] mentioned the bonds of Romanness that joined the remotest city of Lusitania to the farthest military post in the mountains of Bithynia in a uniformity and cohesion that our presence there proved. And thus, just as the soul of every man was a piece of the universal and general spirit – he added – so every city of the Empire, no matter how small or how distant, partook of the genius of Rome.][12]

7   Mário de Carvalho, *Um Deus Passeando pela Brisa da Tarde* (Lisbon: Caminho, 1994), 16.
8   Mário de Carvalho, *A God Strolling in the Cool of the Evening*, trans. Gregory Rabassa (London: Phoenix, 1998), 4.
9   Carvalho, *Um Deus*, 282.
10 Carvalho, *A God*, 234.
11 Carvalho, *Um Deus*, 183.
12 Carvalho, *A God*, 149.

From Emperor Marcus Aurelius's perspective, the location should not matter in the Roman world. However, being so distant from the centre of the empire, Tarcisis is a frontier town, and Lusitania and Hispania are frontier provinces and regions. Early on in the narrative, Rufus, the representative of a new social class, contemptuous of learning and sophistication, expresses this peculiar situation in a very plain way: 'Curvo-me perante Marco Aurélio Antonino. Ele, porém, está em Roma, no centro do Orbe; eu em Tarcisis, no fim do mundo'[13] ['I bow before Marcus Aurelius Antoninus. But he's in Rome, the centre of the Orbis. I'm in Tarcisis, at the far end of the earth'].[14] This being at the 'far end of the earth' becomes a significant topic in *A God Strolling in the Cool of the Evening*: the narrative shows how the 'genius of Rome' is constantly under pressure not only due to the physical presence of barbarians at the empire's borders, but also, and above all, due to the presence of new ways of thinking and of conceiving human life which inevitably touch (either emotionally or rationally) the sophisticated Roman citizens. To those who live in remote places, distant from the centre of Romanness and thus more vulnerable to barbarian influences, the main issue seems to be the cultural menace that must be negotiated in everyday life.

In the Roman-Hispanic setting presented in this novel, the new religious, social and political events are really 'barbarian' practices and beliefs, since they seem to signal a new concept of human dignity and citizenship, more global and encompassing, aiming at protecting (or at least acknowledging) even those who were outside Romanness: the foreigners, the slaves, the uneducated, the unsophisticated. There is a new 'barbarian stance', which becomes more bewildering and more active when perceived in the borderline location depicted in the novel. In the Iberian, or Hispanic margin of the empire, this 'barbarian stance' is both a menace and a motive for reflection about the well-established rules and rituals of Roman identity, as we may notice in one of the dialogues between Lucius Valerius and the

---

13   Carvalho, *Um Deus*, 90.
14   Carvalho, *A God*, 69.

new Christian convert Iunia, vividly addressing their different perspectives on tradition and social practices:

> Depois decidiu-se, levantou para mim os olhos e afrontou-me, brusca:
> – As termas ... os espectáculos ... os banquetes ... os enfeites ... artifícios dos demónios para desviarem as almas de Deus, já que perguntas ...
> – Havia termas no tempo dos meus avós, há termas e balneários desde que Roma é Roma ... e sempre haverá. As termas são uma aquisição da romanidade. Uma das fronteiras entre nós e a barbárie.
> – E quem serão os bárbaros, aos olhos do Deus único?
> [...]
> Tentei apelar ao sentido de cidadania de Iunia e lembrar-lhe o perigo mortal que rondava a cidade. Os bárbaros já se mostravam! Mas Iunia era um templo sem portas. Eu não conseguia descobrir nenhum acesso.
> – Ou mouros ... – discorria ela. – Esses pobres mouros a quem recusam até a sepultura também são criaturas de Deus e deslocam-se a Seu mando.[15]

> [Then she made a decision, raised her eyes to me in a brusque confrontation, and said: 'Baths ... spectacles ... banquets ... adornments ... tricks of the devil to lead souls away from God, since you ask me ...'
> 'There were baths in the time of my forefathers, there have been baths as long as Rome has been Rome ... and there always will be. The baths are one of the advances of Romanness. One of the things that separate us from the barbarians.
> 'And who are the barbarians in the eyes of the one God?'
> [...]
> I appealed to Iunia's sense of citizenship, reminding her of the mortal danger surrounding the city. The barbarians were already on the scene! But Iunia was a temple without doors; I could not find any way in.
> 'The Moors,' she went on. 'Those poor Moors, who are even denied burial, are also God's creatures and are moving under His orders.'][16]

By reverting to the historical roots of Iberian identity within the Latin world, the novel by Mário de Carvalho suggests, on the one hand, the importance of the southern border with the barbarian 'Moors', and, on the other hand, the awareness of the special position of Iberia/Hispania, at the

15   Carvalho, *Um Deus*, 161 and 163.
16   Carvalho, *A God*, 130 and 132.

margins of the 'civilized' world, which makes it therefore more fit to reflect upon the value of Roman, or Romance, characteristics. Even if Iberian identity was mainly shaped by Latin language and customs, the Peninsula's specific borderline location, facing northern Africa and the Atlantic Ocean, grants it a particular exemplarity (and maybe self-consciousness) concerning issues of cultural contact, and the negotiation of differences. This may be particularly relevant if we consider that modern European cultures have evolved in a continuous process of questioning role models and symbolic locations of a common 'centre', which was traditionally identified with Rome.[17] Being consciously distant from the centre, Iberian cultures offer themselves a broader horizon of possibilities in both the incorporation and the critical appreciation of different, often 'marginal', elements.

In the Portuguese cultural discourse of the twentieth century, we come across some rather significant literary images of the Iberian difference within the Romance sphere. The two examples I will now mention show how these images may appear in different discursive contexts (in essays or fiction) but usually tend to propose a similar definition of the Iberian identity by stressing its multiple influences.

In 1935, the Portuguese literary historian and critic Fidelino de Figueiredo presented the myth of Pyrene as the distinctive Iberian symbol, and hence decided to name Pyrene his new essay which aimed at being 'uma introducção á história comparada das literaturas portuguesa e espanhola'[18] [an introduction to the comparative history of Portuguese and Spanish literatures].[19] At the beginning of the essay, Figueiredo explains the title's 'intention', proposing his own version of Pyrene's story – a long, complex

17   Cf. the exhaustive study of the expression and concept 'Rome n'est plus dans Rome' [Rome is no longer in Rome] in European culture, by Christophe Imbert, *Rome n'est plus dans Rome. Formule magique pour un centre perdu* (Paris: Classiques Garnier, 2011).

18   Fidelino de Figueiredo, *Pyrene: ponto de vista para uma introducção á história comparada das literaturas portuguesa e espanhola* (Lisbon: Empresa Nacional de Publicidade, 1935). There is also a Spanish translation of the essay (Madrid: Espasa–Calpe, 1971).

19   My translation, as in all quotations from Figueiredo's essay.

and often inconsistent version of the myth.[20] In Figueiredo's version, Pyrene was a Greek aristocratic maiden who fell in love with Hercules, but had to flee to western lands due to her father's disapproval:

> Fugindo à cólera do pai, [...] Pyrene veio guarecer-se nas montanhas do extremo ocidente, que separam a Gália da Hispânia. Reinava, então, nas terras do cabo do mundo, a dinastia de Tubal. Também Tubal se acolhera a estes confins tranquilos e hospitaleiros.[21]

> [Escaping her father's wrath, [...] Pyrene came to find peace in the far western mountains, which separate Gallia from Hispania. The dynasty of Tubal then ruled the lands of the end of the world. Tubal himself had taken refuge in these peaceful and friendly borders.]

Afterwards, Pyrene became the ruler of Hispania, which led to her being attacked by the monster Geryon, and her eventual death in those mountains which would later come to be named after her:

> Gerião, o monstro tricéfalo da Líbia, vagamundeando por estas apartadas terras, cubiçou-lhe o ceptro e acabou pelo usurpar; e terror tal infundiu à indefesa Pyrene que ela teve de se ocultar numa lapa lôbrega da montanha. [...] Expira a infeliz Pyrene e Hércules levanta-lhe sôbre a montanha um imponente mausoleu de cabeços sôbre cabeços. E deuses e homens, compadecidos, chamaram a êsses montes os Pyreneus ...[22]

> [Geryon, the three-headed monster from Lybia, wandering about these remote lands, envied Pyrene's throne and ended up seizing it from her; the unprotected Pyrene was so frightened she had to hide herself in a dark grotto in the mountain. [...] The unhappy Pyrene dies and Hercules builds her a majestic mausoleum with hills over hills. And the gods and men, compassionate, called those mountains the Pyrenees ...]

According to Fidelino de Figueiredo, the story was not over by then, because Hercules sought revenge and went after Geryon at 'ilha Erythia, para além

---

20 Cf. the short description of 'Pyrénè' in Pierre Grimal, *Dictionnaire de la mythologie grecque et romaine*, 8th edn (Paris: Presses Universitaires de France, 1986), 403.
21 Figueiredo, *Pyrene*, 7.
22 Figueiredo, *Pyrene*, 8.

do Oceano, no extremo da terra'[23] [the island of Erythia, beyond the Ocean, at the far end of the earth]. They fought and Hercules won, thus taking the monster's flock back home to mount Olympus, in 'Grécia luminosa' [bright Greece].[24]

Figueiredo argues that this story may be read as the symbol of love and heroic virtues, which could be seen as the two key elements in Iberian culture. We may question this reading, but discussing its validity is not the point here. Much more relevant are the images used by the author to tell the story of Pyrene, and his vivid expressions concerning places and movements: the Peninsula is repeatedly described as being at 'the end of the world', clearly separated from Europe by huge mountains, and as a rather peaceful land, even if it is also unprotected, vulnerable and open to dispute and attack; the menace to Iberia comes from the south (through the monster from Lybia) and then true victory can only be accomplished beyond the Ocean; finally, the end of the story implies getting some reward (the monster's flock), though it leads to coming back not to the Peninsula but to Greece, i.e., to the symbolic centre, and origin of all identities. Even if Fidelino de Figueiredo does not clearly stress any of these ideas, we may conclude that his version of Pyrene's story builds the ground for a definition of Iberian identity as a relational concept, evolving from several elements, such as a distinctive geographical location, a European cultural matrix, the capacity to overcome some threats coming from the southern border, and a promising Atlantic horizon. All that exists within the Peninsula is hence the outcome of this crossroads of influences.

Some similar images can be found in another Portuguese narrative I shall mention to conclude. 'Joan' is a short-story published in 1953 by the Portuguese essayist Agostinho da Silva.[25] The author's literary works are

---

23   Figueiredo, *Pyrene*, 8.
24   Figueiredo, *Pyrene*, 9.
25   This short-story was first published in the volume: Agostinho da Silva, *Herta. Teresinha. Joan. Três Novelas, ou Memórias de Mateus-Maria Guadalupe* (Lisbon: Portugália Editora, 1953). All quotations come from the latest edition of Agostinho da Silva's complete works: *Estudos e Obras Literárias*, ed. Paulo Borges (Lisbon: Âncora Editora, 2002).

somehow neglected in comparison to his philosophical and controversial writings, but he constitutes a very interesting voice in the Portuguese literary panorama in the middle of the twentieth century, especially in what concerns the representation of cultural identities.[26] The narrative 'Joan' is worth mentioning here precisely because it displays some remarkable images of the Iberian identity as the result of this living at the border, in contact with multiple cultures.

The story's narrator and protagonist Mateus, a Portuguese student at La Sorbonne, in Paris, in the late 1930s, meets some new friends from Great Britain, and repeatedly tries to explain them his Iberian identity. We know, from the beginning, that he feels as though he belongs to the 'Peninsula', with no particular national attachment.[27] Therefore, in the European context, he builds an Iberian self-portrait that, quite significantly, is based upon the mythical and historical relations of Iberian populations with either the Celts or the Arabs. To grasp his friends' attention, Mateus invents some possible identities, deriving their likelihood from Iberia's specificity as a frontier region. First, he evokes his supposed Celtic heritage:

> Então eu [...] me declarei seu compatriota e dei-lhe, com absoluta certeza histórica e etnográfica, um quadro de celtas povoando a Península ocidental, domesticando e afeiçoando às maviosidades do espírito poético as asperezas ibéricas.[28]

> [So I [...] declared myself [Joan's] compatriot and gave her, with absolute historical and ethnographic certitude, the image of the Celts colonizing the western Peninsula, taming and submitting the Iberian rudeness to the tenderness of the poetic spirit.]

Later, Mateus remembers his hypothetical Moorish genealogy:

26 Cf. my article: Ângela Fernandes, 'Imágenes literarias de Portugal y de España en el siglo XX', in Patrizia Botta, coord., Laura Silvestri *et al.*, eds, *Rumbos del hispanismo en el umbral del Cincuentenario de la AIH. Moderna y contemporánea*, vol. V (Roma: Bagatto Libri, 2012), 264–9.

27 When explaining he was homesick, Mateus evokes his 'grande saudade da barulhenta e anárquica Península' [deep nostalgia for the noisy and anarchic Peninsula]. Agostinho da Silva, 'Joan', in Paulo Borges, ed., *Estudos e Obras Literárias* (Lisbon: Âncora Editora, 2002), 129 (my translation, as in all quotations from this short-story).

28 Silva, 'Joan', 132.

Sobre ascendência, contei-lhes uma história de meus avós convertidos pelos capitães de Mafoma, passando calados o Estreito, batendo-se logo em Guadalete, ligeiríssimos à volta dos pesados cavaleiros cristãos e fincando pé nos anfiteatros algarvios como numa Terra Prometida. Fui, para aqueles saxões, neto de poetas e piratas, de furiosos arrábidos e de físicos sábios.[29]

[About my ancestors, I told them a story about my grandparents, converted by the captains of Mafoma, passing quietly through the Strait [of Gibraltar], fighting in Guadalete, all light footed near the heavy Christian knights, and settling themselves in the amphitheatres of the Algarve as in a Promised Land. I was, to those Saxons, the grandson of poets and pirates, of furious monks of Arrábida and of learned physicians.]

In Agostinho da Silva's narrative, the Roman, or the Romance roots of Iberian culture are a mere distant echo. And yet, once again in this literary fiction, the Iberian identity grows from the assertion of a borderline location, at the margin of the probably less adventurous Latin world, and thus incorporates all sorts of barbarian possibilities. This may be a fair conclusion to an essay where I tried to argue that contemporary literary representations of Iberian identity significantly delve into the very tension between the centre and the margins. Above all, the representation of Iberian plural identities seems to entail both the acknowledgement of some distant (Roman) centre and the discussion of local borderline movements or transfers.

Works cited

Carvalho, Helena P. Abreu de, 'A construção do espaço ibérico em época romana. Conceitos, escalas e modelos de desenvolvimento', *Revista de História das Ideias* 31 (2010), 7–23.

29   Silva, 'Joan', 133.

Carvalho, Mário de, *A God Strolling in the Cool of the Evening*, trans. Gregory Rabassa (London: Phoenix, 1998).

——, *Um Deus Passeando pela Brisa da Tarde* (Lisbon: Caminho, 1994).

Cavafy, C. P., *Collected Poems*, ed. George Savidis, trans. Edmund Keeley and Philip Sherrard (Princeton: Princeton University Press, 1992).

Fernandes, Ângela, 'Imágenes literarias de Portugal y de España en el siglo XX', in Patrizia Botta, coord., Laura Silvestri *et al.*, eds, *Rumbos del hispanismo en el umbral del Cincuentenario de la AIH. Moderna y contemporánea*, vol. V (Roma: Bagatto Libri, 2012), 264–9.

Figueiredo, Fidelino de, *Pyrene: ponto de vista para uma introducção á história comparada das literaturas portuguesa e espanhola* (Lisbon: Empresa Nacional de Publicidade, 1935).

——, *Pirene. Introducción a la historia comparada de las literaturas portuguesa y española*, trans. Carmen Muñoz (Madrid: Espasa–Calpe, 1971).

Grimal, Pierre, *Dictionnaire de la mythologie grecque et romaine*, 8th edn (Paris: Presses Universitaires de France, 1986).

Imbert, Christophe, *Rome n'est plus dans Rome. Formule magique pour un centre perdu* (Paris: Classiques Garnier, 2011).

Lourenço, António Apolinário, and Alexia Dotras Bravo, 'Da Ibéria à Hispânia, da Espanha à Ibéria', *Revista de História das Ideias* 31 (2010), 285–301.

Mathisen, Ralph W., and Danuta R. Shanzer, eds, *Romans, Barbarians, and the Transformation of the Roman World* (Farnham: Ashgate, 2011).

Silva, Agostinho da, 'Joan', in Paulo Borges, ed., *Estudos e Obras Literárias* (Lisbon: Âncora Editora, 2002), 129–53.

——, *Herta. Teresinha. Joan. Três Novelas, ou Memórias de Mateus-Maria Guadalupe* (Lisbon: Portugália Editora, 1953).

JON KORTAZAR

Identities in Diverse Societies in the Novel
Bilbao–New York–Bilbao by Kirmen Uribe*¹

One of the most striking passages regarding identity in the novel *Bilbao–New York–Bilbao* (2009 in its Basque edition,² 2010 in its Spanish edition³) by Kirmen Uribe (Ondarroa, Bizkaia, 1970), with which he won the Spanish National Narrative Prize in 2009, appears very early on in the work. The author-narrator interviews his Aunt Maritxu and she tells him a symbolic tale that demonstrates the key notions underpinning how diverse identities will function in the novel:

> 'Your grandmother suffered a lot. During the war, too, she was alone for a year, without her husband. She took into her home an official from Franco's side, Javier, and also a lady whose mother was a prisoner in the women's prison at Saturraran.'
> I frowned.
> 'Yes, I know it's startling to have people from both sides in your home in wartime. But ideas are one thing and the heart is another.'⁴ (26–7) [29]

*   This essay was translated from Spanish by Cameron Watson.
1   This work has been developed within the research project IT 851-13 funded by the Government of the Basque Country. It is also included in the research project 'Hacia una teoría de la Historia Comparada de las literaturas del dominio Ibérico', with reference HUM 2007–62467, funded by the FEDER Funds and directed by Dr Fernando Cabo Aseguinolaza, of the Universidade de Santiago de Compostela. An expanded version of this text will be included in the volume *Meanwhile New York: The Literary Creation of Kirmen Uribe* (Madrid and Frankfurt a.M.: Iberoamericana/ Vervuert), forthcoming.
2   Kirmen Uribe, *Bilbao–New York–Bilbao* (Donostia: Elkar, 2009).
3   Kirmen Uribe, *Bilbao–New York–Bilbao*, trans. Ana Arregi (Barcelona: Seix Barral, 2010).
4   Translator's note: for economic reasons, references will be included in the text. References in parentheses refer to the Spanish edition and in brackets to the first Basque

'Ideas are one thing and the heart is another.' This brief note will serve as a guide in our journey through the work and its conception of identity.

I. Interconnected identities during the time of the first generation

Aunt Maritxu's short narration refers to the time of the Spanish Civil War. As we know, the novel shifts between three (although I contend that it should be counted as four) generations in Kirmen Uribe's family. The first is embodied by Granddad Liborio, about whom the following is stated:

> About my grandfather I don't know too much. Liborio Uribe. By the time I was born he was dead and our father didn't talk to us a lot about his father. He wasn't big on the past, himself. A seaman by nature, he preferred to look to the future. About the people in our mother's family, on the other hand, yes: we know a thousand tales from Mother's side. (17) [19]

The time of Granddad Liborio is constructed, then, through the narrations of women in the family in such a way that in this novel, which has been accused (in my opinion erroneously) of minimizing the role of women, it is they who personify the principal role of creating stories in that first moment. The second generation is represented by the father of author-narrator Kirmen Uribe, the third by the same autofictional author, and the fourth, which I see and do not want to overlook, is represented, as in any good sailor, by the future outlook symbolized by Unai, the son of the author-narrator's wife.

edition. When no references in brackets are included, it means that the text has only been published in the Spanish edition of the book. This edition was translated from an as yet unpublished second Basque edition, which incorporated several additions to the original text by Kirmen Uribe. All citations from *Bilbao–New York–Bilbao* in English are taken from a forthcoming edition of the work translated from the second Basque edition by Elizabeth Macklin, which will incorporate these additions.

That first time is that of a community created which, without relinquishing its identity, is able to engage in dialogue and create a tolerant society, despite living either in wartime, like the narrator's grandmother and Liborio's wife, or in the postwar era.

Before beginning my analysis, it is worth noting that there are two narrative levels in which the interconnected identities of diverse societies will be located: at the level of familial and anonymous characters, as in the case of the narrator's grandfather and grandmother, and at the level of historical characters which mainly involve the architect Bastida, the painter Arteta, and the politician Prieto. It is through them that the conditions are established for the creation of a society that carries out a series of dialogues during a difficult moment, thus creating an interconnected society in its approaches that is not only based on a cry from the heart.

a) *The level of familial and anonymous people*

After having referred to the case of the grandmother who takes in an official from Franco's side into her home, which at this moment is paradigmatic, and the daughter of a jailed republican, given that the Saturraran jail served as a jail for women from the faction that was loyal to the Republic, one might put forward a series of cases in which the characters think differently yet share a common biography. The text expands on page 143 [169] and with the particular form of Kirmen Uribe's narration new information about the characters is added in a game of memory and recall that never remembers in the same way, so that when one returns to a passage and tells it a second time, it is recalled in a different way. This enriches the passage with new data and thereby humanizes the characters:

> There were two other people who'd been given houseroom. Both of them spent their days at the jail at Saturraran. One was the military man Javier and the other was Carmen, from Asturias, the daughter of a prisoner ... I don't know the exact circumstances but Communist Party people had told Carmen to go to that North Street house. I don't know who her contact would have been, who would have sent her there. (143–4) [169]

The message that life is above any ideology is underscored time and time again. This is also when people with different ideologies forget about such differences in order to create an environment of peaceful coexistence. This occurs when speaking about Liborio and his fellow in-law Anparo:

> All during those long days when Liborio was bedridden our grandmother Anparo, his fellow in-law, would come to visit him. Even though Anparo was an ardent Basque nationalist, she'd sit at Liborio's bedside every afternoon and read him the Francoist press. I can imagine Grandmother's way of reading, like that of a child, slow, stressing each syllable. Every once in a while, Anparo would quit reading and light into Liborio: 'What lies your friends keep telling. This is the last time I'm reading you this nonsense.' Liborio would smile at her with his eyes. He knew for a certainty Anparo was kidding. He knew for a certainty that the next afternoon too, Anparo would go to visit him and read him the newspaper. (176)

While it is true that familial relations are not always so peaceful and, in the case of the grandmother and her mother-in-law, the relationship (in which an attempt is made to smooth over the problems) ends up being less idyllic, the grandmother wants a friendly rapport with her Carlist mother-in-law, allowing her to name her second daughter:

> She left her second daughter's naming to her mother-in-law, however. They had been furious for ages because of politics. The mother-in-law was a traditionalist and our grandmother was a nationalist. To calm the waters and get their relationship on a better footing she told her mother-in-law that she'd be picking the name for the baby. Her mother-in-law, however, was not so forgiving. She called the baby Margarita, the name of the traditionalists' ladies auxiliary. (65) [76]

Nevertheless, there is an acceptance of opposites in the treatment between the narrator-character and his grandfather, Liborio. In a metafictional narrative passage, the author contemplates why he chose his paternal as opposed to his maternal grandfather when there were so few stories about him. The narrator affirms that, deep down, he made the decision because he was ideologically different, and because he was able to create through him a network of complicity, and understanding, if not comprehension:

The allegedly good and openhanded man, was in jail, apparently, for having come down on the side of the fascist uprising. At first I found that hard to take. I couldn't comprehend it.

But then I saw that in a person's life the surrounding terrain takes on great weight and that those surroundings condition the decisions that get made. [168]

When I first took up the idea of the novel, I found the Granddad Liborio character simultaneously attractive and uncomfortable. My own grandfather had himself come down on the side of the fascist uprising, on the side of that movement which brought those bloodbaths into being. I could have spoken, no doubt about it, of my other grandfather, Mother's father. Hipolito Urbieta, a calm and canny man [...]. Still and all, for the novel Liborio was far more attractive to me. A person full of contradictions, who sparked so many questions in me. (141–2)

In the citation there is a moment in which the author makes a confession. The word 'contradictions' does not fit the portrait he paints of Liborio, given that he is coherent in his outlook. However, it does contradict the position maintained by the author, but not his own.

Whatever the case, either out of discomfort or out of attraction, there is a passage in Liborio's life that dignifies him. When the massacre of the prisoners in the Larrinaga jail in Bilbao is being narrated, right in the middle of the Spanish Civil War, Liborio manages to flee and make his way toward the rebel lines. At that moment:

As he was going up Begoña, however, a skinny little fellow named Jose Luis Meler who was escaping along with him was hit by sharpshooters.

Liborio took him up in a fireman's carry and bore him to a safe place. (128) [140]

Meler promised to help Liborio rise up the social scale, but Liborio never wanted anything: 'Jose Maria Meler, the fellow Liborio saved from Larrinaga jail, promised Liborio he'd help him obtain a good position in society, and would get money for him too, if he wanted. But Liborio never asked him for any money at all' (142–3) [168–9].

The circle between the two comrades, and perhaps the word is ambiguous here, closes at the moment of Liborio's suffering. Then Meler appears once more to show his gratitude by paying for the burial of his saviour (176).

b) *The level of historical characters*

If at the first level of characters the phrase '[i]deas are one thing and the heart is another' served as a pretext for creating those interconnected identities, at the second core of analysing the complex identity of the historical characters in the novel the basic phrase, the motto for creating understandings, would be '[t]hey all of them held different ideological beliefs but admired one another' (175) [200]. An ideology and admiration that are found, are intertwined, and come undone within the circle of three key figures in the artistic and political history of the Basque Country: between Ricardo Bastida, one of the most important architects in prewar Bilbao, and Aurelio Arteta, an exemplary painter who learned much from cubism and was close to the historical avant-gardes. Ricardo Bastida, who is the focus of the narration, would also be in contact with the socialist politician Indalecio Prieto.

Initially, the novel centres on the creative work of Ricardo Bastida, a traditionalist and conservative, and Aurelio Arteta, a nationalist and innovator. The chapter that relates their relationship is titled, significantly, 'Two Friends'; the same name as Granddad Liborio's boat, one of the first enigmas that serves as a form of union in the text. If Liborio was one of the friends, then who was the other? This is the question that leads to an investigation that turns out to be false. The boat was named by its previous owners before Liborio bought it. The two friends are not, therefore, Liborio and another person, but Bastida and Arteta, who develop a relationship that begins with the painting of a mural in Bastida's house. It continues with a project to create murals for the Bank of Bilbao in Madrid, and carries on with an assignment for the Logroño seminary, a key development, given that the author-narrator has the correspondence between both of them regarding this task. He thus states that: 'Reading the letters you see clear as day what Arteta and Bastida were like. They were totally different from each other' (53) [61]. And yet they were still friends, even though Arteta was agnostic and Bastida took part in the Eucharistic Congress in Chicago in 1926. In the correspondence between Arteta and Bastida, which develops from page 51 onward [chapter 7], artistic doubts and processes in the Logroño seminary are recounted. If there was a major difference between Bastida and Arteta, this was overcome in their collaboration on artistic projects. Arteta painted the buildings Bastida designed by means of huge murals. The difference between Bastida and Indalecio Prieto was greater still, and yet, personal affinity and friendship overcame ideological differences. The narrator points this out clearly when Bastida sent some religious images sketched by Arteta, in a clear attempt to draw him into his religious faith:

> He knew that Prieto was an agnostic and didn't believe in those things, but that's exactly why he went on sending them [...].
> It was a game between them, one of them a monarchist and the other a socialist. Prieto was vastly amused by Bastida's lifelong attempt to turn him into a believer. (90) [106]

And then in the palimpsest that is the whole work, there are transcribed phrases from Prieto's diary in which the socialist politician talks about his friendship with Bastida.

As regards the interconnected nature of situations and personal friendships, the passage that recounts Bastida's visit to Prieto in his exile in Saint-Jean-de-Luz in 1948 is important. Curiously, their topics of conversation are personal (childhood memories, religious subjects) and professional (the plans both had for Bilbao that were cut short by the war) in nature (page 115).

The narrator underscores the consequences Bastida had to put up with as a result of their friendship, and at this moment the subject becomes political:

> The relationship he had with Prieto created big headaches for Bastida. Despite his being the architect of the bishop's residence and a member of the Catholic Action association, the Francoists denounced Bastida and he lost his position and his salary in the Bilbao municipal government. (116)

When he speaks about Bastida in this passage, one finds one of the clearest condemnations of strong identities, as opposed to interconnected identities: 'He [Bastida] immediately felt trapped between the two sides. For some people he was too conservative, for others the friend of socialists' (116). In the same way that José Luis Meler went to visit Liborio at the moment of

his greatest pain, the three friends repeat the same ritual; they go to visit
their friend at the moment of his greatest pain or death:

> Ricardo Bastida died on November 15, 1953. Bastida had learned that Indalecio Prieto
> was feeling poorly and wanted to pay him a visit in Mexico, since Arteta too was an
> emigré there. But on the plane he fell ill and had to return. Just as soon as he reached
> the Mexico City airport he got another flight back home. (115) [149]

> One of the first to go see the body [of Arteta] was Indalecio Prieto, who was also in
> Mexico in those years. Prieto truly marvelled at Arteta.[5] (127) [149]

It is a similar situation when recounting the case of the socialist Tomás
Meabe's death, whom he helped with money earned from selling his paint-
ings (175 [200]), a moment in which the narrator combines the two phrases
used here in this overview of the first generation:

> They all of them held different ideological beliefs but admired one another.
>   I recalled that saying of Aunt Maritxu's, likewise, about the people Grandmother
> Ana had in her home during the war. 'Ideas are one thing and the heart is another.'
> (175) [200]

II. The discovery of the other in the second generation

In the descriptive overview offered here, I would highlight a crucial idea
in each of the generational periods presented in the novel. The second
generation is represented by the mother and father of the character narrator Kirmen Uribe. In this section I would like to emphasize two key
ideas: the changing identity experienced by this generation, told through
female characters, and the importance of the other, recreated through the
anecdotes of the narrator's father.

---

5   Translator's note: the second sentence here has only been published in the Spanish
     edition. It was translated into English from the unpublished second Basque edition.

The first feature of identity associated with this generation is the rapid process of laicization and loss of traditions, in a swift process of modernization that is signalled in passing (although significantly) in the text:

> Her generation was perhaps the one that underwent the most changes. Raised in the straitened society of the postwar, they suddenly had to fathom the ideas of the '68 revolution. Mother herself has said to me more than once, they went from working in Christian communities to being Marxists in a just few months. (66) [76]

Alongside this rapid change, that generation also maintains a certain syncretism, because despite its modern features, it accepts some traditional beliefs, like those defended by aunt Margarita:

> But inside them the two worlds were both very much alive. And precisely because of that, even though she was the trade-union rep at the cannery, Aunt herself took care of setting up the créche at Christmastime and would take us up to the Antigua hermitage on foot, and tell us that one of the images in the hermitage, that of the Nazarene, was miraculous. (66) [76]

Together with change and syncretism, an identity is offered through the image of the father that must both discover and respect the other. There are two levels of this signification in the narration. Firstly, there is a narrative level in which the actions related show a respect for the other. This occurs when telling the story of how his father is detained for illegal fishing, and the subsequent trial in which he is declared not guilty. After the trial, everyone – the accused and the witnesses – must return together in a small plane.

> Everyone who'd taken part in the trial was on the flight together from Stornoway to Glasgow. It was such a small aircraft they all ended up in conversation. One of the pilots from the Malvinas told our dad, in English, smiling, You know you were there. Dad smiled right back at him. (132) [147]

So then, the official truth, not guilty, clarifies the real truth: the father was guilty. Yet the smile between both of them not only recognizes this reality, but it accepts above all the other.

At a second level, the narrator underscores the importance of the other at a symbolic or allegorical level and also in small spaces, as if the novel's message would like to highlight the fact that different people should respect the other, given that they live in small spaces, as is the case of the Basque Country. We should see these references in light of the importance of respecting the other. The two metaphors are taken from the seafaring world and in one situation the need to count on others is highlighted. In this case it is a carpenter on wooden ships or the machinist in the new vessels:

> At one time it was carpenters on fishing boats. That in the era of the sailing ships. It was essential to have carpenters on the crew. If there was some breakup, if the mast went awry, if there was no carpenter aboard the vessel was sunk. And so it was that there were usually three or four carpenters on sailing ships. And there was always a contest between the master and the head carpenter. The shipmaster tended to want to go faster, to put the mast's resistance to the test. The carpenter, though, tended to want to go slower, wanted to take good care of the boat, to get into port in one piece. I've often thought we all have the same contest going on in us. That we do have a shipmaster who wants to take risks and then the carpenter, who'd prefer to maintain the reservoirs, to play it safe.
>
> Later it was the machinists who took the carpenters' place. And the contest went on exactly the same, down to the present day. The machinist wants to take care of the machine, so that it won't overheat. The shipmaster wants to navigate using the whole of the machine. (94–5) [110–11]

Despite the personal interpretation suggested by the narrator, 'I've often thought we all have the same contest going on in us', I believe that the need for and difference with the other conforms to a higher level, precisely because of its symbolic nature.

That dialectic with the other is demonstrated in a most effective way in the passage in which the narrator travels with his mother to find the 'other' in his father in Stornoway. An old harbourmaster, Angus MacLeod, was responsible for arresting and helping (once more the dialectic with the other) fishermen who had been fishing illegally. A long time had gone by since then, and I think this fact is very important – the passage of time to justify the dream Angus still has in the story: to visit the Cantabrian coast, to do the journey that the narrator Kirmen Uribe's father did in reverse:

> Angus's dream was to get to know the Cantabrian coast. [...]
>   The situation was weird. Dad's alleged enemy, that man who'd taken Basque boats in under guard, was now wanting to go to the Basque Country. As we'd gone to get to know Stornoway, he wanted to get to know our home place. (164) [187]

This passage is extremely important because it demonstrates a harmony between adversaries, a unity of different people, reconciliation, an important word in the current Basque political panorama, although only after the passage of time.

III. Postmodern and global identities in the third generation

The third generation to which the autofictional narrator Kirmen Uribe belongs is presented as a bearer of characters fitting a postmodern and global identity. Naturally, a good deal of attention should be paid to the configuration of this identity, because it does not just identify a generation but, as will be addressed later in more detail, the remaining identities (such as, for example, the interconnected identities of the first generation) are defined from this base, from this postmodern vision, even when they are not part of a postmodern but rather a traditional society. Yet Kirmen Uribe's postmodern identity outlook rubs off on other identities, from the point of view that defines his own identity, within the identity parameters suggested by Diego Bermejo.[6]

In the first place, this is an identity that travels. Already during the description of the first flight from Frankfurt to New York in 2003, the narrator meets an Indian. 'I remember when we went in 2003 I became aware of a girl who had an Indian look about her' (60) [70]. This reference, which will extend to the importance or not of coincidences, is important because

---

6   Diego Bermejo, 'Identidad, globalidad y pluralidad en la condición posmoderna', in Diego Bermejo, ed., *La identidad en sociedades plurales* (Anthropos) (Barcelona: Universidad de la Rioja, 2011), 15–76.

it locates the author-narrator character within the globality of different forms of identity on his journeys, initially pointing out its external form and aspect. Of course, an internationally-minded writer like Kirmen Uribe must maintain a globalized identity, as he demonstrates unsurprisingly in chapter 11, 'The Käsmu Gravestones', in which he describes a writers' meeting in Estonia. The variety of identities, joined in the literary texts that they all cultivate, leads to them meeting together at a moment in which different voices and different languages can come together. It is true, however, that this encounter among poets in different languages, and therefore that hint of international harmony, can only take place in an idealized and very specialized setting, although the text does attempt to correct this ideal reference point immediately through a story about the Malvinas/Falklands War: with speakers of the same language, Welsh, fighting on different sides – in other words, national identity prevailing over linguistic identity.

The third generation's identity is driven by two elements that reinforce its features. One is travel. The novel takes place during a transatlantic flight, in other words, in the worst possible space in which to develop any action. The other is the importance of the media.

Yet the decision to locate the action in a closed space, a plane, a ship, in parallel to traditional ships, boats, is undertaken from the writer's consciousness, as the following note about his intentions (described in a very metaliterary way) testifies to:

> I laid out the project of the novel to Fiona. The idea had gone on evolving, and finally I'd be setting everything on a flight between Bilbao and New York. How else would I speak about three generations of a family without going back to the nineteenth-century novel. I told her about the process of writing the novel and in bits, in very small bits, stories of the three generations. (136) [155]

Travel is not a specific feature of this third generation. The Bastidas (father and son) had journeyed to the Americas before Kirmen Uribe. And the second generation, of course, is a generation that had spent its whole life travelling for professional reasons. But the third generation travels more and further. They are more global.

The importance of new media and the impact of the Internet on the novel is a topic that will be treated in another chapter. Yet it is evident and a near manifesto is proclaimed on the subject:

> Our small cultures had to get renewed. The ways of doing things renewed. To adapt to the times. The medium has changed. Nowadays it's not just books. Right there, you've got your new technologies. And who's on the receiving end has changed too. No one was writing solely for the fellow members of their own community now. The world's smaller. (101) [118]

As regards the globality of this identity, one should bear in mind another moment that recalls a plural identity in which writers and artists meet. This is the dinner in New York described on pages 152 and thereafter [chapter 17]. It is attended by the poet, Elizabeth Macklin, the hosts, José Fernández de Albornoz, a doctor, and Scott Hightower, a professor of literature, the professor Mark Rudman, the poets Marie Ponsot and Phyllis Levin, and the Czech filmmaker Vojtěch Jasný.

It is perhaps the most cosmopolitan moment (and I use the word carefully, because it does not mean the same thing as global) in the novel. Yet at the same time, it is the moment in which global identity reaches its highest point, because there are clear references to gender identity, maternity, and adoption by homosexual couples.

This postmodern global identity of the third generation is under threat from the strong identity of Basque nationalism. There are two passages in which reference is made to this identity through the activity of ETA. The first is about the day it declares one of its ceasefires, which was thought to be a definitive declaration.

> The news of ETA's last ceasefire caught me in Madrid on March 24, 2006. A friend called me on my mobile. He was overjoyed, 'What we'd been hoping for years on end has finally happened', is what he said. (175) [200]

But that hope was cut short, broken, and an attack on the Ertzaintza (the Basque police force) police station in Ondarroa on 21 September 2008, is described. This is also a case of personal testimony, reflected in his preoccupation for his relatives and friends, but also from a collective outlook:

I look at the housewife who lives across from me. She's begun gathering up the glass. Her husband was killed by the paramilitaries in 1980. He was pro-independence. Her daughter was in my class. We weren't older than ten. That was the first time I was conscious of the rawness of the conflict. [...]
    This fall I'll turn thirty-eight. I've lived the whole of my life with this. Thirty-six years with a conflict and only two or three with some peace. How few. (191–2) [218]

On the 2003 trip the narrator travelled with a young Indian, yet on this trip he accompanies Renata, an African-American. The understanding between different people will be key to the global perception of the novel, but especially as regards the fourth generation.

IV. The fourth generation: shared identities looking toward the future

Kirmen Uribe and Renata Thomas, sitting next to one another in a plane, each of them with a boat called 'Dos Amigos' [Two Friends] in order to carry out the narration. The humble fisherman from Ondarroa and the slave ship that became a freedom ship (107) [123] in that series of dual reflecting images that so abound in the novel; two people from different races who reflect on stereotypes.

    One of the most emblematic scenes regarding the image of identities in the book takes place in front of Vojtěch: two girls from Ondarroa, one a white child and the other Senegalese are communicating:

He stood watching the children who were playing in a meadow beneath the tower. [...] The children who were playing there were two little girls. One of them black and the other white. Both of them born in the town. They were catching butterflies, with a sheet [...] those two little girls who'd gone to catch butterflies were using the same language [Basque], but to play in. Even the one who was the daughter of Senegalese. (198–200) [229–31]

The scene which Vojtěch describes as 'marvelous', and defines as the 'most natural' scene he has ever filmed, represents shared identity, the accepted difference that is the fundamental thesis of the novel.

There is, moreover, another scene in which accepted otherness represents integrated identity; it is just that this takes place in the virtual world of PlayStation games. I am referring to Unai's idea to sign Drogba, a black soccer player who plays for Chelsea, to Athletic Bilbao. Athletic has a well-known philosophy of only signing players who have been born or raised in soccer clubs from the Basque Country, and maintains this as a strong sign of its identity: there is endless debate over whether foreign players should be signed and from here, in a parodic way, signing a black player would be a dual negation of that touch of identity Unai is undertaking, but only in fiction. For this reason, the Basque daughter of a Senegalese sailor represents in this fourth generation the potential to hope for a future integration of identities.

Works cited

Bermejo, Diego, 'Identidad, globalidad y pluralidad en la condición posmoderna', in Diego Bermejo, ed., *La identidad en sociedades plurales* (Anthropos) (Barcelona: Universidad de la Rioja, 2011), 15–76.

Uribe, Kirmen, *Bilbao–New York–Bilbao* (Donostia: Elkar, 2009).

——, *Bilbao–New York–Bilbao*, trans. Ana Arregi (Barcelona: Seix Barral, 2010).

HELENA BUFFERY

Iberian Identity in the Translation Zone

In a previous essay on the politics of reading Iberia,[1] I drew on Spivak's[2] figure of the reader-as-translator to explore the construction of Iberian identity in translation, defending the need for more translational awareness in the teaching of modern foreign languages and cultures in UK Higher Education. The case study included there focused on processes of inter-cultural translation, examining the way in which the limits of identity are constructed and negotiated in the shuttle between one language and another. It approached the problem of *Reading Iberia* primarily from an inter-national, intercultural perspective, taking arguably one of the most stereotypical figures of Iberia, that of the gypsy flamenco dancer, and ana-lysing the dynamics of identity and resistance brought into play in one par-ticular rewriting, Francesc Rovira-Beleta's 1963 film *Los Tarantos*.[3] Whilst my analysis attended to some aspects of the multicultural and plurilingual space constructed within the film, it did not really address the implications of this intracultural diversity for contemporary cultural analysis. Such questions were formulated more directly in Kathryn Crameri's essay in the same volume, on 'Teaching and Researching the "Other Cultures" of Spain',[4] and have become the focus for considerable debate over the past

1   Helena Buffery, 'The Rat Trap?: The Politics of Translating Iberia', in Helena Buffery, Stuart Davis, and Kirsty Hooper, eds, *Reading Iberia: Theory/History/Identity* (Bern: Peter Lang, 2007), 22–42.

2   Gayatri Chakravorty Spivak, 'The Politics of Translation', in *Outside in the Teaching Machine* (London: Routledge, 1993), 179–200.

3   Francesc Rovira-Beleta, dir., *Los Tarantos* (perf. Carmen Amaya, Antonio Gades, etc.) (Barcelona: DVD. Divisa, 2004 [1963]).

4   Kathryn Crameri, 'Reading Iberias: Teaching and Researching the "Other Cultures" of Spain', in Helena Buffery, Stuart Davis, and Kirsty Hooper, eds, *Reading Iberia: Theory/History/Identity* (Bern: Peter Lang, 2007), 209–25.

decade, particularly within Anglo-American Hispanism.[5] More generally, this debate is framed by increasing questioning of the validity of national models in understanding identity and culture, pointing to the limitations they place on any understanding of modes of cultural representation and reproduction.

Much of this questioning has taken place from within postcolonial and more recently globalization studies, leading to increasing embracement of postnational or 'world' cartographies and a recognition of identities that is relational, responsive and layered. Yet the frame I have found most useful, and which I propose to consider further here, continues to be that of cultural translation, in particular Emily Apter's notion of the translation zone[6] as a space of shifting borders and encounters between different languages, cultures and communities. Indeed, I would like to argue that her formulation is of particular relevance in describing the Iberian space: not only as a space of contact and competition between different languages, cultures and communities, but also in its production of multiple and overlapping views of the relationship between language, identity and space. Apter's reinflection of the map of Comparative Literature in terms of the translation zone, concerned particularly with sites that are 'in-translation', speaks to more recent sociolinguistic research querying the validity of the national language model so prevalent in Western Europe.[7] The perceived self-evidence of a link between language and identity formerly attributed to minority or stateless languages and cultures, has come to be seen as most prevalent in multilingual spaces like those found in the Iberian Peninsula. More than the study of influences or common cultural trends that have become characteristic of Peninsular Comparative Literature, I would here like to propose an approach that attends to the construction of identity in translation, ranging from scrutiny of the processes and products gener-

5   See especially Mabel Moraña, ed., *Ideologies of Hispanism* (Nashville: Vandebilt University Press, 2005).
6   Emily Apter, *The Translation Zone. A New Comparative Literature* (Princeton and Oxford: Princeton University Press, 2006).
7   Eric A. Anchimbe, ed., *Linguistic Identity in Multilingual Spaces* (Cambridge: Cambridge Scholars Publishing, 2007).

ated in the movement from source to target text (in context) to the more metaphorical understanding of 'translational' research as attending to the performative, the in-between and the cross-disciplinary. It is my intention here to present the bracketed inter-relation between these two notions of 'in-translation' as opening a space for critical reevaluation and intervention in debates about the changing relationships between the diverse languages and cultures of the Iberian Peninsula. My analysis will focus primarily on examples related to Catalan culture, but all of them suggest the benefit of such an intracultural lens.

Looking at the specific case of Catalan identity within the Iberian translation zone, it immediately becomes apparent how processes of translation have been determinant in the construction of Catalan identity, whether in parallel with other European nations and vernaculars, through translation from classical languages, incorporation of the texts of Western European tradition, or through the Herderian readings of national culture associated with the nationalist movements of the late nineteenth and early twentieth century. Indeed, following calls for analysis of the role of translation in the post-romantic revival of Catalan culture in key organs like *Els Marges*, the *Revista de Catalunya* and *Història de la literatura catalana* in the 1980s,[8] there were a plethora of new editions, anthologies and studies of translation, often drawing on descriptive or sociological approaches such as those formulated by Even-Zohar[9] and Toury.[10] As might be expected from a polysystem perspective, these studies revealed how the process of translation was identified by early twentieth-century Catalan writers and intellectuals as key to the achievement of cultural prestige. The text displayed below, for instance, by Josep Carner (1884–1970), responds to the

8   Lluis Cabré and Marcel Ortin, 'Aproximació a Josep Carner, traductor (els anys de l'Editorial Catalana: 1918–1921)', *Els Marges* 31 (1984), 114–25; Joan Fontcuberta i Gel, 'Als cinquanta anys de "L'Art de traduir" de C. A. Jordana', *Revista de Catalunya* 36 (1989), 119–30; Josep Murgades, 'El Noucentisme', in Joaquim Molas, ed., *Història de la literatura catalana*, vol. IX (Barcelona: Ariel, 1988).

9   Itamar Even-Zohar, *Papers in Historical Poetics* (Tel Aviv: Porter Institute, 1978).

10   Gideon Toury, *In Search of a Theory of Translation* (Tel Aviv: Porter Institute for Poetics and Semiotics, 1980).

Biblioteca Popular dels Grans Mestres [Popular Library of Great Masters] enterprise to translate the complete works of Shakespeare in the 1900s in the following utopian terms:

> Perquè el català esdevingui abundós, complexe, elàstic, elegant, és necessari que els mestres de totes les èpoques i tots els països siguin honorats amb versions a la nostra llengua [...]. Perquè la literatura catalana es faci completa, essencial, illustre, cal que el nostre esperit s'enriqueixi amb totes les creacions fonamentals. Com podria ésser sumptuós un palau, sense els hostes!

> I certament mai allò que sigui absolut autoctonisme – i per lo tant parcial humanitat – pot senyorejar l'univers [...]. Per fortificar-se un, i viure esplèndidament, necessita quelcom semblant a acaparar la riquesa de la sang agena, convertint-la en estrènua saba personal, multiplicant sempre els esforços per intensificar aqueix exclusivisme heroic i genial de fer afluir a la pròpia essència totes les deus inestroncables de la vida.[11]

> [So that Catalan might become abundant, complex, elastic and elegant, it is necessary that the masters of all the ages and all the nations should be honoured with versions in our language [...]. So that Catalan literature might be made complete, essential and illustrious, it is necessary that our spirit be enriched with all the essential creations. How could the palace be sumptuous without the guests!

> And there is no doubt that nothing that is absolutely autochtonous – and hence of partial humanity – can rule the universe [...]. To strengthen oneself, and live in splendour, one needs to be able to collect and store the riches of foreign blood, converting it into a strenuous personal sap, and to always multiply one's efforts to intensify the heroic and inspired exclusivism that is to make all the irrepressible springs of life flow into one's personal essence.][12]

---

11   Josep Carner, 'Del Shakespeare en llengua catalana [1907]', in Iolanda Peligrí and Núria Nardi, eds, *El reialme de la poesia de Josep Carner* (Barcelona: Edicions 62, 1982), 56. This passage from Carner has been cited in other studies of the importance of translation for the construction of Catalan national identity, most notably in Lawrence Venuti's 'Local Contingencies: Translation and National Identities', in Sandra Bermann, ed., *Nation, Language and the Ethics of Translation* (Princeton and Oxford: Princeton University Press, 2005), 177–202.

12   Unless otherwise stated, all translations are my own. Note that my translation of 'la pròpia' as 'one's personal' is not entirely satisfactory, and fails to reflect the more general use of 'pròpia' in contemporary Catalan as connoting attachment to the local

Translation here becomes a mode of internationalization, and indeed the choice of Shakespeare, and the particular preeminence claimed for Catalan as a language suited to Shakespeare's genius, becomes a way of distinguishing the Catalan language and culture from the more inward-looking attitude associated at the time by Catalan intellectuals with Castilian centralism.[13] Of course, this is a narrative that can be traced through other figures and motifs right up to the present day, as I myself explored in considering the translation and reception history of *Shakespeare in Catalan*.[14]

Translation has also been viewed as central to the visibility of Catalan culture, as can be seen in the image used for a 2010 exhibition about Catalan literature in translation that was held in Barcelona, 'Ficcions enfora!' [Fictions for Export], based on a photograph of the kind of shipping containers to be found in the city's Zona Franca. Elsewhere, in his groundbreaking study *El malestar en la cultura catalana*,[15] Josep-Anton Fernàndez has investigated how the lack of legitimating mirrors outside Catalonia (especially at the level of the Spanish state media and politics, where he argues there has been little concern with representing the diversity of cultures that share the same geographical space) has contributed to current identity crises. Indeed, as the 2010 exhibition showed, recent cultural critique and policy has proved more sensitive to the role of translation in the processes of recognition and identification that contribute to the formation of identity and community. Empirical studies like that of Arenas

---

identity, whether understood as regional or national. It might equally be translated as 'one's own' or 'our own', 'proper' or 'our proper'. What is important to note is how the notion conflates the individual and the personal with the collective and the communitarian.

13   A particularly illuminating example is the reading Joan Maragall (1860–1911) makes of *Hamlet* post-1898, in which he associates the Prince of Denmark with the weakness and lack of decision of Spain, whereas his own sympathies lie with Fortinbras. Joan Maragall, 'Hamlet', in *Obres completes. Edició definitiva*, vol. XV (Barcelona: Edimar, 1929–55), 131–6.

14   Helena Buffery, *Shakespeare in Catalan: Translating Imperialism* (Cardiff: University of Wales Press, 2007).

15   Josep-Anton Fernàndez, *El malestar en la cultura catalana* (Barcelona: Quaderns Crema, 2008).

and Škrabec[16] explore the landscape of translation from Catalan into other languages, exposing recent shifts in Catalan cultural policy towards internationalization through book fairs and publishing networks, engaging professional translators, mediators and performers to sell Catalan literary wares. Yet they have also pointed to the 'relative lack of interchange between literature written in the different official languages of Spain', concluding that 'Spanish, a majority language does not work as a bridging language to access other languages via translation'.[17]

An excellent example of this problematic can be observed in the dynamics of translation, and especially self-translation, of peripheral literary narratives within the Iberian space: how different authors travel (or not) within their own space due to both temporal and spatial dislocation. Carme Riera (1948–) is a case in point, also explored by Fernàndez,[18] who reveals how she shifts in self-representation and self-identification according to the language of expression. What he attributes to a process of slippery and deliberate mistranslation and denial of belonging to the Catalan space in order to become more acceptable to a Spanish-speaking audience is, I think, far more complex, revealing the kind of nuanced negotiation of diverse identities that is at the centre of her creative output. If I cite her here, it is because her work helps to reflect the complex dynamics of identity construction within the Iberian space, which itself must be seen relationally, in terms of its geographical borders and international language communities and markets. In her self-translation of *Cap al cel obert* [Towards the open sky],[19] for instance, as *Por el cielo y más allá*,[20] Riera makes quite extensive changes to the content of the book, including the addition of an epilogue especially for the Spanish-language reader. In doing this, as I

16   Carme Arenas and Simona Škrabec, *La literatura catalana i la traducció en un món globalitzat*, with English trans. Sarah Yandell (Barcelona: Institut Ramon Llull, 2006).
17   Arenas and Škrabec, *La literatura catalana*, 77.
18   Fernàndez, *El malestar*.
19   Carme Riera, *Cap al cel obert* (Barcelona: Cercle de Lectors, 2000).
20   Carme Riera, *Por el cielo y más allá*, trans. Carme Riera (Madrid: Alfaguara, 2001).

have argued elsewhere,[21] she reveals the need to explain the cultural and historical context in far more detail to a non-Catalan speaking reader, whilst at the same time indicating her awareness that she is writing for two different traditions.

The novel tells the story of a nineteenth-century Mallorcan *xueta*, Maria, who travels with her sister to Cuba. Through an elaborate series of cases of mistaken identity, she ends up married to the father of the man to whom her deceased sister had been betrothed; is betrayed by his family who take her for a money-grabbing threat to their inheritance; is accused of treason against the metropolitan government due to a poem she writes in which she self-identifies with Cuba; and is either executed or escapes with a suspected white slave trader in a rather flamboyant 'balloon of romance'. More important than Maria's story, however, is the mirror the novel sets up between the two island landscapes and between the parallel struggles for different degrees of self-determination in Cuba and Catalonia. Through this frame the reader is able to observe how the complex layerings of affiliation and identification accumulated and inscribed in Maria's writings and on her body become prone to simplistic manipulation by competing nationalist politics.

In many ways, the Spanish-language epilogue serves to confirm certain readings of the novel, such as that of Fernando Valls,[22] which see its primary critique to be directed against the identity politics of a contemporary Catalan nationalism perceived to be excessively exclusive. Indeed, in some ways the epilogue might be read as singling out the Iberian periphery's role in colonial domination, as opposed to that of the metropolitan centre:

> Con *Por el cielo y más allá* intento pagar una deuda con mi abuela y con la isla de Cuba, a la que tantos mallorquines emigraron hasta bien entrado el siglo XX. También trato de reflexionar sobre la historia de nuestro pasado y las contradicciones de nuestro presente, que nos abocan a la más absoluta desmemoria. No hace tanto que fuimos

21 Helena Buffery and Laura Lonsdale, 'Invisible Catalan(e)s: Catalan Women Writers and the Contested Space of Home', in Xon de Ros and Geraldine Hazbun, eds, *A Companion to Spanish Women's Studies* (London: Boydell & Brewer, 2011), 287–300.

22 Fernando Valls, 'Primera lectura de *Cap al cel obert*', in Lluisa Cotoner, ed., *El espejo y la máscara: veinticinco años de ficción narrativa en la obra de Carme Riera* (Barcelona: Destino, 2000), 305–17.

emigrantes y también negreros. La Cataluña *rica i plena* y el industrializado País Vasco, por ejemplo, se forjaron, en gran parte, con capital proveniente de los ingenios esclavistas, y aunque no nos guste, quizá el hecho de reconocerlo nos permitirá ser más generosos y tolerantes con los inmigrantes, con cuantos son diferentes o, simplemente, no piensan lo mismo que nosotros.[23]

[With *Towards an Open Sky* I try to repay a debt to my grandmother and to the island of Cuba, to which so many Mallorcans emigrated until well into the twentieth century. I also try to reflect on the history of our past and the contradictions of our present, which lead us to total amnesia. It's not so long since we were emigrants and in some cases slave traders. The Catalonia *rica i plena* [rich and complete] and the industrialized Basque country, for example, were built, to a great extent, with capital from mills run on slave labour, and though we might not like it, perhaps if we recognized it we could be more generous and tolerant towards immigrants, and towards those who are different to, or who simply think differently from ourselves.]

However, the use of second person plural forms throughout this excerpt makes such simplistic constructions of identity far more difficult to justify. Instead, it might be argued that the epilogue brings all of these different identities – Catalan, Basque, Mallorcan – into a shared space that includes the Spanish-language reader. It all depends on how we read the 'nosotros' and 'nuestro' here – who is the us, who the them? – drawing attention once more to the process of construction of identity in translation. Ultimately, Riera's decision to make her message about the ambivalent legacy of nineteenth-century nationalism so much more explicit for the Spanish-speaking reader indicates that she is aware that they might not make the connection otherwise, due to ignorance of the Catalan cultural landscape.

A similar issue can be found in the, I would say, 'failed' translation of Albert Boadella's *Trilogia catalana* comprising *Ubú president, els últims dies de Pompeia, La increïble història de Dr Floit i Mr Pla* and *Daaalí* – for the Spanish-language Cátedra edition of 2006, put together by Milagros Sánchez Arnosi.[24] Here, in the introduction and notes especially, can be seen the way in which translation can be used to define, construct and fetishize

---

23   Riera, *Por el cielo*, 442.
24   Albert Boadella, *Trilogía catalana*, ed. Milagros Sánchez Arnosi (Madrid: Cátedra, 2006).

difference through the drawing of boundaries and the reproduction and confirmation of stereotypes. Of course, satire (like humour more generally) is notoriously difficult to translate due to its dependence on spatially and temporally contiguous cultural knowledge (and hence to its rootedness in a cultural and linguistic community). However, the footnotes in the Cátedra edition are particularly instructive about the ways in which peripheral identities are construed through translation into Spanish. In the examples that follow, for instance, we can see the process by which the critique of Jordi Pujol central to the satirical and political effect of *Ubú president* is generalized to include all Catalanists, who are always described as Catalan nationalists within the edition, and – ultimately – all Catalans. The proverb, 'de fuera vendrán y de tu casa te echarán', for instance, is explained without citing any sources to be a:

> Lema xenófobo, racista y fascista en contra de la inmigración. Hay que recordar que Pujol hizo unas polémicas declaraciones sobre los inmigrantes en las que alertaba a los catalanes del peligro que suponía el mestizaje con la llegada masiva de los inmigrantes. Además, su esposa los criticó por vivir en Cataluña y los acusó de imponer sus costumbres y religión.[25]

> [Xenophobic, rascist and fascist saying against immigration. It should be remembered that Pujol made some controversial declarations about immigrants in which he warned Catalans of the dangers of miscegenation with the arrival of mass migration. Furthermore, his wife criticized them [i.e. immigrants] for living in Catalonia and accused them of imposing their customs and religion.]

On the same page, reference to a television company called 'Telestrés' is glossed as a reference to TV3, the Catalan channel inaugurated in 1983, before adding the more ideologically-motivated interpretation that '[e]s un canal favorable a los nacionalistas y en el que Pujol apareció constantemente durante doce años'[26] [it is a channel that is favourable to the nationalists and on which Pujol appeared constantly for twelve years]. Further on, the Catalan writer Francesc Puigpelat is identified as a 'Spanish'

25 Boadella, *Trilogía*, 92.
26 Boadella, *Trilogía*, 92.

novelist, whose obsession with Boadella's satire of Catalan nationalists led him to write an article criticizing the dramatist.[27] The significance of the Catalan flag, the *senyera*, is downplayed in another footnote by citing its provenance to be that of the kingdom of Aragon,[28] whilst a satirical reference to J. B. Pulla is glossed as denoting J. B. Culla, described as a 'catedrático de historia contemporánea que forma parte de aquellos historiadores dedicados a la búsqueda de razones científicas que justifiquen el catalanismo nacionalista'[29] [a contemporary history professor who forms part of that group of historians dedicated to finding scientific proof to justify nationalist Catalanism].

Alongside the tagging of all manifestations of Catalan cultural identity as nationalist, Sánchez Arnosi, in her notes to *Ubu presidente*, systematically corrects this 'erroneous' sense of difference by ethnotyping all Catalan artists, writers, journalists and politicians cited in *Ubú president* as Spanish, as in the case of Puigpelat above. The systematic downplaying and ridiculing of any Catalan sense of difference within the edition ultimately means that the footnotes contribute to map the space of Catalan identity as an artificially 'constructed' one, with no basis in reality.

To my surprise, this strategy seemed to be far more arbitrary and haphazard in the annotation of the final play in the trilogy, *Daaalí*, leading me to explore whether there was any underlying pattern to the way in which epithets were applied. Closer analysis revealed that more 'universal' writers and artists, such as Velázquez and Lorca, did not seem to require 'location' in terms of identity at all. In the notes to this play, furthermore, the reappearance of the identity category of Catalan, denied to the figures cited in the earlier plays, was limited to certain artists only, and is generally used to distinguish them as inferior, provincial and 'putrescent':

27   Boadella, *Trilogía*, 93.
28   Boadella, *Trilogía*, 93.
29   Boadella, *Trilogía*, 109.

Figure	Description	Translation	Page
Gaudí	arquitecto español (1852–1926), representante del modernismo catalán	Spanish architect, representative of Catalan Modernism	94
Arturito Mas*	Diminutivo irónico para referirse al político español	Ironic diminutive to refer to the Spanish politician	96
Font i Sabaté**	Danza popular catalana [...]. Su autor fue Josep Font i Sabaté: compositor español (1903–1964)	Popular Catalan dance [...]. Its author was Josep Font i Sabaté: Spanish composer (1903–1964)	
Fortuny	Pintor catalán (1838–1874) de escenas costumbristas ambientadas en el siglo XVIII [*sic*]	Catalan painter (1838–1874) of costumbrista scenes set in the eighteenth century [*sic*]	359
Josep Pla	Escritor español (1897–1981)	Spanish writer† (1897–1981)	378
Tapioles	Boadella ha caricaturizado el nombre del pintor informalista catalán ...	Boadella has caricatured the name of the informalist Catalan painter [Tàpies]	394
Salvador Espriu	escritor español (1913–1985)	Spanish writer‡ (1913–1985)	403
Miró	pintor catalán (1893–1983) [...]. Para Dalí, la mayor parte del arte catalán era putrefacto	Catalan painter [...]. For Dalí, most of Catalan art was putrescent	414

*   Artur Mas is the current President of the Catalan Generalitat.
**   This figure is mentioned in a footnote about the *sardana* (Boadella, *Trilogía*, 105).
†   Pla, of course, if controversial, is one of the most emblematic and canonical Catalan writers.
‡   Of the writer most commonly associated with Catalan cultural resistance to Franco.

Accumulatively, it becomes apparent how in the process of translation from Catalan to Spanish here, Catalan identity is both marked as different and redefined as subordinate. This strategy is justified in a later note, appealing to Dalí's own attitude to relations between Catalonia and Spain: 'Dalí dejó como heredero universal al Estado español y no a la Generalitat de Cataluña, a pesar de los intentos de Pujol, por el que, por cierto, Dalí no tenía demasiado simpatía'[30] [Dalí made the Spanish state the universal heir of his work and not the Catalan Generalitat, in spite of the endeavours of Pujol, of whom, as it happens, Dalí was not particularly fond].

Of course, Boadella himself is a particularly controversial figure today, who does not shy from publicly attacking Catalan linguistic and cultural policy, presented as a threat to the kind of bilingual, antinormative space celebrated within many of his works with Els Joglars. However, the case discussed above reveals the ways in which Boadella's self-avowed 'counter-cultural' stance depends on the construction of the kind of impermeable intersubjective limits that do not fully reflect the everyday flow between diverse bodies and languages characteristic of the contemporary – globalized – Catalan landscape. Indeed, the theatrical landscape of Barcelona itself, for many years criticized for its lack of openness to non-Catalan productions,[31] has become increasingly sensitized to the diversity of its audiences. The first decade of the twenty-first century has seen a proliferation of spaces dedicated to new practitioners and practices, the fostering of theatre and performance networks at regional, inter-regional, European and transnational levels, and imaginative attempts by publicly-funded theatres to engage with the diversity of audiences that inhabit contemporary urban space. Finally, I would like to take a brief look at ways in which representation of Iberia as a plurilingual and multicultural landscape is coming to affect how we might view identity in translation in the multilingual city

30   Boadella, *Trilogía*, 467.
31   Lourdes Orozco, *Teatro y política en Barcelona: 1980–2000* (Madrid: Publicaciones de la ADE, 2007).

space of Barcelona today, and with the increasing influence of what Marvin Carlson would call a 'heteroglossic' stage.[32]

The play with which I would like to end this discussion – *V.O.S.* (short for Versió Original Subtitulada [Subtitled Original Version]) – was devised by director and dramaturg Carol López (1969–) from a series of improvised sessions with actors around a skeleton scenario. Supported by the Teatre Lliure, which itself has spent the past decade exploring its relationship with multiple and diverse theatre audiences in Barcelona, Catalonia and networks involving other Spanish and European theatres, it was first performed in the Espai Lliure in January 2005. Like a number of other plays produced over the past decade (including many directed and/or devised by López herself), *V.O.S.* overtly sets out to explore multilingual spaces, revealing the different processes of intersubjective negotiation produced in the translation between languages. In López's published diary of the creative process,[33] which itself shifts between Catalan and Spanish, she reveals parts of the intertextual map underlying the play: from the workshops, readings, shows and sensations she experienced on a training course in Buenos Aires in August 2004 to the relationships developed with her actors and production team during rehearsals in Barcelona. The basic premise of the play is the impossibility of lasting love, the paradox of contemporary relationships: '[C]uando no se tiene se echa de menos y cuando se tiene se echa de más'[34] [when you don't have one you miss it, and when you have one it's too much]. But this is merely used as a base from which to explore the different performative possibilities such a scenario presents, through interaction with the different actors – Àgata Roca, Paul Berrondo, Andrés Herrera and Vicenta N'Dongo – and their and her different ideas, thoughts, desires and languages, in a palimpsest that constantly re-inscribes their shifting and responsive individual versions onto the same space.

32 Marvin Carlson, *Speaking in Tongues. Languages at Play in the Theatre* (Ann Arbor: University of Michigan Press, 2006).

33 Carol López, 'Notas en versión original', *Documents de dansa i teatre* 5 (2005), 46–57.

34 López, 'Notas', 46.

Improvisación escena de enamoramiento de ANDER y CLARA: él le regala algo que
ha escrito. Le regala sus palabras. Me parece muy romántico. Contaremos la historia
de amor a través de una libreta.

 ¿Y si ANDER está escribiendo la historia que estamos viendo? CLARA recoge
mesa mientras le comenta que la historia no se entiende porque no la está contando
de forma lineal. Lo que hemos visto hasta ahora es lo que CLARA ha leído.[35]

[Improvisation of scene where Ander and Clara fall in love: he gives her something
he's written. He gives her the gift of his words. I find this very romantic. We'll tell
the story of their love through a notebook.

 What if Ander is writing the story we are seeing? Clara clears the table, saying that
the story isn't clear enough because he's not telling it in a linear fashion. Everything
we've seen until now is what Clara has been reading.]

The final script was produced as a result of further feedback from open
rehearsals, producing a polyphonic and plurilingual comedy that moved
between Catalan, Spanish, Basque and English, and incorporated a wide
range of local, intracultural and global cultural references: from Barcelona
street names to Basque football chants to games based on contemporary
Hollywood cinema in translation. López's primary concern with the process
rather than the story or scenario – 'Que se vea el proceso en el montaje.
¿Cómo enseñar que lo importante es el proceso?'[36] [Let the process be seen
in in the staging. How to reveal the importance of the process?] – provided a particularly compelling window on to the fluid and performative
nature of identity, one that clearly connected with contemporary audiences, becoming the major hit of the 2004–5 season.[37] Instead of fixing
and fetishizing the limits between different Iberian cultures, contemporary
plays like that of López explore the diverse processes of cultural negotiation
between language, identity and space: '[L]a idea de que todos los espacios
convivan en uno y cada cual tenga el suelo que necesita configurando un
mosaico de diferentes suelos es algo que tenía en mente'[38] [the idea that

35   López, 'Notas', 53–4.
36   López, 'Notas', 49.
37   It was also awarded the Premio Butaca for Best Short Play, Best Director and Best
     Actress in a Supporting Role for Àgata Roca.
38   López, 'Notas', 47.

all spaces are contained in one space and that everyone has the space they need, configuring a mosaic of different spaces is what I had in mind]. They reveal the translation zone that is contemporary Iberia.

Works cited

Anchimbe, Eric A., ed., *Linguistic Identity in Multilingual Spaces* (Cambridge: Cambridge Scholars Publishing, 2007).

Apter, Emily, *The Translation Zone. A New Comparative Literature* (Princeton and Oxford: Princeton University Press, 2006).

Arenas, Carme, and Simona Škrabec, *La literatura catalana i la traducció en un món globalitzat*, with English trans. Sarah Yandell (Barcelona: Institut Ramon Llull, 2006).

Boadella, Albert, *Trilogía catalana*, ed. Milagros Sánchez Arnosi (Madrid: Cátedra, 2006).

Buffery, Helena, *Shakespeare in Catalan: Translating Imperialism* (Cardiff: University of Wales Press, 2007).

——, 'The Rat Trap?: The Politics of Translating Iberia', in Helena Buffery, Stuart Davis, and Kirsty Hooper, eds, *Reading Iberia: Theory/History/Identity* (Bern: Peter Lang, 2007), 22–42.

——, and Laura Lonsdale, 'Invisible Catalan(e)s: Catalan Women Writers and the Contested Space of Home', in Xon de Ros and Geraldine Hazbun, eds, *A Companion to Spanish Women's Studies* (London: Boydell & Brewer, 2011), 287–300.

Cabré, Lluis, and Marcel Ortin, 'Aproximació a Josep Carner, traductor (els anys de l'Editorial Catalana: 1918–1921)', *Els Marges* 31 (1984), 114–25.

Carlson, Marvin, *Speaking in Tongues. Languages at Play in the Theatre* (Ann Arbor: University of Michigan Press, 2006).

Carner, Josep, 'Del Shakespeare en llengua catalana [1907]', in Iolanda Peligrí and Núria Nardi, eds, *El reialme de la poesia de Josep Carner* (Barcelona: Edicions 62, 1982), 54–6.

Crameri, Kathryn, 'Reading Iberias: Teaching and Researching the "Other Cultures" of Spain', in Helena Buffery, Stuart Davis, and Kirsty Hooper, eds, *Reading Iberia: Theory/History/Identity* (Bern: Peter Lang, 2007), 209–25.

Even-Zohar, Itamar, *Papers in Historical Poetics* (Tel Aviv: Porter Institute, 1978).

Fernàndez, Josep-Anton, *El malestar en la cultura catalana* (Barcelona: Quaderns Crema, 2008).

Fontcuberta i Gel, Joan, 'Als cinquanta anys de "L'Art de traduir" de C. A. Jordana', *Revista de Catalunya* 36 (1989), 119–30.

López, Carol, 'Notas en versión original', *Documents de dansa i teatre* 5 (2005), 46–57.

Maragall, Joan, 'Hamlet', in *Obres completes. Edició definitiva*, vol. XV (Barcelona: Edimar, 1929–55), 131–6.

Moraña, Mabel, ed., *Ideologies of Hispanism* (Nashville: Vandebilt University Press, 2005).

Murgades, Josep, 'El Noucentisme', in Joaquim Molas, ed., *Història de la literatura catalana*, vol. IX (Barcelona: Ariel, 1988).

Orozco, Lourdes, *Teatro y política en Barcelona: 1980–2000* (Madrid: Publicaciones de la ADE, 2007).

Riera, Carme, *Cap al cel obert* (Barcelona: Cercle de Lectors, 2000).

——, *Por el cielo y más allá*, trans. Carme Riera (Madrid: Alfaguara, 2001).

Rovira-Beleta, Francesc, dir., *Los Tarantos* (perf. Carmen Amaya, Antonio Gades, etc.) (Barcelona: DVD. Divisa, 2004 [1963]).

Spivak, Gayatri Chakravorty, 'The Politics of Translation', in *Outside in the Teaching Machine* (London: Routledge, 1993), 179–200.

Toury, Gideon, *In Search of a Theory of Translation* (Tel Aviv: Porter Institute for Poetics and Semiotics, 1980).

Valls, Fernando, 'Primera lectura de *Cap al cel obert*', in Lluisa Cotoner, ed., *El espejo y la máscara: veinticinco años de ficción narrativa en la obra de Carme Riera* (Barcelona: Destino, 2000), 305–17.

Venuti, Lawrence, 'Local Contingencies: Translation and National Identities', in Sandra Bermann, ed., *Nation, Language and the Ethics of Translation* (Princeton and Oxford: Princeton University Press, 2005), 177–202.

ESTHER GIMENO UGALDE

Polyglot Iberia – or What Is the Place for Iberian Languages in Current Cinema? Presence (and Absence) of Iberian Languages in Cinema

I. Introduction

The present work focuses on the role of Iberian languages in cinema and on how these are represented in an ever more globalized cinema industry. In other words, this chapter aims to analyse the presence and absence of the different Iberian languages in cinema. Although my essay mainly concentrates on the cinema produced in Spain, where for obvious reasons language diversity becomes more evident, it also provides some illustrative examples from Portuguese cinema in order to offer a more encompassing Iberian perspective.

I argue here that it is not possible to deal with the presence of Iberian (minority) languages in cinema without considering other aspects related to cinematic language choice such as a) the notable presence of English in Iberian cinemas, b) the increasing multilingualism in films, and c) the obvious prevalence of Spanish over the regional languages of Spain.[1] This essay will therefore also focus on all these questions. As I would like to illustrate

---

1   Due to the limited scope of this article, I explicitly exclude from my analysis the presence on screen of other Spanish or Portuguese accents, which undoubtely exist in many films about immigration from the former colonies. Nevertheless, I would like to mention a few recent films in which filmmakers give voice to e.g. Latin American, African or Brazilian characters such as *Princesas* [Princesses] and *Amador* (Fernando León de Aranoa 2005 and 2010) or *No Quarto da Vanda* [In Vanda's Room] (Pedro Costa 2000).

with this essay, my main thesis is that one currently finds different filmic tendencies (not necessarily contradictory) in the Iberian Peninsula. Global tendencies do not exclude local tendencies, rather the opposite: their interplay can form 'glocal' hybridities, which have been very prolific in recent cinema. As Ana Sedeño, in her essay on transnational cinema, points out:

> [L]o multicultural también juega entre los intersticios. La globalización no genera lógicas unidireccionales (desde los grandes centros de producción hasta los minoritarios o periféricos) sino bidireccionales [...].[2]

> [The multicultural element also plays in the interstices. Globalization does not generate unidirectional logics (from the big centres of production to the minoritarian or peripheral ones), but bidirectional ones.][3]

I advocate the study of cinema from a similar approach – although centred upon the Peninsula and its languages – as Shohat and Stam do when defending the need to carry out a 'polycentric, dialogical and relational analysis of visual culture existing in relation to one another'.[4] The polycentric, dialogical and relational perspective I propose here will be twofold: a) external, with regard to the relationship between cinema made on the Iberian Peninsula and that from abroad, and b) internal, identifying the relationship between the cinema of the various areas of Iberia.

Furthermore, as this essay aims to highlight, the analysis of Iberian cinemas problematizes – at least indirectly – the question of what constitutes Iberian Studies or – more exactly – what we should understand by Iberian Cultural Studies. Since language in cinema is not as essential as it is in literature or theatre, the study of cinema offers 'a more encompassing

---

2   Ana Sedeño Valdellós, 'Cine transnacional: nuevas formas de entender el cine en su dimensión globalizada', *El Ojo que Piensa. Revista Virtual de Cine Iberoamericano* 3 (January–June 2011) <http://www.elojoquepiensa.net/elojoquepiensa/index.php/articulos/162> accessed 4 March 2012.

3   Unless otherwise stated, all translations are my own.

4   Ella Shohat and Robert Stam, 'Narrativising Visual Culture. Towards a Polycentric Aesthetics', in Nicholas Mirzoeff, ed., *The Visual Culture Reader* (London: Routledge, 1998), 46.

alternative to the traditional philological approaches'[5] which have been traditionally used to define and delimit different (Iberian) literatures. Thus, this wider notion allows me here to discuss the situation of cinema spoken in Iberian languages, but also to address my interest both in multilingualism and other languages such as English.

II. The increasing presence of English in Iberian cinemas

It is nothing new to affirm that English has gained a place as an international language of communication and a language of academic exchange, but it is perhaps not so evident that this tendency is also increasing in the cinematic discourses of the Iberian Peninsula. It is a fact that over the last ten years there has been an increasing interest in filming in English, since there are more and more Spanish and Portuguese filmmakers who have decided to shoot their films in this language. Whereas – as should be illustrated in the next section – multilingualism on screen is often linked to aspects such as the filmmakers' place of origin and their inter- and transcultural experiences or linked to certain themes (e.g. geographical or cultural displacements), the preference for English by many (but not only) young directors is, in most cases, a simple commercial question or a more 'global way' of understanding cinema. This recent trend has not gone unnoticed by the media. *The Hollywood Reporter* dedicated an article in May 2011 devoted to this phenomenon, which was entitled: 'Juan Carlos Fresnadillo and Rodrigo Cortes are among a new wave of directors following in Alejandro Amenabar's footsteps'. And it added: 'With the Nicole Kidman-starrer *The*

---

5   José Colmeiro, 'Imagining Galician Cinema: Utopian Visions?', in Kirsty Hooper and Manuel Pug Morux, eds, *Contemporary Galician Cultural Studies. Between the Local and the Global* (New York: MLA, 2011), 203–4.

Others, Alejandro Amenabar broke ground for innovative Spanish story-tellers who are savvy in genre and comfortable in English'.[6]

After his first two films (*Tesis* [Thesis] 1996, *Abre los ojos* [Open Your Eyes] 1997), Alejandro Amenábar shot a film in English – *The Others* (2001) – which brought him international fame, and some years later made his second international film (*Agora* 2009), again in English. Following Amenábar's example, for the adaptation of the novel *Los crímenes de Oxford* – written by the Argentine writer Guillermo Martínez – the Basque director Alex de la Iglesia tried his luck with English (*The Oxford Murders*, Álex de la Iglesia 2008) and Juan Antonio Bayona, the director of *El orfanato* [The Orphanage] (2007), has currently presented his first film in this language, *The Impossible* (2012), starring Naomi Watts and Ewan McGregor and based on a real story of one family's experience of the 2004 tsunami in Thailand.

But not all these examples are exclusively in English: one also finds mul-tilingual echoes in *The Frost* (2009) by the Catalan filmmaker Ferran Audí, a film which combines English, Norwegian and Spanish dialogues. Based on the *Lille Eyolf* [Little Eyolf] (1894) by the great dramaturge Henrik Ibsen, but situated in contemporary Norway, the film narrates the story of Rita and Alfred, a couple in crisis after the accidental death of their only son. In Audí's adaptation the couple is bi-national – the Spanish Rita and the Norwegian Alfred – and the dialogues in different languages (English, Spanish and Norwegian) produce a realistic effect. These examples, among many others, are helpful to illustrate the increasing presence of English on the Spanish screen, sometimes also in combination with other languages.

Nonetheless, it is important to emphasize that, for commercial rea-sons, horror films, thrillers or science fiction have traditionally been the genres in which the international language *par excellence* has been most widely used:[7] *The Others* (Amenábar 2001), *Darkness* (Jaume Balagueró 2002), *Fragile* (Jaume Balagueró 2005), *Buried* (Rodrigo Cortés 2010),

6   Pamela Rolfe, '5 Spanish Filmmakers Ready to Crack the Global Market', *The Hollywood Reporter* (15 May 2001) <http://www.hollywoodreporter.com/news/5-spanish-filmmakers-ready-crack-188491> accessed 10 February 2012.
7   <http://blogs.terra.es/blogs/cine/archive/2007/06/26/Directores-espa_F100_oles_2C00_terror-en-ingl_E900_s.aspx> accessed 5 February 2012.

Red Lights (Rodrigo Cortés 2011), *28 Weeks Later* (Juan Carlos Fresnadillo 2007) or *Intruders* (Juan Carlos Fresnadillo 2011)[8] are just a few examples of a cinematic genre – horror/thriller – with clear commercial purposes, both domestically and abroad. As far as Portugal is concerned, I would like to mention the case of *Contraluz* [Backlight] (Fernando Fragata 2009, Portugal/USA), a science-fiction film shot in English and starring, among others, Joaquim de Almeida. Despite its meager success, the film was advertised as 'o primeiro filme em Hollywood de um realizador português' [the first Hollywood movie of a Portuguese director].[9]

In recent Portuguese cinema there are also examples of films shot partially or totally in English such as *Second Life* (Miguel Gaudêncio/ Alexandre Valente 2009), *Star Crossed – Amor em Jogo* (Mark Heller 2009) or *Arte de Roubar* [The Art of Stealing] (Leonel Vieira 2008). Even though, in the first two cases, the presence of non-Portuguese male protagonists justifies and makes plausible a predominant diegetic presence of English, it is quite surprising that, though most of the characters are Portuguese, Brazilian and Spanish actors, *Arte de Roubar* was shot entirely in English.[10] As Leonel Vieira himself admitted, the main reason to use English in his film was the desire to internationalize it and to make it accessible to the non-lusophone audience. However, both the incredibility of the plot – located in Alentejo but using North American imaginaries reminiscent of Tarantino's or the Cohen brothers' cinema – and the unrealistic use of English were reasons for the poor box office receipts of the film, which failed to achieve the success aspired by its filmmaker.

---

8   A film shot in London, Madrid and Segovia <http://www.rtvcyl.es/Noticia/2D852636-9AB2-E7C7-F33A857C85FA7CCF/intruders/rodada/segovia/abrira/festival/san/Sebastian> accessed 10 February 2012. Fresnadillo has also shot other thrillers such as *Intacto* [Intact] (2001), in a bilingual (English/Spanish) soundtrack.

9   <http://www.cinemaportugues.info/2009/08/contraluz-backlight/> accessed 23 February 2012.

10 Júlia Garraio, 'O futuro do cinema português passa pelo inglês? Sobre alguns recentes caminhos da cinematografia portuguesa', in Kathrin Sartingen and Esther Gimeno Ugalde, eds, *Perspectivas Actuais na Lusitanística: literatura, cultura, cinema, língua* (München: Meidenbauer, 2011), 118.

Outside the mainstream, the experience abroad of some filmmakers has sometimes resulted in projects in which the use of English can be explained by reasons of script or cast. One could think here about some postmodern Catalan comedies such as *Honey, I Sent the Men to the Moon* (1997) or *Costa Brava or Family Album* (1995) by Marta Balletbò-Coll. The latter, for instance – described by Epps as a 'transnational lesbian love story'[11] – tells the love story involving a Catalonian performing artist/tour guide and an Israeli engineer brought up in Boston. The voice-over of the main character, Anna, closes the film with a romantic, happy ending that unavoidably reminds us of Zygmunt Bauman's concept of 'liquid identities',[12] when the sociologist refers to flexible, fluctuating and changing identities in a postmodern and global world:

> What a miracle! We'll make it together to the US. I will start a new life, together. I have always suspected there was a God; now, I know this one and it is a Goddess, fifty per cent catholic and fifty per cent Jewish and she understands Catalan people. [...] As soon as we get to San Francisco, I'll start getting information about Engineers without Frontiers, just in case corporate America disappoints sensitive Montserrat and, as soon as I get to N.Y. city with my monologue, I am going to buy myself a sesame bagel with cream cheese at the bagel store on one hundred and tenth at Broadway. One thing I'm sure of: is that we are both going to miss Barcelona and Girona and the Costa Brava.[13]

Further examples of Spanish directors filming in English could be some comedies by the Catalan Maria Ripoll:[14] *The Man with Rain in his Shoes* (1998), shot in London, or *Tortilla Soup* (2001) about the Hispanic community in Southern California. Or *Sublet* (1991) by Chus Gutiérrez, also shot in English and dealing with the experiences of a young girl from Madrid who decides to move to New York. To sum up, what all these films have in

---

11   Brad Epps, 'Echoes and Traces: Catalan Cinema, or Cinema in Catalonia', in Jo Labany and Tatjana Palvovic, eds, *Companion to Spanish Cinema* (London: Blackwell Press, 2013), 68.

12   Zygmunt Bauman, *Liquid Modernity* (Cambridge: Polity Press, 2000).

13   Quotation from the film *Costa Brava or Family Album*.

14   <http://www.mariaripoll.com/> accessed 23 February 2012.

common – besides their language choice – is the fact that they focus on themes related to the experiences of displacement and could, in a sense, be categorized as 'migration films'.[15]

And yet, despite the increasing number of English-spoken films by Spanish and Portuguese directors, it is surprising that the only Iberian film-maker who has been able to consolidate a professional career in English is the Catalan Isabel Coixet, who paradoxically is one of the most well-known directors of current Spanish cinema. As Brad Epps emphasizes, Coixet can be considered 'the master of a shrewd Catalan internationalism in which English, not Spanish, is the language of preference',[16] having shot five of her seven feature films partially or entirely in English: *Things I Never Told You* (1996), *My Life Without Me* (2003), *The Secret Life of Words* (2005), *Elegy* (2008) and *Map of the Sounds of Tokyo* (2009). Without doubt, Coixet belongs to a filmmakers' generation whose cinema is characterized by a way of 'thinking globally and acting globally too'.[17] As in the case of Isabel Coixet, the reasons for filming in English are not only economic and cultural globalization but also, as Lim Dennis points out, physical mobility. Actually, her films – very often co-productions – are not only shot in English but also located in different places of the planet such as Oregon (USA), Vancouver (Canada), Belfast (Ireland) or Tokyo (Japan) and with a crew (both artistic and technical) of different nationalities. This is probably the reason why her work has been defined as 'cine "nómada"' [nomadic cinema], in which 'predomina la diferencia, la diversidad y las identidades alternativas a nivel genérico, étnico, cultural, sexual' [differ-

15   According to Wahl, '[m]igration films emphasize the process of adaptation or integra-tion, whether successful or not, to a foreign society and language'. Chris Wahl, '"Du Deutscher, toi Français, You English: Beautiful!" – The Polyglot Film as a Genre', in Miyase Christensen and Nezih Erdogan, eds, *Shifting Landscapes: Film and Media in European Context* (Newcastle: Cambridge Scholars Publishing, 2008), 340.

16   Epps, 'Echoes and Traces', 70.

17   Lim Dennis quoted in María Camí-Vela, 'Cineastas españolas que filman en inglés: Isabel Coixet', in Pietsie Feenstra and Hub Hermans, eds, *Miradas sobre pasado y presente en el cine español (1990–2005)* (Amsterdam and New York: Rodopi, 2008), 182–3.

ence, diversity and alternative identities on gender, ethnic, cultural and sexual levels prevail].[18]

III. Polyglot screens, between the local and the global

The tendency described in the previous section and present in many feature films produced in the Iberian Peninsula since the mid 1990s finds its counterpart in another growing tendency, also resulting from globalization: namely, the increasing use of multilingualism in cinema.

Cultural and language contact as well as certain themes (such as migration, the setting of allophone communities in other places or in exile) promote multilingual fictional representations, since bi- and multilingual communities tend to depict their linguistic diversity in fictional representations such as literature, theatre, television or cinema.[19] Thus, the contact among languages and cultures – as a result of globalization, migration and the increase in co-productions (both European and transnational) – have favoured the spread of bi- and multilingual films over the last decade.

In this context, the most paradigmatic example of polyglot (global and transnational) cinema is probably the metaphoric *Babel* (2006) by the Mexican filmmaker Alejandro González Iñárritu, a film which

> weaves four stories set in different parts of the world: urban Tokyo, the Moroccan countryside, and the USA–Mexican border. Chance and misunderstandings, generated by characters who communicate in different languages, with distinct cultural assumptions and prejudices, make all the characters victims of despair and distress.[20]

18   Camí-Vela, 'Cineastas espanõlas', 182–3.
19   For pragmatic reasons and due to the limited scope of this article I only focus on feature films and explicitly exclude documentary film productions.
20   Luisela Alvaray, 'Are We Global Yet? New Challenges to Defining Latin American Cinema', *Studies in Hispanic Cinemas* 8/1 (2011), 81.

As Berger and Komori point out, 'subtitled in order to make it accessible to its audiences, *Babel* can be considered not only a modern cinematographic interpretation of the Babel metaphor, but also a representative example of polyglot cinema'.[21]

Despite the dominance of English and the Hollywood industry, language diversity has become a common feature for some representatives of independent cinema in the USA such as Jim Jarmush (*Night on Earth* 1991; *The Limits of Control* 2009) or some exilic and diasporic European filmmakers such as Toni Gatlif (French filmmaker who is originally Argelian and the director of multilingual films such as *Latscho drom* [Safe Journey] 1993 or *Gadjo dilo* [The Crazy Stranger] 1997) or Radu Mihăileanu (Romanian-French filmmaker and director of the multilingual *Train de vie* [Train of Life] and *Va, vis et deveins* [Live and Become]).

Language contact has also been an important trait of *beur* cinema and chicano cinema since the 1970s and 1980s and it is also a main characteristic of the younger *cinéma du banlieu* and Turkish-German cinema. Just to give an example, many films have focused on the Turkish community in Germany since the beginning of the 1990s. As Christine Heiss points out, in these films 'codemixing and codeswitching from standard German to Turkish, *Türkendeutsch*, or to a combination of German dialect or regional variety and *Türkendeutsch* is quite frequent. *Türkendeutsch* is

---

21   Verena Berger and Miya Komori, 'Introduction: Moving Pictures from a Modern Babel', in Verena Berger and Miya Komori, eds, *Polyglot Cinema. Migration and Transcultural Narration in France, Italy, Portugal and Spain* (Münster: LIT Verlag, 2011), 7. However, in their analysis the authors do not mention the problem represented by multilingual films such as *Babel* when screened in a country such as Spain, where films are usually dubbed into Spanish. *Babel* was indeed released in most Spanish cinemas in the dubbed version, losing thus its metaphoric character (Cristian Marín Gallego, *La traducción para el doblaje de películas multilingües: Babel*, Master thesis in Audiovisual Translation [Las Palmas: Universidad de las Palmas de Gran Canarias, 2007]) and its central tenet which is, as they emphasize, 'the representation of language diversity as its protagonists experience it'. Berger and Komori, 'Introduction', 9.

often used to mark characters or to obtain a humoristic effect in comedies'.[22]
Recent successful examples of Turkish-German cinema are *Gegen die Wand*
[Head-On], *Auf der anderen Seite* [The Edge of Heaven] (Fatih Akin
2004 and 2007), both dramas, and the comedy *Almanya, Willkommen in
Deutschland* [Almanya, Welcome to Germany] (Yasemin Samdereli 2011).

To sum up, the so-called 'cinéma du métissage', the 'accented cinema',[23]
the 'diasporic cinema'[24] and of course the rise of European and international co-productions have brought about an increase of cultures on the
screen resulting in even more transnational, multicultural and polyglot
screens. Though this classification could be arguable, Tessa Dywer[25] and
Chris Wahl[26] consider 'polyglot cinema' as a genre and define it as a cinema
'marked by the naturalistic presence of two or more languages at the level
of dialogue and narrative'.[27]

The multilingual tendency, however, is not only present in Europe
but also noticeable in Latin America. In recent years indigenous people
are playing an increasing role in cinema since Latin-American filmmakers are conferring them both a visual and acoustic presence (through real

22   Christine Heiss, 'Die Stilisierung von Türkendeutsch im Film und das Problem der
     Synchronisation ins Italienische', *InTRAlinea* 12 (2010) <http://www.intralinea.it/
     volumes/eng_more.php?id=902_0_2_0_M74%> accessed 4 March 2012.
23   Hamid Naficy, *An Accented Cinema. Exilic and Diasporic Filmmaking* (Princeton:
     Princeton University Press, 2001). The 'accented cinema', which is often bi- or mul-
     tilingual, is defined in the *Migrant and Diasporic Cinema in Contemporary Europe*'s
     website as 'an aesthetic response to the experience of displacement through exile,
     migration and diaspora. Accented cinema comprises different types of cinema made
     by exilic, diasporic, and postcolonial ethnic and identity film-makers who live and
     work in countries other than their country of origin (Naficy 2001: 11ff)' <http://
     www.migrantcinema.net/glossary/term/accented_cinema/> accessed December
     2011.
24   <http://www.migrantcinema.net/glossary/term/diasporic_cinema/> accessed April
     2012.
25   Tessa Dywer, 'Universally Speaking: Lost in Translation and Polyglot Cinema',
     Fictionalising Translation and Multilingualism, special issue of *Linguistica
     Antverpiensia New Series* 4 (2005), 295–310.
26   Wahl, 'Du Deutscher', 334–50.
27   Dywer, 'Universally Speaking', 296.

voice in vernacular language) in their films. Thus, a significant number of recent, successful films can be attested in which different indigenous languages (e.g. Quechua, Mapuche, Guarani, Aymara) interact in different ways with the dominant language (Spanish): *Play* (Alicia Sherson 2005), *Madeinusa* (Claudia Llosa 2005), *El niño pez* [The Fish Child] (Lucía Puenzo 2009), *La teta asustada* [The Milk of Sorrow] (2009), *Zona Sur* [Southern District] (Juan Carlos Valdivia 2009) are good examples. Even though Berger refers specifically to 'migrant cinema', her words equally match the aforementioned tendency in Latin-American film:

> [F]ilmmakers are not only creating a distinctive *spoken language*, but also uncovering hegemonic discourses while allowing the immediacy of *subaltern voices* (Spivak 1998) to be heard. Their filmic text thus maintains the linguistic habits of the speakers in order to confer authenticity on the multicultural societies being visualised.[28]

In the European context there are also examples of multilingual co-productions such as *Land and Freedom* (Ken Loach 1995) or the well-known comedy *L'auberge espagnole* [Pot Luck] (Cédric Klapisch 2002). Within the Iberian context films like *Transe* [Trance] (Portugal, France, Italy, Russia 2006), the successful film by the Portuguese filmmaker Teresa Villaverde, or the comedy *Mortinho por Chegar a Casa* [Dying to Go Home] (Carlos da Silva/George Sluizer 1996) – shot in Portuguese, Dutch and English – can be given as examples of successful multilingual films. Although it is an increasing tendency, Júlia Garraio reminds us that:

> O uso de uma língua que não a portuguesa tão pouco é um fenómeno inédito na cinematografia nacional, sobretudo em co-produções. Oliveira rodou vários filmes parcial ou totalmente em francês e inglês: entre outros, *O Convento* (Portugal/França, 1995), *Viagem ao Princípio do Mundo* (Portugal/França, 1997), *A Carta* (Portugal/França/Espanha, 1999), *Vou para Casa* (Portugal/França, 2001).[29]

---

28 Verena Berger, 'Voices against the Silence: Polyglot Documentary Films from Spain and Portugal', in Verena Berger and Miya Komori, eds, *Polyglot Cinema. Migration and Transcultural Narration in France, Italy, Portugal and Spain* (Münster: LIT Verlag, 2011), 211; emphasis in the original.

29 Garraio, 'O futuro', 117.

[The use of a non-Portuguese language is not an unprecedented phenomenon in national cinema, especially in co-productions. Oliveira shot several films partially or totally in French or English: among others, *O Convento* (Portugal/France, 1995), *Viagem ao Princípio do Mundo* (Portugal/France, 1997), *A Carta* (Portugal/France/ Spain, 1999), *Vou para Casa* (Portugal/France, 2001).]

Similarly, there are previous examples in Spanish cinema such as the comedies *¡Vente a Alemania, Pepe!* [Come to Germany, Pepe!] (Pedro Lazaga 1971), *Españolas en París* [Spaniards in Paris] (Roberto Bodegas 1971) or *La línea del cielo* [Skyline] (Fernando Colomo 1984). All these examples depict the cultural and linguistic displacement of Spanish characters living abroad, which is 'translated' at the acoustic level into polyglossic screens.[30]

Migrant figures are portrayed in some examples of recent Portuguese cinema such as the aforementioned *Transe* (Teresa Villaverde 2006) or *América* (João Nuno Pinto 2010). Villaverde's film, spoken in Russian, Portuguese and Italian, paints an uncomfortable picture of Europe in which Sonia, a young Russian woman, leaves St Petersburg behind in search of a better life. However, Sonia's travels through Europe, which terminate in Portugal, only bring misery and exploitation. Immigration is also the main theme of *América*, which tells the story of Liza, a young immigrant Russian girl married to a small-time crook called Vítor. Taking advantage of the wave of immigrants, he turns their house in a marginal district of Lisbon into a halfway home. Vítor's Andalusian ex-wife (played by María Barranco) is behind the scam and falsifies passports for illegal immigrants from Russia and Africa. In this nightmare Liza meets Andrei, a young Ukrainian, with whom she falls in love, and sees him as a way out of her rapidly deteriorating life. Spoken in Russian, Portuguese, Spanish and Creole, this black comedy can be interpreted as a European dystopian version of the 'American dream'. Defined by its filmmaker as a 'babel de nacionalidades, razas e historias

---

30   In her excellent paper on Spanish emigration cinema Miya Komori analyses *¡Vente a Alemania, Pepe!*, *Españolas en París* and *Un franco, 14 pesetas* [One Franc, 14 Pesetas] (Carlos Iglesias 2006). Miya Komori, 'Going North: Language and Cultural Contact in Spanish Emigration Cinema', in Verena Berger and Miya Komori, eds, *Polyglot Cinema. Migration and Transcultural Narration in France, Italy, Portugal and Spain* (Münster: LIT Verlag, 2011), 193–210.

cruzadas' [Babel of nationalities, races and crossed stories], *América* reflects Nuno Pinto's effort to rethink immigration, since – in his view – Portugal and Spain see their identity as something static.[31]

The impact of immigration to Spain, especially from North Africa, as well as the contact and conflict between different cultures and languages, have also been reflected in many Spanish films of the last few decades. As an example of the diversity of voices, films such as *Las cartas de Alou* [Letters from Alou] (Montxo Armendáriz 1990), *Susanna* (Antonio Chavarrías 1996), *Saïd* (Llorenç Soler 1999)[32] or *Retorno a Hansala* [Return to Hansala] (Chus Gutiérrez 2008), among others, can be cited. As occurs in real life, language use in realistic cinema also carries a social charge and implies different values. Cristina Martínez-Carazo describes these aspects in great detail:

> With respect to the language use, the displaced characters oscillate between two linguistic codes: their mother tongues and Spanish with a marked accent, an accent that, besides its phonetic peculiarities, carries a social charge. Behind the communication is hidden a series of added values such as social class, level of education, degree of integration, ethnicity and place of origin. The sensation of alienation that is derived from language is thus doubled: on the one hand we hear the accent of the immigrant when he/she speaks Spanish, and on the other, the presence of the mother tongue of characters, generally still incomprehensible to the Spanish audience [...].[33]

Geographical travel, although not necessarily related to the topic of immigration, can also result in polyglot cinematic projects. This is, for instance, the case of *Caótica Ana* [Chaotic Ana] (2007), Julio Medem's feature film after his controversial documentary *La pelota vasca* [The Basque Ball] (2003). Perhaps his most ambitious project, *Caótica Ana* – defined by Paul

---

31   <http://www.20minutos.es/noticia/875803/0/> accessed 15 March 2012.
32   In the case of *Susanna* and *Saïd*, shot and set in Barcelona at the end of the twentieth century, Catalan also has an important diegetic impact. In contrast to the other examples, they are trilingual films.
33   Cristina Martínez-Carazo, 'Immigration and Plurilingualism in Spanish Cinema', in Verena Berger and Miya Komori, eds, *Polyglot Cinema. Migration and Transcultural Narration in France, Italy, Portugal and Spain* (Münster: LIT Verlag, 2011), 159.

Julian Smith as an 'aesthetic odyssey'[34] – is spoken in Spanish, English, French, Berber and Arabic and was shot in different places with an international artistic crew (Spanish, British, German and French):

> Medem shot in Ibiza, where Ana lives and paints in a cave with her German father (Matthias Habich); in Madrid, where she joins an artists' commune at the invitation of enigmatic patron Justine (an underused Charlotte Rampling); in the Canaries, whose sand dunes stand in for the Western Sahara, the native land of Ana's first lover, the exiled Said (Nicolas Cazalé), and, finally and for the first time, in the U.S., where Ana works as a New York waitress.[35]

IV. Polyglot Iberian cinema – or what is the place for Iberian languages in current cinema?

Considering the global panorama – where both English hegemony and multilingualism have become increasingly solid tendencies on our screens – depicted in the previous sections of this essay, one should ask oneself what the role of Iberian languages is in cinema produced in Spain and Portugal and what the future for less extended languages such as Catalan, Galician or Basque is in Iberian cinematographies. In other words: what are the possibilities for these languages to become present in our cinemas? What are their possibilities of gaining recognition from the audience or being projected internationally? In the last part of this chapter I would like to throw some light on these questions by offering a general view of the presence (and absence) of Iberian languages in current cinema, with a special emphasis on Catalan cinema.

The imposition of Spanish during the Franco regime frustrated any chance of making cinema in any language other than Spanish, although

---

34   Paul Julian Smith, 'Chaotic Ana', *Film Quarterly* 61/2 (2007), 30.
35   Smith, 'Chaotic Ana', 30.

there were a few exceptions.[36] Brad Epps describes perfectly the panorama of Catalan cinema during the dictatorship:

> Arguably nowhere – other than the political, juridical, and military system, of course – was such monolingual imposition more doggedly in evidence than in the area of cinematic production, where only a handful of films, and almost always with great difficulty, were allowed to express themselves in Catalan. When they were allowed, as with the Argentine Tulio Demicheli's *La herida luminosa/La ferida lluminosa/The Wound of Light* (1956), Rafael Gil's *Siega verde/Verd madur/Green Harvest* (1960, but not appearing in Catalan until 1967), Armando Moreno's *Maria Rosa* (1964), Josep Maria Font's *En Baldiri de la costa/Baldiri from the Coast* (1968), Francesc Rovira Beleta's *La llarga agonia dels peixos fora de l'aigua/La larga agonía de los peces fuera del agua/The Long Agony of Fish out of Water* (1970), or Vicente Lluch's *Laia* (1971), it was usually in highly controlled dubbed or double versions, with screenings delayed or limited to smaller towns.[37]

After Franco's death the debates on the possibility of developing new cinematographies different from the Spanish model were opened.[38] In this context, for instance, the first symposium of Basque cinema (*Jornadas de Cine Vasco* 1976)[39] and the cinema section within the Catalan Congress of Culture (*Congrés de Cultura Catalana* 1977) took place. The linguistic question was obviously not excluded from the debates on cinema but the original enthusiasm about the possibility of creating cinematographies in Euskara[40] or Catalan soon waned in the face of reality. The lack of tra-

---

36   In the case of Basque cinema, one should also mention the documentary *Ama Lur* [Motherland] (Néstor Basterretxea/Fernando Larruquert 1968) which marked a turning point in its renaissance.

37   Epps, 'Echoes and Traces', 51–2.

38   Undoubtedly, the discussions about the *novo cinema galego* [new Galician cinema] at the Ourense film festival (*I Semán de Cine en Orense*), celebrated in 1973, set a precedent. See Colmeiro, 'Imagining', 204.

39   In these sessions 'Basque cinema was defined as one made by and for Basques, made in Euskara, which dealt with Basque issues and demonstrated a Basque aesthetic, still to be developed'. Barry Jordan and Rikki Morgan-Tamosunas, *Contemporary Spanish Cinema* (Manchester and New York: Manchester University Press, 1998), 183.

40   In the Basque context some people such as Juan Miguel Gutiérrez (filmmaker), Pío Caro Baroja (Pio Baroja's nephew) and especially Antton Ezeiza defended the need to make films in the Basque language.

dition, the lack of a solid industry, the fact that many 'local' filmmakers moved to the Spanish capital or the commercial inviability of films spoken in languages other than Spanish were some of the reasons that explain why neither cinema in Basque nor in Galician nor (to a less extense) in Catalan have gained a foothold. Nevertheless, it should be emphasized that, in contrast to Basque or Galician cinema, the situation of Catalan cinema is rather special: whilst most Catalan cinema has continued to be filmed in the Spanish language, films in the Catalan language have been constantly produced throughout the 30 years of democracy.

With some notable exceptions – *Ikuska* [Watching],[41] the adaptation in TV format of three of the canonical novels of Basque literature (*Ehun metro/Cien metros* [One Hundred Metres],[42] *Zergatik panpox/¿Por qué panpox?* [Why Panpox?],[43] *Hamaseigarrenean aindanez/Al parecer sucedió la decimosexta vez* [Apparently on the Sixteenth Time][44]) and other examples such as *Kareletik/Por la borda* [Overboard] – during the 1980s the majority of Basque filmmakers shot their movies in Spanish: e.g. Imanol Uribe, Montxo Armendáriz, Pedro Olea or Enrique Urbizu. But at the same time they were responsible for the recognition and prestige of the new Basque cinema in Spain and abroad. This is especially true for the generation which followed: e.g. Jaime Bajo Ulloa, Julio Medem or Álex de la Iglesia.

As Kepa Sojo rightly points out in his article about Basque cinema,[45] the cinema of Medem, Bajo Ulloa and De la Iglesia is so personal that it has nothing to do with Basque culture or identity, save very few exceptions.

41 A series of shorts co-ordinated by Antton Ezeiza (1978–84) and filmed entirely in Euskara.
42 Alfonso Ungría's adaptation (1985) from the homonymous novel (1976) by Ramon Saizarbitoria.
43 Novel written by Arantxa Urretabizkaia (1979) and adapted for the cinema by Xabier Elorriaga (1985).
44 A cinematographic adaptation (1985) by Anjel Lertzundi of his own novel published in 1983.
45 Kepa Sojo, 'El reto del cine vasco', *Euskonews* (September 2005) <http://www.euskonews.com/0314zbk/gaia31402es.html> accessed 4 March 2012.

Even those who have dealt with more 'Basque' topics or have situated the *plots* in Euskal Erria have tended to shoot in the Spanish language: *Tasio* (1984),[46] *Akelarre* (1984), *Vacas* [Cows] (1992), *Yoyes* (2000), etc. And only the fictional documentary *La fuga de Segovia* from Imanol Uribe's 'political trilogy' – *El proceso de Burgos* [The Burgos Trial] 1979, *La fuga de Segovia* [Escape from Segovia] 1981, *La muerte de Mikel* [The Death of Mikel] 1984 – was partly shot in Euskara.[47] In a short chapter devoted to Basque cinema, Barry Jordan and Rikki Morgan-Tamosunas clearly express that:

> While Basque in origin, most Basque directors tend to live and work outside the region. Moreover, even if they have been asked to produce versions in euskera [...], their films nearly all tend to be shot, distributed and exhibited in Castilian.[48]

Perhaps for this reason a broader definition of Basque cinema has prevailed, as described by the above-mentioned scholars:

> The notion of Basque cinema has become a broadly accepted category, even though (for obvious reasons of commercial viability), the vast majority of films do not exploit the Basque language, euskera. In other words, the concept of Basque cinema does not rely fundamentally on a linguistic imperative for its identity and standing.[49]

46 Strangely enough, despite the fact that Armendariz has always claimed that films should be made in Euskara, all his films, including the adaptation from Atxaga's novel *Obabababakoak* (1988), are shot in Spanish.

47 The fictional documentary *La fuga de Segovia* is spoken in Euskara and Spanish. Carlos Roldán Larreta, 'Euskera y cine: Una relación conflictiva', *Fontes Linguae Vasconum: Studia et Documenta* 71 (1996), 167. 'En la película de Uribe los presos hablan entre sí en este idioma respondiendo a una realidad que se dio en la cárcel de Segovia. El haber hecho hablar en euskera a los funcionarios hubiera sido ridículo' [In Uribe's film, prisoners talk among themselves using that language to represent a reality that existed in the prison of Segovia. Talking to the guards in euskera would have been ridiculous] (Roldán Larreta, 'Euskera y cine', 168).

48 Jordan and Morgan-Tamosunas, *Contemporary Spanish Cinema*, 182.

49 Jordan and Morgan-Tamosunas, *Contemporary Spanish Cinema*, 182.

In the new millennium most of the Basque filmmakers still make films in Spanish,[50] although they do not exclude other languages such as English or even polyglot versions. As already mentioned, De la Iglesia used English for the cinematic version of Martínez's novel *Los crímenes de Oxford*, while Medem's *Caótica Ana* is a paradigmatic example of polyglot cinema, since it is spoken in Spanish, English, French, Berber and Arabic. Similarly, for *Room in Rome* (2010), Medem's last work, the Basque filmmaker opted for English with few dialogues in Spanish, Italian and Russian. Loosely based on the Chilean *En la cama* [In Bed] (Matías Bize 2005), *Room in Rome* tells the romantic story of two young women, the Spanish Alba and the Russian Natasha, who meet in a hotel in Rome for 12 hours.

Whilst the younger generation of Basque filmmakers – people like Kepa Sojo (*El síndrome de Svensson* [The Svensson's Syndrome] 2006), Nacho Vigalondo[51] (*Los cronocrímenes* [Timecrimes] 2007, *Extraterrestre* [Alien] 2011) or Borja Cobeaga (*Pagafantas* [Friend Zone] 2009, *No controles* [Love Storming] 2010) – also seems to give preference to the Spanish language when making their films,[52] a renewed interest for cinema in Euskara can be observed. According to the information given by the Association of Independent Audiovisual Production Companies of the Basque Country (IBAIA),[53] from 2005 to 2011 a total of 18 feature films were shot partly or entirely in Basque, undoubtedly a milestone for Basque cinema in Euskara.[54]

---

50   Alex de la Iglesia (e.g. *La comunidad* [Common Wealth] 2003, *Crimen ferpecto* [Ferpect Crime] 2004, *Balada triste de trompeta* [The Last Circus] 2010, *La chispa de la vida* [As Luck Would Have It] 2012), Helena Taberna (e.g. *La buena nueva* [The Good News] 2008), Montxo Armendáriz (e.g. *Silencio roto* [Broken Silence] 2001, Obaba 2005), Julio Medem (e.g. *Lucía y el sexo* [Sex and Lucia] 2001).

51   Vigalondo is Cantabrian, but he did his cinematographic training in the Basque Country.

52   Koldo Serra has made an international production shot in English and Spanish entitled *El bosque de las sombras* [The Backwoods] (2006).

53   I would like to thank IBAIA for this valuable information: <www.ibaia.org>.

54   *Aita* [Father] (José María de Orbe 2010) also includes a few scenes in Euskara. However, most of the film is spoken in Spanish since its main character, Luis Pescador, does not speak Basque. 2005 is also the production year of the TV-movie *Zeru horiek/*

Titles such as *Aupa Etxebeste!* [Hi, Etxebeste!] (2005), *Kutsidazu bidea, Ixabel/Enséñame el camino, Isabel* [Show Me the Way, Isabel] (2006),[55] *Eutsi!/¡Resiste!* [Resist] (2007), *Zorion perfektua/Felicidad perfecta* [Perfect Happiness] (Jabi Elortegi 2009), *80 Egunean/En 80 días* [In 80 Days] (2010) or *Izarren argia/Estrellas que alcanzar* [Stars to Wish Upon] (2010), *Arriya/La piedra* [The Stone] (2011), *Mugaldekoak/Operación Cométe* [The Cométe Operation] (2011), *Urte berri on, amona!/¡Feliz año, abuela!* [Happy New Year, Grandma!] (2011) are part of what I call here a modest 'boom' of Basque original soundtrack. In this context, however, it should be highlighted that even though they are normally classified as Basque original soundtracks, most of them include some scenes and dialogues in Spanish (or even in languages other than Basque) or are even bilingual (Euskara/Spanish). This is obviously not surprising if we take into account that cinema tends to represent fiction as close as possible to reality and this also affects language representation, since language contact is very common in many Spanish autonomous regions such as the Basque Country, Galicia or Catalonia, which are officially bilingual.

From the mid-1970s and during the 1980s cinema in Catalan experienced a modest 'boom' in all topics and genres. One could mention here the 'local' comedies of Francesc Bellmunt or Ventura Pons or films with certain commercial success which recovered the historical memory of Catalonia such as *Companys, procés a Catalunya* [Catalonia on Trial] (Josep Maria Forn 1978) – spoken mainly in Catalan and Spanish but with some scenes in French and German – can be mentioned. But without a doubt, as Martí-Olivella highlights,

---

Esos cielos [Those Skies] (2005), an adaptation of Atxaga's novel in which 'se rodó en euskera por los actores vascos y se dobló a los que no lo hablaban' [Basque actors were filmed in Basque, and those who did not speak it were dubbed]. Jon Kortazar, 'Novela vasca y cine', *Encuentros en Verines. Casona de Verines, Pendueles (Asturias)* (2008) <http://www.mcu.es/archivoswebmcu/verines/pdf/334.pdf> accessed 4 March 2012.

55   Adaptation of Joxean Sagastizabal's novel, written in 1994. According to Kortazar, 'probablemente el libro que más ejemplares ha vendido en la literatura actual vasca' [it is probably the book that sold the most copies in the current Basque literature]. Kortazar, 'Novela vasca'.

since the great public and critical success of *La plaça del diamant* (Diamond Square, 1982) many new and veteran filmmakers have attempted filmic adaptations of literary texts. The list is considerable but there is no other Catalan director who has better reclaimed this cine-lit tradition in order to subvert it from within than Ventura Pons.[56]

The veteran Ventura Pons – who has adapted some of the most relevant authors of Catalan literature such as Quim Monzó, Sergi Belbel, Ferran Torrent, Josep Maria Benet i Jornet, Lluïsa Cunillé and Lluís Anton Baulenas – deserves therefore special mention. Throughout his extended career – his last film dates from 2012 – Pons has translated into images a total of thirteen works of contemporary Catalan literature: *Puta misèria* [Fucking Misery] (1989), *El perquè de tot plegat* [What's It All About] (1994), *Actrius* [Actresses] (1996), *Carícies* [Caresses] (1997), *Amic/Amat* [Beloved/Friend] (1998), *Anita no perd el tren* [Anita Takes a Chance] (2000), *Amor idiota* [Idiot Love] (2004), *Animals ferits* [Wounded Animals] (2005), *La vida abysmal* [Life in the Abyss] (2006), *Barcelona (un mapa)* [Barcelona. A Map] (2007), *Forasters* [Foreigners] (2008), *A la deriva* [Adrift] (2009) or *Mil cretins* [A Thousand Fools] (2011). Although most of his works have a Catalan original soundtrack, some of them can be classified as bi- or multilingual films, as will now be illustrated.

Following the play by Lluïsa Cunillé (*Barcelona, mapa d'ombres* 2004), Pons not only respects its original dialogues, almost identical to Cunillé's work, and its narrative structure – though introducing some modifications such as the use of flashbacks or the exterior scenes with Gaudí's Sagrada Família [Sacred Family] as background – but also Cunillé's language choice.[57] As in the original, dialogues of the different scenes take place in Catalan, except for some scenes in Spanish, when Ramon (Josep Maria Pou), the main male character, speaks with the young Argentinian woman (María Botto), who rents a room in their flat in Barcelona's Eixample district.

56   Jaume Martí-Olivella, 'Catalan Cinema: An Uncanny Transnational Performance', in Dominic Keown, ed., *A Companion to Catalan Culture* (Woodbridge, Suffolk, UK, and Rochester, NY: Tamesis, 2011), 198.

57   Lluïsa Cunillé, 'Barcelona, mapa d'ombres', in *Deu peces* (Barcelona: Edicions 62, 2008), 383–448.

In contrast to the literary works written solely in Catalan such as *Anita no perd el tren* and *Amor idiota* – the first based on a monologue and the second on a novel written by Baulenas – Pons's adaptations are bilingual, both Catalan and Spanish sharing a balanced presence. Even though from a linguistic point of view the cinematographic 'translations' differ in great measure from the original novels, since the latter are written exclusively in Catalan, the director manages to stage the bilingualism used in Catalonia today in quite a realistic manner. Another interesting example of Pons' cinema is *Animals ferits* (2005), based on some short stories from Jordi Puntí's *Animals tristos* [Sad Animals] (2002). Here Ventura Pons transforms the Catalan texts into a polyglot film set in a post Olympic and modern Barcelona, in which characters not only switch from Spanish into Catalan but in which other subaltern voices such as non-peninsular varieties of Spanish – namely Peruvian, Mexican and Argentinean – and even Quiche can also be heard.

Just like *Animals ferits*, *L'illa de l'holandès* [The Dutchman's Island] (2000) by Sigfrid Monleón is an example of a multilingual film based on a literary work originally written in Catalan. Monleón's adaptation of the homonymous novel by the Valencian author Ferran Torrent uses Catalan, Spanish and French to tell a story located on a Mediterranean island in the late 1960s. From the linguistic point of view, *L'illa de l'holandès* is also an interesting cinematic attempt to represent the internal linguistic variety of the Catalan language by giving voice to other dialects that are different from the Barcelonian central dialect.[58]

In this new millennium both Catalan cinema and cinema in Catalan are experiencing a significant peak and have obtained much success both in Spain and abroad. Coinciding with the 'coming-of-age of Catalan cinema,'[59] new generations of filmmakers such as Marc Recha (*Dies d'agost* [Some Days in August] 2006, *Petit indi* [Little Indi] 2009), Cesc Gay (*Ficció*

---

58 Other significant examples are *El mar* [The Sea] (2000) or *Pa negre* [Black Bread] (2010) by Agustí Villaronga, based respectively on the homonymous novels of Blai Bonet and Emili Teixidor.

59 Martí-Olivella, 'Catalan Cinema', 188.

[Fiction] 2006, *V.O.S.* 2009), Albert Serra (*Honor de cavalleria* [Honour of the Knights] 2006) or Mar Coll (*Tres dies amb la família* [Three Days with the Family] 2009), etc. have contributed to bestowing prestige on cinema in the Catalan language and to internationalizing Catalan cinema.[60] For younger generations, Catalan seems to be a normalized language[61] which they introduce in their films as they use it in other daily life contexts. But with the same ease with which they speak other languages, their characters also express themselves in Spanish or French. *L'arbre de les cireres* [The Cherry Tree] (1998), *Pau i el seu germà* [Pau and His Brother] (2001), *Les mains vides/Les mans buides* [Empty Hands] (2003) – all three by March Recha – or *Tres dies amb la família* (2009) by Mar Coll are spoken in Catalan and French or even in both languages combined with Spanish.

As I stated elsewhere, bilingualism as well as multilingualism is becoming one of the principal distinctive traits of contemporary Catalan cinema.[62] The increasing number of bilingual films – especially since the beginning of the new millennium – also reveals that this is a growing tendency in Catalan cinema: *Joves* [Youth] (2003), *Ficció* and *V.O.S.* [Original Version with Subtitles] (2006 and 2009), *El coronel Macià* [Colonel Macià] (2006), *Salvador* (2006), *Les dues vides d'Andrés Rabadán* [The Two Lives of Andrés Rabadán] (2008), *La mosquitera* [The Mosquito Net] (2010), etc. are just a few examples of this new trend.[63] Whereas, by using different narrative strategies, most of these films realistically represent typical Catalan and Spanish language contact in today's Catalonia, *El coronel Macià* and *Salvador* – the first set in the first three decades of the twentieth century and the second in the last months of Franco's dictatorship – depict a linguistic panorama which can be defined as diglossic.

60   Other films like *Salvador* by Manuel Huerga (2006) or *Elisa K.* by Judith Colell and Jordi Cadena (2010) can be mentioned.
61   I use here the adjective 'normalized' as it is conventionally applied in Sociolinguistics.
62   Esther Gimeno Ugalde, 'Bilingüisme i diglòssia al cinema català contemporani: *El coronel Macià* (Josep Maria Forn) i *Salvador* (Manuel Huerga)', *Journal of Catalan Studies* (2011), 305–24.
63   This new trend in cinema produced in Catalonia is to some extent visible in other Iberian cinemas such as in Galician cinema.

If the situation of cinema in the Basque language seems to a certain extent to be desperate, cinema in Galician cannot be described in more positive terms. As in the case of Basque cinema, the best-known Galician cinema, inside and outside Galicia, is that spoken in Spanish. Successful films identified by the audience as Galician movies[64] such as *La lengua de las mariposas* [Butterfly's Tongue] (1999), *El lápiz del carpintero* [The Carpenter's Pencil] (2002) – both based on Manuel Rivas' literary work: *¿Qué me queres, amor?* [What Do You Want from Me, Love?] (1995) and *O lapis do carpinteiro* (1998), written originally in Galician – *Los lunes al sol* [Mondays in the Sun] (2002) or *Celda 211* [Cell 211] (2008) are spoken in Spanish. As Colmeiro perfectly describes:

> Although Galician language remains a fundamental aspect of Galician cultural identity, the language used in the films cannot be a meaningful distinctive marker. Most feature films shot in Galicia, with some notable exceptions, are filmed in Spanish and then dubbed into Galician in a postproduction for their general release in Galicia, as the dubbing in Galicia is required to obtain production subsidies and be shown on Television de Galicia (TVG).[65]

This is partly due to historical reasons since cinema in Galician has enjoyed a relatively short life. Indeed, *Urxa* (Carlos Aurelio López Piñeiro/Alfredo García Pinal 1989) and *Sempre Xonxa* [A Woman Forever] (Chano Piñeiro 1989) are the two first feature films in Galician, both shot at the end of the 1980s.[66] Similar to the Basque case, after almost inexistent production in

64   Whether because of the origin of the director, the location, the subject matter, the artistic/technical team or the cast.
65   Colmeiro, 'Imagining', 205.
66   In contrast, cinema spoken in Catalan dates back to the 1930s with *El Cafè de la Marina* [The Marina Café] (1933–4) by Domènech Pruna, a film based on the homonymous play by Josep Maria de Segarra written that same year. According to information provided by a contemporary, the Catalan version of the film was screened in most parts of Catalonia as well as in Majorca, Valencia and the Catalan-speaking region of France. Josep Maria Caparrós, 'El cine catalán durante la Renaixença', in Sergi Alegre *et al.*, *El cine en Cataluña. Una aproximación histórica* (Barcelona: PPU, 1993), 26. The Spanish version of the film was not screened in Madrid until 1941, although in other capitals such as Bilbao it was screened in 1934. Cf. Joaquim

the Galician language during the 1990s, there is evidence of some remarkable efforts to make films in this language in the new millennium.

In recent years there has been a tendency to make bilingual movies such as *Rafael* (Xavier Bermúdez 2011) or the comedies *Era outra vez* [Once Upon Another Time] (2000) or *Días de voda* [Wedding Days] (2002), both part of Pinzás' Dogma 95 trilogy, which also includes *El desenlace* [The Outcome] (2005), the latter only spoken in Spanish.[67] Cinema in Galician seems to have reached a climax most recently with the success of three films partly spoken in Galician at the Málaga Film Festival in 2011: *Crebinsky* (Enrique Otero 2011), *Doentes/Enfermos* [Sick People][68] (2011) and the documentary *Radiografía dun autor de tebeos* [X-Ray of an Author of Comics] (Marcos Nine 2011). To some extent this fact confirms what the producer Farruco Castromán called the '*Pa negre*-effect': 'Con *Pa negre* transmitiuse que unha película noutra lingua que non sexa español pode funcionar en salas. Isto demostra que o cine está cambiando' [*Pa negre* [Black Bread] sent the message that a film in a language other than Spanish can do good in the box office. This shows that cinema is changing].[69] Indeed, the success of a film shot entirely in Catalan proves that cinema spoken in languages other than Spanish can also be a commercial hit in Spain[70] and be recognized both in the most important festivals of our country (e.g. Goya Awards, San Sebastian International Film Festival) and abroad (e.g. Academy Awards in Hollywood).

On the other hand, the polyglot character of *18 comidas* [Life is Served] (Jorge Coira Nieto 2010) or *Crebinsky* (Enrique Otero 2011) confirms the

---

Romaguera i Ramió, dir., *Diccionari del cinema a Catalunya* (Barcelona: Enciclopèdia Catalana, 2005), 132.

67   There are also few monolingual Galician soundtracks such as the TV-movie *A mariñeira* [The Fisherwoman] (X. Anton Dobao 2007).

68   Based on the homonymous play of the Galician playwright Roberto Vidal Bolaño.

69   Quoted in Alfonso Pato, 'A primavera do cinema en galego', *El País* (25 March 2011) <http://elpais.com/> accessed 10 January 2012.

70   Takings according to the Ministry of Education, Culture and Sport: 2.650.327,55 Euro <http://www.mcu.es/bbddpeliculas/cargarFiltro.do?layout=bbddpeliculas &cache=init&language=es> accessed 16 January 2012.

hypothesis that multilingualism is an increasing tendency in other Iberian cinematographies, not only in Catalan cinema. The dramatic comedy *18 comidas* – mainly spoken in Spanish but including some dialogues in Galician, English and Macedonian – depicts a modern and multilingual Santiago de Compostela, whereas *Crebinsky* is undoubtedly a more daring project: 'A beautiful, fable-like film with touches of magic realism and slapstick silent comedy, *Crebinsky* creates the sense of a distinctive if long-lost world'.[71] Set in the World War II period *Crebinsky* narrates a surreal story played by American soldiers, Nazis, Franco's soldiers and Galician natives and is shot in Galician, English and German, with some dialogues in Russian and Spanish.

V. Concluding remarks: towards a normalization of Iberian languages in cinema

Cinema still represents one of the leading forms of transmission of values and of construction of shared imaginary referents for a cultural or linguistic community. The dependence of European societies regarding the USA-American mainstream is obvious and at the same time it is one of the weaknesses of European cinema.[72] Cinema in Iberian languages has to compete not only with the hegemony of English, but also with the dominance of Spanish – both in a political and demolinguist sense. For different reasons – of a historical, political and, last but not least, commercial nature – Iberian languages have not consolidated themselves in cinema in recent decades. In contrast to the overwhelming number of Spanish original soundtracks, the relatively scarce number of films with Basque, Galician and, to a lesser extent, Catalan original soundtracks confirms

---

71   <http://www.filmlinc.com/films/on-sale/crebinsky> accessed March 2012.
72   Antoni Ferrando and Miquel Nicolás, *Història de la llengua catalana* (Barcelona: UOC, 2005), 460.

that the normalization process of Iberian languages remains an unresolved matter in cinema. Nevertheless, in recent years some attempts to make cinema in Iberian languages – other than Spanish and Portuguese – can be observed, thus illustrating a growing tendency that confers more value on cinema spoken in less extended or non-state languages.

The fact that four films – from a total of eleven – participating in the official section of the Festival de Cine de Málaga (2011)[73] were bi- or multilingual projects spoken in Basque, Galician or Catalan and that the winner of the 2012 edition was a bilingual Catalan film (*Els nens salvatges* [The Wild Children] by Patricia Ferreira) is a clear sign that we are witnessing an important change towards the representation and recognition of Iberian languages in cinema.[74] Undoubtedly, the resounding success of *Pa negre* by Agustí Villaronga in the last Goya awards and the fact that the Academia de Cine Español, for the first time in its history, selected a film spoken in Catalan to represent Spain in the Oscar awards – together with Almodóvar's *La piel que habito* [The Skin I Live In] (2011) and Zambrano's *La voz dormida* [The Sleeping Voice] (2011) – establishes an unprecedented event in the cinema being produced in Spain and may be an indicator of a new future for cinema produced in other Iberian languages.

I would like to conclude this essay by mentioning a further symbolic (but probably very noteworthy) example of the increasing presence (or perphaps normalization) of Iberian languages on screen – I am referring, of course, to the porn industry. Although it can be perhaps interpreted as

---

73 The following full-length films were competing in the official section: *¿Para qué sirve un oso?* [What is the Use of a Bear?] (Tom Fernández), *Amigos* [Friends] (Borja Manso/Marcos Cabotá), *Arriya/La piedra* (Alberto Gorritiberea), *Catalunya über alles* [Catalonia Above All] (Ramon Termens), *Cinco metros cuadrados* [Five Square Metres] (Max Lamcke), *Crebinsky* (Enrique Otero), *Doentes/Enfermos* (Gustavo Balza), *El hombre de las mariposas* [The Butterfly Man] (Maxi Valero), *En fuera de juego* [Offside] (David Marqués), *Hora menos* [Hour Less] (Frank Spano) and *Open 24 h* (Carles Torras).

74 *Arriya/La piedra* was shot in Euskara and Spanish, *Doentes* is bilingual Galician-Spanish, *Open 24 h* Catalan-Spanish, *Crebinsky* is a multilingual film and *Catalunya über alles* is a bilingual soundtrack, Catalan-Mandinga with some dialogues in Castilian.

a provocative example, its inclusion in this context is also appropriate for two reasons: first of all, because Culture Studies should be today understood as a discipline that encompasses different practices belonging both to high and popular culture.[75] And secondly, for a more pragmatic reason, because this example can give us the key to understand to what extent we are witnessing a normalization of Iberian languages in the film industry and, in a broader sense, a normalization of the different cultures of the Iberian peninsula. *Les exxcursionistes calentes* [The Hot Female Hikers] (1999) by Conrad Son is the very first porn film shot in a Catalan original soundtrack and thus the very first in an Iberian language other than Spanish or Portuguese. As Josep-Anton Fernàndez points out:

> [E]ls discursos que la pel·lícula evoca no es limiten a la llengua i la política cultural: *Les exxcursionistes calentes*, pel seu títol i per la seva ambientació (a la comarca de la Cerdanya, al Pirineu català), ressona amb la tradició de l'excursionisme, que és un dels pilars històrics de la cultura del catalanisme, tant amb la Renaixença com amb el Modernisme, com més tard amb el moviment escolta. Tant és així, que no seria extravagant argumentar que el vídeo pornogràfic de Conrad Son marca l'entrada simbòlica de la cultura catalana en l'edat adulta [...].[76]

> [The discourses which this film evokes are not limited to language and cultural politics: *Les exxcursionistes calentes*, from its title and setting (in the region of Cerdanya, in the Catalan Pyrenees) links to a tradition of hiking which is one of the historical foundations of Catalanism, from the Renaixença to the Modernism, to the later Scout movement. Such is the case that it wouldn't be excessive to argue that Conrad Son's pornographic video marks the passing of Catalan culture into adulthood.]

Something similar is the case with *O divino ferrete* [The Hot Branding-Iron], a project by various producers who, with a clear intention to contribute to

---

75   In his book *After the Great Divide* (1986) Huyssen states in fact that postmodernism is a new cultural condition in which the modern separation between high and popular cultures ceases to exist. Andreas Huyssen, *After the Great Divide: Modernism, Mass Culture, Postmodernism* (Bloomington, IN: Indiana University Press, 1986).

76   Josep-Anton Fernàndez, 'De *Les Exxcursionistes calentes* a *Elegies de Bierville*, i vice-versa: els Estudis Culturals', in Mercè Pirconell and Margalida Pons, eds, *Literaratura i cultura: aproximacions comparatistes* (Barcelona: Lleonard Muntaner, 2009), 62.

the normalization of the Galician language, aim to bring to fruition the first porn film shot entirely in Galician.[77] As with Son's film, set in rural Catalonia, this Galician film – not yet finished – tells a pornographic story set in a rural area. It is probable that, because of their symbology, these perhaps unconventional examples illustrate more clearly the increasing acceptance being experienced in today's cinematographic industry of 'minority' Iberian languages. It still remains open if in the next few years I will be able to report on the existence of the very first porn film in the Basque language …

Works cited

Alvaray, Luisela, 'Are We Global Yet? New Challenges to Defining Latin American Cinema', *Studies in Hispanic Cinemas* 8/1 (2011), 69–86.

Bauman, Zygmunt, *Liquid Modernity* (Cambridge: Polity Press, 2000).

Berger, Verena, 'Voices against the Silence: Polyglot Documentary Films from Spain and Portugal', in Verena Berger and Miya Komori, eds, *Polyglot Cinema. Migration and Transcultural Narration in France, Italy, Portugal and Spain* (Münster: LIT Verlag, 2011), 211–25.

——, and Miya Komori, 'Introduction: Moving Pictures from a Modern Babel', in Verena Berger and Miya Komori, eds, *Polyglot Cinema. Migration and Transcultural Narration in France, Italy, Portugal and Spain* (Münster: LIT Verlag, 2011), 7–12.

Camí-Vela, María, 'Cineastas españolas que filman en inglés: Isabel Coixet', in Pietsie Feenstra and Hub Hermans, eds, *Miradas sobre pasado y presente en el cine español (1990–2005)* (Amsterdam and New York: Rodopi, 2008), 179–91.

Caparrós, Josep Maria, 'El cine catalán durante la Renaixença', in Sergi Alegre *et al.*, *El cine en Cataluña. Una aproximación histórica* (Barcelona: PPU, 1993), 11–38.

Colmeiro, José, 'Imagining Galician Cinema: Utopian Visions?', in Kirsty Hooper and Manuel Pug Morux, eds, *Contemporary Galician Cultural Studies. Between the Local and the Global* (New York: MLA, 2011), 204–20.

77   <http://www.odivinoferrete.com/>.

Cunillé, Lluïsa, 'Barcelona, mapa d'ombres', in *Deu peces* (Barcelona: Edicions 62, 2008), 383–448.

Dywer, Tessa, 'Universally Speaking: Lost in Translation and Polyglot Cinema', *Fictionalising Translation and Multilingualism*, special issue of *Linguistica Antverpiensia New Series* 4 (2005), 295–310.

Epps, Brad, 'Echoes and Traces: Catalan Cinema, or Cinema in Catalonia', in Jo Labany and Tatjana Palvovic, eds, *Companion to Spanish Cinema* (London: Blackwell Press, 2013), 50–80.

Fernàndez, Josep-Anton, 'De *Les Exxcursionistes calentes* a *Elegies de Bierville*, i viceversa: els Estudis Culturals', in Mercè Pirconell and Margalida Pons, eds, *Literaratura i cultura: aproximacions comparatistes* (Barcelona: Lleonard Muntaner, 2009), 61–91.

Ferrando, Antoni, and Miquel Nicolás, *Història de la llengua catalana* (Barcelona: UOC, 2005).

Garraio, Júlia, 'O futuro do cinema português passa pelo inglês? Sobre alguns recentes caminhos da cinematografia portuguesa', in Kathrin Sartingen and Esther Gimeno Ugalde, eds, *Perspectivas Actuais na Lusitanística: literatura, cultura, cinema, língua* (München: Meidenbauer, 2011), 113–28.

Gimeno Ugalde, Esther, 'Bilingüisme i diglòssia al cinema català contemporani: *El coronel Macià* (Josep Maria Forn) i *Salvador* (Manuel Huerga)', *Journal of Catalan Studies* (2011), 305–24.

Heiss, Christine, 'Die Stilisierung von Türkendeutsch im Film und das Problem der Synchronisation ins Italienische', *InTRAlinea* 12 (2010) <http://www.intralinea.it/volumes/eng_more.php?id=902_0_2_0_M74%> accessed 4 March 2012.

Huyssen, Andreas, *After the Great Divide: Modernism, Mass Culture, Postmodernism* (Bloomington, IN: Indiana University Press, 1986).

Jordan, Barry, and Rikki Morgan-Tamosunas, *Contemporary Spanish Cinema* (Manchester and New York: Manchester University Press, 1998).

Komori, Miya, 'Going North: Language and Cultural Contact in Spanish Emigration Cinema', in Verena Berger and Miya Komori, eds, *Polyglot Cinema. Migration and Transcultural Narration in France, Italy, Portugal and Spain* (Münster: LIT Verlag, 2011), 193–210.

Kortazar, Jon, 'Novela vasca y cine', *Encuentros en Verines. Casona de Verines, Pendueles (Asturias)* (2008) <http://www.mcu.es/archivoswebmcu/verines/pdf/334.pdf> accessed 4 March 2012.

Marín Gallego, Cristian, *La traducción para el doblaje de películas multilingües: Babel*, Master thesis in Audiovisual Translation (Las Palmas: Universidad de las Palmas de Gran Canarias, 2007).

Martí-Olivella, Jaume, 'Catalan Cinema: An Uncanny Transnational Performance', in Dominic Keown, ed., *A Companion to Catalan Culture* (Woodbridge, Suffolk, UK, and Rochester, NY: Tamesis, 2011), 185–206.

Martínez-Carazo, Cristina, 'Immigration and Plurilingualism in Spanish Cinema', in Verena Berger and Miya Komori, eds, *Polyglot Cinema. Migration and Transcultural Narration in France, Italy, Portugal and Spain* (Münster: LIT Verlag, 2011), 157–71.

Naficy, Hamid, *An Accented Cinema. Exilic and Diasporic Filmmaking* (Princeton: Princeton University Press, 2001).

Pato, Alfonso, 'A primavera do cinema en galego', *El País* (25 March 2011) <http://elpais.com/> accessed 10 January 2012.

Roldán Larreta, Carlos, 'Euskera y cine: Una relación conflictiva', *Fontes Linguae Vasconum: Studia et Documenta* 71 (1996), 163–76.

Rolfe, Pamela, '5 Spanish Filmmakers Ready to Crack the Global Market', *The Hollywood Reporter* (15 May 2001) <http://www.hollywoodreporter.com/news/5-spanish-filmmakers-ready-crack-188491> accessed 10 February 2012.

Romaguera i Ramió, Joaquim, dir., *Diccionari del cinema a Catalunya* (Barcelona: Enciclopèdia Catalana, 2005).

Sedeño Valdellós, Ana, 'Cine transnacional: nuevas formas de entender el cine en su dimensión globalizada', *El Ojo que Piensa. Revista Virtual de Cine Iberoamericano* 3 (January–June 2011) <http://www.elojoquepiensa.net/elojoquepiensa/index.php/articulos/162> accessed 4 March 2012.

Shohat, Ella, and Robert Stam, 'Narrativising Visual Culture. Towards a Polycentric Aesthetics', in Nicholas Mirzoeff, ed., *The Visual Culture Reader* (London: Routledge, 1998), 27–49.

Smith, Paul Julian, 'Chaotic Ana', *Film Quarterly* 61/2 (2007), 30–4.

Sojo, Kepa, 'El reto del cine vasco', *Euskonews* (September 2005) <http://www.euskonews.com/0314zbk/gaia31402es.html> accessed 4 March 2012.

Wahl, Chris, '"Du Deutscher, toi Français, You English: Beautiful!" – The Polyglot Film as a Genre', in Miyase Christensen and Nezih Erdogan, eds, *Shifting Landscapes: Film and Media in European Context* (Newcastle: Cambridge Scholars Publishing, 2008), 334–50.

Notes on Contributors

MARIA FERNANDA DE ABREU is Associate Professor at the Faculty of Social and Human Sciences, New University of Lisbon, where she co-ordinates the area of Spanish Studies. She founded and currently directs the Institute of Iberian and Ibero-American Studies, and she is a member of the Centre for the History of Culture, at the New University of Lisbon. Her research areas include Portuguese Literature (nineteenth century), Hispanic Literatures and Comparative Literature. Her main publications include *Cervantes no Romantismo Português: cavaleiros andantes, manuscritos encontrados e gargalhadas moralíssimas* (1994) or 'De que lado o espelho? Das teorias às práticas comparatistas no estudo das relações literárias entre Portugal e Espanha' (2007).

MARIA GRACIETE BESSE graduated in Romance Philology at the University of Lisbon, Faculty of Arts, and got her PhD at the University of Poitiers, with a study on the Portuguese author Alves Redol. She is currently full Professor at the University of Paris – Sorbonne, Paris IV, Chair of the Portuguese department and Adjunct-Director of the UFR on 'Iberian and Ibero-american Studies'. She founded and directs the seminar on 'Lusophone Studies' at the CRIMIC (Centre de Recherches Interdisciplinaires sur les Mondes Ibériques et Contemporains), at the Sorbonne. Her main publications include *Cultures lusophones et hispanophones: penser la relation* (org.) or *Les Grands récits: miroirs brisés? Les Grands récits à l'épreuve des mondes ibériques et ibéro-américains* (2010).

HELENA BUFFERY came to University College Cork in 2010 from the University of Birmingham where she was a senior lecturer in Hispanic Studies. Her principal teaching and research interests include contemporary Hispanic theatre and performance, Translation Studies and Catalan Studies. She has published widely in these areas, including recent volumes on Shakespeare in translation (translated as *Shakespeare en català*, 2010), exile theatre and performance (*Stages of Exile*, 2011) and *Barcelona: Visual Culture, Space and Power* (2012), co-edited with Carlota Caulfield. She has a long-standing interest in the different aspects and instances of intercultural contact that characterize the Hispanic world and is commited to analysis of Iberian and Hispanic cultural production from a comparative, translational perspective. Recent work in this area includes a co-edited volume on *Reading Iberia*, with Stuart Davis and Kirsty Hooper (2007), and she is contributing the Catalan sections to a forthcoming *Cultural History of Modern Literatures of Spain* for Polity.

CÉSAR DOMÍNGUEZ is Associate Professor of Comparative Literature and Jean Monnet Chair at the University of Santiago de Compostela, where he holds appointments in the Department of Literary Theory and Comparative Literature and the Department of Art History. His teaching and research focus upon theory of Comparative Literature, Comparative Literary History, Comparative European Literature, Comparative Studies in Medieval Literatures, and (Early) World Literature. In addition to numerous articles and books on these topics, he is Co-editor of the ICLA Co-ordinating Committee's two-volume *Comparative History of Literatures in the Iberian Peninsula*. As for professional services, he is chair of the ICLA Research Committee, member of the ICLA Co-ordinating Committee, Officer of the European Network for Comparative Literary Studies, Vice-President of the SELGYC, and member of the Academia Europaea. He is now working on projects devoted to the EU and the idea of European literature and a comparative history of medieval literatures in a world context under the aegis of the ICLA.

ÂNGELA FERNANDES is Assistant Professor at the Romance Literatures Department, Faculty of Arts, University of Lisbon. She got her PhD in Literary Theory at the same university in 2009. At the Centre for Comparative Studies, University of Lisbon, she co-ordinates the research project DIIA – Diálogos Ibéricos e Ibero-Americanos [Iberian and Ibero-American Dialogues], on the dialogues between Iberian and Ibero-American literatures and cultures. Her research interests include Literary

Theory, Comparative Literature and Modern Spanish Literature. She is the author of *Os Efeitos da Literatura: algumas questões de arte e de moral* (2004) and co-editor of *Diálogos Ibéricos e Iberoamericanos: actas del VI congreso internacional de ALEPH* (2010). Her recent publications include 'As relações portuguesas de Ramón Gómez de la Serna' (2010) and 'Imágenes literarias de Portugal y de España en el siglo XX' (2012).

DEREK FLITTER is Professor in Hispanic Studies at the University of Exeter. He works principally on Spanish literature and ideas of the nineteenth and early twentieth century. His publications include the monographs *Spanish Romantic Literary Theory and Criticism* (1992) and *Spanish Romanticism and the Uses of History: Ideology and the Historical Imagination* (2006). He has published widely on many aspects of Spanish Romanticism and its relationship with other periods of Spanish and broader European literary history, and on the Galician *Rexurdimento*. He is to co-edit a forthcoming collection of essays on the poet José de Espronceda, and is currently completing a monograph on eschatology in Spanish Romantic drama.

ESTHER GIMENO UGALDE is currently a Visiting Scholar in the Department of Romance Languages and Literatures at Harvard University where she is working on a project about multilingualism and polyphony in Catalonian/Iberian cinema, funded by the Max Kade Foundation NY and the Austrian Academy of Sciences. A graduate of the University of Vienna, she first taught at the same institution as a Lecturer and in 2009 was appointed Assistant Professor (non-tenure track). She also lectures at the *Universitat Oberta de Catalunya* and was a Visiting Lecturer at the University of Freiburg in Germany. In the academic year 2013/2014 she will join Boston College as an Assistant Professor. Esther Gimeno is the author of *La identidad nacional catalana. Ideologías lingüísticas en la Cataluña de 1833 a 1932* (2010). Recent work on Iberian and Hispanic Studies from a comparative perspective includes the co-edition of a book on Spanish and Latin American Women Filmmakers (forthcoming 2013) and a volume on literary and cultural relationships between Portugal and Catalonia (forthcoming 2013).

JON KORTAZAR is a multidisciplinary intellectual who develops his activity in multiple areas, from his work as a Professor of Basque Literature at the University of the Basque Country or as a Visiting Professor at the University of Santiago de Compostela, to his published collaborations in different mass media. The Galician PEN Club granted him the 2008 Rosalía de Castro Award for his published essays, and in 2009 he received the Lauaxeta Prize offered by the Diputación de Bizkaia as recognition of his whole work. He was also a Patron of the National Library and Vicepresident of Eusko Ikaskuntza – Sociedad de Estudios Vascos (2005–2008). Jon Kortazar is the author of several studies on Basque Literature, such as *Euskal literatura XX. mendean* (1990–2003), *Luma eta lurra* (1997), or *La narrativa vasca, hoy. Una mirada desde la postmodernidad* (2003). He is the co-ordinator of *Egungo euskal literaturaren historia*, a history of Basque contemporary literature in eight volumes, currently under development.

JOHN MACKLIN is Professor of Hispanic Studies and Head of the School of Modern Languages and Cultures at the University of Glasgow. A graduate of Queen's University, Belfast, he first taught in the University of Hull and in 1987 he was appointed Cowdray Professor of Spanish at the University of Leeds, where he was successively Head of Department, Head of School, Dean of Arts, Dean of the Research School in the Humanities, and Pro-Vice-Chancellor. He was Principal and Vice-Chancellor of the University of Paisley, after which he returned to Hispanism. His main research interests are in the fields of early twentieth-century fiction, especially Modernism, on which he has published several books and numerous articles and chapters. He has also co-authored a language text *¡Qué bien!*, bilingual editions of three of Cervantes' *Exemplary Novels*, as well as Unamuno's *Abel Sánchez* and *Niebla*. He has written on contemporary Spanish narrative and on two Portuguese dramatists. He is currently editing a *Companion to Unamuno*.

GABRIEL MAGALHÃES graduated in Modern Languages and Literatures, Portuguese and Spanish Studies, at the University of Lisbon, Faculty of Arts. He got his PhD at the University of Salamanca with a dissertation entitled *Garret and Rivas: Romanticism in Spain and Portugal* (2009). He worked at the University of Salamanca and is currently Professor at the

Department of Arts, in the University of Beira Interior. He was the Director of the Portuguese and Spanish Studies undergraduate course, and led the research project RELIPES (Linguistic and Literary Relations between Portugal and Spain since the Beginning of the Nineteenth Century). On Iberian topics, he also published the volume *Estar Entre* (2007) and *Los secretos de Portugal: peninsularidad e iberismo* (2012). As a novelist, he won the Prize 'Revelação' from the Portuguese Association of Writers with *Não Tenhas Medo do Escuro* (2009), and has recently published *Madrugada na Tua Alma* (2011).

FERENC PÁL studied Hungarian, Russian and Spanish Literature at Eötvös Loránd University in Budapest between 1968 and 1975, and in 1978 he entered the Portuguese Department at that same University, where he co-organized the Department of Portuguese and Brazilian Studies. He has taught several courses on nineteenth- and twentieth-century Portuguese and Brazilian literature. He has developed a research career on the reception of Portuguese and Brazilian literature, and on the works of Eça de Queirós, whose *O Mistério da Estrada de Sintra* (1886) he published on a translated version. He also published Fernando Pessoa's poetry in Hungarian, and translated some of José Saramago's novels. He is currently the Director of the Departament of Portuguese at Eötvös Loránd University, and Vice-Dean for International Affairs of the Faculty of Arts.

SANTIAGO PÉREZ ISASI was awarded a PhD in Spanish Literature by the University of Deusto in 2009 and is currently a postdoctoral researcher at the Centre for Comparative Studies of the University of Lisbon, where he is developing the project 'Portugal na Ibéria: mapa das relações literárias peninsulares (1870–1930)' [Portugal in Iberia: Mapping Peninsular Literary Relations] funded by FCT, the Portuguese Foundation for Science and Technology. Santiago Pérez Isasi is member of the research group DIIA – Diálogos Ibéricos e Ibero-Americanos [Iberian and Ibero-American Dialogues], at the Centre for Comparative Studies. His most recent publications include 'Imágenes de la Península Ibérica en la historiografía romántica europea' (2012) or 'The Concept of Spanishness in 19th-century Literary Historiography' (2013).

TERESA PINHEIRO has been a Professor of Iberian Studies at the Chemnitz University of Technology since 2004. She graduated from the universities of Cologne and Lisbon in German and Portuguese Studies and was awarded her PhD in Cultural Anthropology at the University of Paderborn in 2002. Her research fields are Iberian Cultural Studies, Emigration, Representations of Collective Identity, Discourses on Republics in Portugal and Spain, Nation-Building in Catalonia, Iberian Concepts of Europe. Her most recent publications include *Peripheral Identities: Iberia and Eastern Europe between Dictatorial Past and European Present* (co-edited with Beata Cieszynska and Eduardo Franco, 2011) and *Iberische Europa–Konzepte. Nation und Europa in Spanien und Portugal seit dem 19. Jahrhundert* (2009).

JUAN M. RIBERA LLOPIS, PhD in Romance Philology (1985), is a Lecturer in Catalan Philology at the Complutense University of Madrid. His research interests include the Comparative Study of Iberian Literatures, a topic on which he has taught courses at Doctorate and Master level. He has presented papers on this matter in conferences such as the regular meetings of AILLC, SELGyC or AHLM, and published several studies on literary history and criticism. Some of his most relevant publications are *Literatura catalana, gallega y vasca* (1982), 'Relaciones gallego-catalanas (1920–1939): materiales y propuestas para su estudio' (2000–2001, in collaboration with O. Rodríguez) or 'Literaturas galega e catalá desde 1939: Para unha comparación da narrativa histórica. II' (in *Bases metodolóxicas para unha historia comparada das literaturas de Península Ibérica*, 2004).

LEONARDO ROMERO TOBAR is Professor of Spanish Literature at the University of Zaragoza; he has taught in different Spanish Universities, such as Complutense University of Madrid, University of Santiago de Compostela or Carlos III University of Madrid, as well as in other countries. He was Vice-President of SELGyC and Co-founder of the Spanish Society of Bibliography. He has published both medieval (mostly hagiography) and modern texts (Larra, Espronceda, Bécquer, Clarín, Valera, Baroja, Valle-Inclán) and has written studies on nineteenth-century Spanish narrative (*La novela popular española del siglo XIX*, 1976), Romanticism

(*Panorama crítico del romanticismo español*, 1994; *La lira de ébano. Escritos sobre el Romanticismo español*, 2009), epistolary literature (he is the editor of the eight volumes of Valera's letters), literary history (*La literatura en su historia*, 2006; *Literatura y Nación*, 2008), travel literature (*Libros de viaje, realidad vivida y género literario*, 2005), Larra's journalistic works (*Dos liberales o lo que es entenderse*, 2007).

JÜRI TALVET is a graduate of Tartu University in English philology (1972) and a PhD by Leningrad (St Petersburg) University (1981, with a dissertation on the Spanish Golden Age picaresque novel). He has over several decades taught Western literary history (from 1992 as a Chair) at Tartu University, where he founded and directed the area of Spanish Studies (from 1992/1993). He chaired the Estonian Association of Comparative Literature from 1994 to 2010 and has edited its annual international journal *Interlitteraria* since 1996. As a writer (a member of the Estonian Writers' Union since 1984), he has published a number of books of poetry and essays. He has been active as a translator of (mainly) Spanish and Latin-American literature (*Lazarillo de Tormes*, Quevedo's poems, Gracián's *Oráculo manual*, Calderón's *La vida es sueño* and *El gran teatro del mundo*, etc.). As a researcher, he has published *Hispaania vaim* (1995) and *Tõrjumatu äär* (2005), as well as more than a hundred essays and articles on literature and culture in American, Estonian, Spanish and Russian journals.

ROBERTO VECCHI is Associate Professor in Portuguese and Brazilian Studies at the University of Bologna, where he holds the Chair in Portuguese Literature and Brazilian Literature. Head of the Postcolonial Study Centre (CLOPEE), he is also Co-ordinator of the Iberian PhD programme of the University of Bologna where he is responsible for the branch of Portuguese and Brazilian Studies. In Portugal, he is Fellow Researcher at the CES – Centre for Social Studies of the University of Coimbra, with projects on trauma, war and colonial violence and at the ELAB – Laboratory of Advanced Literary Studies of the New University of Lisbon. In Brazil, he is CNPq Fellow Research at the University of Campinas and São Paulo and in UK is Honorary Professor (2012–2015) of

Lusophone Studies at the School of Cultures, Languages and Area Studies at the University of Nottingham. Lastest books: *Excepção Atlântica. Pensar a Literatura da Guerra Colonial* (2010) and with Margarida Calafate Ribeiro (orgs) *Antologia da Memória Poética da Guerra Colonial* (2011).

Index

.

Hispanic Studies: Culture and Ideas

Edited by
Claudio Canaparo

This series aims to publish studies in the arts, humanities and social sciences, the main focus of which is the Hispanic World. The series invites proposals with interdisciplinary approaches to Hispanic culture in fields such as history of concepts and ideas, sociology of culture, the evolution of visual arts, the critique of literature, and uses of historiography. It is not confined to a particular historical period.

Monographs as well as collected papers are welcome in English or Spanish.

Those interested in contributing to the series are invited to write with either the synopsis of a subject already in typescript or with a detailed project outline to either Professor Claudio Canaparo, Department of Iberian and Latin American Studies, School of Arts, Birkbeck College, 43 Gordon Square, London WC1H 0PD, UK, c.canaparo@sllc.bbk.ac.uk, or to Peter Lang Ltd, oxford@peterlang.com.

Vol. 1   Antonio Sánchez
          Postmodern Spain. A Cultural Analysis of 1980s–1990s Spanish
          Culture. 220 pages. 2007.
          ISBN 978-3-03910-914-2

Vol. 2   Geneviève Fabry y Claudio Canaparo (eds.)
          El enigma de lo real. Las fronteras del realismo en la narrativa del
          siglo XX. 275 pages. 2007.
          ISBN 978-3-03910-893-0

Vol. 3   William Rowlandson
          Reading Lezama's *Paradiso*. 290 pages. 2007.
          ISBN 978-3-03910-751-3